DATE DUE			

MODERN GERMAN NATIONALISM

MODERN
GERMAN NATIONALISM

by

ABRAHAM ASHKENASI

A Halsted Press Book
Schenkman Publishing Company
JOHN WILEY & SONS
New York—London—Sydney—Toronto

Copyright © 1976 by Schenkman Publishing Company
3 Mt. Auburn Place, Cambridge, Mass. 02138

Distributed soley by Halsted Press, a Division
of John Wiley & Sons, Inc. New York

Ashkenasi, Abraham.
Modern German Nationalism.

1. Germany, West—Politics and Government
2. Nationalism—Germany—History. I. Title.
DD259.4.A77   320.9'43'085   75-33702

0470-03492-0

forget that elections have been won in the past by Germans seeking to carry out "peaceful" policies. Weimar offered a good case in point. The so-called Erfüllung-politicians were able to consistently maintain themselves in office and in 1928 the SPD had the chancellorship as well. There is not in Germany today that kind of hardening of public opinion, especially for some two million voters who swing their votes to cause one to expect continued consistency in support of international reformism. It is not only that the SPD may not be internally solid enough to maintain that kind of policy or to give the guarantee that these policies will be continued in a fashion commensurate with electoral success. The SPD's hold on the electorate is tenuous. The real or imagined popular fears of the domestic reforms desired by elements in the party weaken the SPD. Tepid friends have jumped from the party bandwagon before and determined enemies have known how to play on social fears with national images. In addition Willy Brandt's position in the party was certainly a fluke of history. I have analyzed his seizure of control from his Berlin bastion in a period of very low party fortunes and his contributions to the SPD's complete change in political stands in the late fifties and early sixties in another book "Reform Party and Foreign Policies", published in Germany. It would be euphoric indeed to count on his influence in the SPD outlasting his position of organizational predominance in the SPD and/or his physical presence as chancellor. The facility with which he was removed from power by an unholy constellation of inner-party manipulation, and national fears expressed by his political enemies (many analyzed in this book) bear out the force of this argument. Brandt fell because the treaties were not as immediately successful as many had hoped. He fell because he was suddenly vulnerable to a whole series of darkly atavistic national fears that could be exploited by determined conservative nationalist elements in German political life. One does not have to accept Herbert Wehner's claim that Brandt was catipulted from office after the '73/74 Guillaume spy affair by an attempted "coldly calculated rightest putsch", to realize that spies have come in and out of Germany's cold war since the 1940's with regularity, without that kind of repercussion. The fact is that the seeds of distrust lie deep in the SPD as well, and although the party has always had its eloquent idealists, its inner party power machinations have scarred its history. In addition organizational retrenchments have usually reflected political timidity and retreat. This is probably the case now, and the hopeful results of the 1972 federal national that German state. This means that South Germany, Germany below the Main-line, retains strong elements of conservatism. It is also interesting to note that it is in Bavaria and in Baden-Württemberg that the pragmatic facists of the National Democratic Party (the term will be discussed fully later) were electorally successful in Protestant areas. The extensive chapter on the NPD gives a further analysis of this phenomenon. The NPD – as we can see in table 1 – practically disappeared as a national party and is no longer an electoral factor in Germany. This development justifies some of the theoretical assumptions made in this book and written before the recent elections. Nationalist and/or authoritarian conservative German voters, more security conscious than adventurist, in the sense that the Nazis were adventurist in the thirties, have not lost their national motivation. On the contrary they have assimilated into the CSU in Bavaria and the CDU in Baden-Württemberg and so have also strengthened the position of modern German nationalism within these two parties, strengthened the nationalist element within these two state organisations and strengthened these state organisations within the union. This development is especially obvious in Bavaria where protestant German nationalists left the NPD to vote for the CSU. CSU-pluses of 5.4 percent in Ansbach, vote percentage increases that lay high over the 0.7 percent achieved for Bavaria as a whole are correlated to NPD losses of 5.8 percent in Ansbach (from 7.0 percent to 1.2 percent). Much the same with slightly lower CSU gains but with comparable NPD losses could be said for cities like Bayreuth, Trlangen or Kaufbeuren. In addition the CSU seems to have held its own or increased by less than 1 percent in cities like Hof or Nürnberg thanks to the decimation of the Bavarian NPD. What this probably means is that hard-core conservative voters have now been assimilated by the CSU in Bavaria and to a lesser degree by the CDU in Baden-Württemberg. Recent land elections indicate that to a lesser extent the same phenomenon can be observed in all German States. In addition there was before, and after Brandt's fall a general swing of about 4 percent away from the SPD in all German land elections between 1972 and mid 1975, so that the 1972 returns no longer completely reflect popular sentiment. The SPD and to a slightly lesser extent the FDP had assimilated the so-called swing-voters, who, given a less favorable foreign and domestic constellation for the SPD/FDP, swung back to a nationalist CDU/CSU. In addition the increased strength of conservative factions within the

CDU above the Main-line, although not as profound as in Baden-Württemberg or Bavaria, still reflect the trend, and was galvanized by election success. This phenomenon was obvious all over Germany. Liberal, or employee wing Union candidates did not do well in the federal elections and have not done well subsequently within the party. In Hess, however, Alfred Dregger, who plays a strong nationalist card and is a close political associate of CSU leader Franz-Josef Strauss, was able to achieve the highest vote percentage for the CDU in an election in Hess since the end of the war. He led his CDU to an increase of 1.9 percent and a percentage of 40.3 percent in Hess. It is obvious here, as well, that the CDU picked up NPD voters. In a previous NPD stronghold, in a strong center of German nationalism in Northern Hess, Grünberg, the NPD lost 9.9 percent and the CDU gained 8.4 percent. And in nearby Alsfeld the NPD lost 5.9 percent and the CDU gained 5.4 percent. In contrast in Rheinland-Pfalz, a state with a structure much like Baden-Württemberg in miniature, the SPD was able to come within .9 percent of the CDU and its relatively liberal leader Helmut Kohl. The exception to this trend in the national election was Schleswig-Holstein and Lower Saxony where the CDU was simply badly beaten. Interestingly enough this area housed the old-fashioned NPD organisations with their penchant for 1930's ideological panegyrics.

TABLE 2

'72 ELECTIONS

Percent Returns by state	SPD	CDU	FDP
Bremen	58.1	29.5	11.1
Schleswig-Holstein	48.6	42.0	8.6
Hamburg	54.4	33.3	11.2
North-Rhine Westphalia	50.4	41.0	7.8
Lower Saxony	48.1	42.7	8.5
Rheinland-Pfalz (Palatinate)	44.9	45.8	8.1
Hess	48.5	40.3	10.2
Saar	47.9	43.4	7.1
Baden-Württemberg	38.9	49.8	10.2
Bavaria	37.8	55.1	6.1

Recent land elections in these states have, however, strengthened conservative elements in the CDU and have somewhat evened out the political differences between north and south Germany, although they remain important. In addition, in City States like Hamburg and Berlin significant swings to Conservative Security and inevitably Nationalized oriented candidates were noted. By and large then it was the conservative and potentially nationalist element within the Union that was strengthened more than the CSU. Again developments within the CDU/CSU Union reflect this rehardening of attitudes toward inner reform and corallarily international compromise inside the Union to some extent in the country.

This book's long last chapter analyses various aspects of the CSU. It is our conclusion that the CSU represents the type of organisation and the type of ideology one can expect from modern German nationalism. The CDU's nationalism is far more subtle than the analysts in modern German liberal periodicals like the "Zeit" or the "Spiegel" express. The weakness of modern journalistic analysis of the CSU have been well illustrated by Alf Minzel in his article on structural change in role of the CSU in Ossip K. Flechtheims new book "Parties in the Federal Republic". Minzel's conclusions are that the CSU has to remain stucturally regional, that it has to maintain its basic Bavarian social and ideological character and that its conceived role is simply that of a bulwark of christian middle-class thought and social organisation (in what it perceives as a Europe threatened by communist inundation). These points if we accept them all, do not make the CSU any less nationalist in the sense that we have defined nationalism in this book. For it is just this combination of regionalism, as well as categorical, moral middle-class imperative, christian righteousness and modern organisational structure which makes the party a typical modern nationalist party. This is especially true when brought into the context of the CSU's close connections to the German managerial leadership elite and capitalist structure. Indeed, this tie was strengthened in the '72 election year. The interlocking directorate, CSU, as to big business has been analyzed to some extent in the chapter on the CSU in this book. The late Wolfgang Pohle carried out a central role in this development. Pohle's death, however, has not hindered the CSU, and especially its leadership under Franz-Josef Strauss, in establishing itself as the party of German industry. Men like Gisbert Kley of Siemens, Rolf Rodenstock, the important optics industrial captain and various industrial magnets from the Flick and Hoeschst concerns are closely associated with the CSU. One of the major manipulators of the association of the CSU and

Secretary of the CDU, Dr. Konrad Kraske, a member of the liberal wing of the Union pointed out in a long article in the CDU's "Deutsche Monatsblatt", many of the long-range reasons for the Union's defeat in the election and indeed many of the long-range developments that should weaken nationalism in its old fashioned form in Germany. Interestingly enough this analysis was a defensive measure against the CSU and its allies, and scored the CDU as a conservative national party. Kraske understood, as many in the CDU began to understand, that it had become fashionable for young people to vote for the SPD or FDP. Two out of three first-voters in Germany gave their votes to the German ruling coalition in the 72 elections. In addition a large percentage of Germans eligible to vote for the first time, actually voted. In an election in which 91.2 percent of the population voted, approximately 85 percent of the eligible first-voters cast their ballots. A second major cause for the CDU defeat was the steady deminishing of the old-fashioned, self-employed middle-class in various areas of Germany. Farmers, self-employed craftsmen, small businessmen etc. are giving way and an increasingly large percentage of the population is becoming employed by major economic organisations and the state. What the Germans called dependent employees as opposed to independent self-employed people in the economic process are increasing as is the trend towards urbanization. For the time being much of this new middle-class opts for the FDP and to a decreasing lesser extent towards the SPD. At least both parties and especially the FDP showed voter increases in percentage in this area. The general increase in tolerance, generally among younger Germans, and the decrease in old-fashioned nationalist positions in Germany generally is analysed in chapter 3 of this book. Nevertheless there is a fertile ground for a new kind of nationalism analysed in this book, and as was pointed out above, these new SPD and FDP votes are not firm. Communal and land elections after the Federal national '72 elections and state-wide land elections before the Federal elections have as we have seen indicated as much. There has on the other hand been a constant post-war 30 to 40 percent acceptability of nationalism among German voters. This may be one of those magic numbers that are used by social scientists and that I am afraid have been also used in this book, to try and pinpoint the popular appeal of ideologies and political movements. On the other hand a long historical tradition seems to justify this kind of an assessment of German nationalism. In addition, one can probably say that this figure is currently a good approximate assessment for all western industrial societies. France and Britain in the 1970's have given excellent examples of this type of modern nationalism. It is bound to business interests, atavistic attitudes, general insecurity, and moral and political conservatism. Both the Heath and Pompidou governments were strongly tainted by it. But nationalism in Western Europe is not as potentially dangerous as the German breed of the same cat; it has not been as volatile in this century. Moreover Germany is Europe's critical mass. When Germany is quiet, everything around it can evidence relative turmoil and Europe as a whole retains its basic stability. On the other hand slght increases in Germany's "instability" or even independence are potent variables. Increases in West European national foreign policy egoism along with Eastern European intransigence endanger not only the SPD and can topple a towering figure like Willy Brandt, but endanger German stability and stoke old flames with newly fashioned rods. Domestic instability in Germany has often been a function of foreign instability; economic nationalism in Europe can lead a resuscitation of old arguments in a new garb. Violent propagation and engagement vary; acceptability of these arguments seems to be fairly constant. In addition there seem to be a hard-core of 10 percent to 15 percent in Germany who are exceptionally nationalistic, and who can be counted on to drive on the rest under the proper conditions.

These terms will be defined in some length later in the book. But for the purpose of this introduction it suffices to open them to intellectual exploration and to hope that the optimistic trends of not only the last federal national election in Germany but of the last ten years, and indeed, some might say the entire postwar period are per vasive enough to wipe out the influence of the uncomfortable geographic, economic and political realities of post-war Europe and the atavism of a historical and philosophical tradition that still pervades and shapes mens' minds.

Contents

MODERN GERMAN NATIONALISM

I

Nationalism and Past and Future Conflicts

There seems to be no doubt that the years since the French Revolution, what historians call the modern period, have been marked by the ascendancy of two messianic political movements: socialism and nationalism. Socialism is a political ideology with clear-cut intellectual boundaries within a theoretical framework, developed from Saint-Simon via Marx and Lenin into the current period and with a clear body of socio-economic thought. Nationalism remains diffuse. Attempts at definition, both by the purveyors of nationalistic ideas and by more dispassionate political scientists, have been legion. The analysis has followed historically descriptive, philosophical lines as well as politically definitive, or sociological lines. All these attempts have been fruitful, but none has been able to pin down this particular phenomenon. Nationalism is a chameleonlike messianic movement that, over 150 years, has consistently changed colours. The most obvious of these changes is the one commented upon by Carlton Hayes, the doyen of scholars of nationalism, as early as 1926; Hayes described the change in nationalism around the year 1848 from emancipatory nationalism — a nationalism based on the emancipatory movements of revolutionary bourgeois Europe after the French Revolution — and the nationalism of that same bourgeoisie after 1848, which might be called establishment nationalism. Establishment nationalism became more and more a force utilized by European elites to maintain control over their societies. This change in nationalism and nationalism's political utilization is illustrated very well and systematically by Richard Rosecrance in his book *Action and Reaction in World Politics*.[1] The use of nationalism as a regulatory feature of nineteenth- and twentieth-

3

century domestic systems and its function as an inspirer of action within these systems show some of the contradictions in the role and function of nationalism.

Within one given political system, various competitive usages and interpretations of one nationalism complicate analysis. Furthermore, although functionally nationalism's role was to provide the integrational organizational myth for stabilized consensus, as well as increased internal international efficiency and enhanced international political mobility for the nation state, its normative power was so great that it could be manipulated not only by leadership elites but by would-be usurpers. In addition, nationalism could be used to subvert more efficient functional processes in order to preserve certain socioeconomic elites and/or destroy or control modernizing or reforming political and social groups and ideas. The German experience gives excellent examples of these functions of nationalism. Historically, there seems to be no doubt that nationalism was a great mover in nineteenth-century Europe. There also seems to be no doubt that it had a kind of life of its own i.e., as much as the leadership groups, especially after 1848, attempted to control their populations through nationalism there was a strong tendency to fall into leadership traps. The national leadership itself was unable to ride the tiger that it had unleashed. (Bismarck's fall from power is a good example.) This is probably true because of one major function of nationalism: its messianic character, its mystical quality. The fact that it appeared fullblown, as it were, on the world scene in the nineteenth century as a philosophical, chiliastic concept, does not mean that it was not two centuries in the making in Western Europe. It does mean, however, that the sudden breakup of previous social forms gave rise to a need for new binding myths, in the sense that R. M. MacIver described them in his book *The Web of Government* — myths that bind masses of people to action, mystiques without which societies are probably unthinkable. For the English historian A. J. Toynbee and the French Catholic philosopher J. Maritain these myths represent a religious essence necessary for any civilization.[2] For Maritain the impetus seems to be the human need for religion and religiosity per se. Toynbee's ideas correspond more closely to MacIvers, and Toynbee furthermore deals with the concept of establishment, growth, modification, and dissolution of civilizations. The ubiquity of state religions and/or state ideologies is simply another way of saying that integrative myths either vary and develop with the needs of societies and leadership elites, or those societies (civilizations) crumble before the penetration of new, modern, political and/or social inputs. These can be internal or external in structure, but it is always the inability to learn and absorb and/or modify to fit the belief structure that causes violent socio-political ruptures.

It is perhaps helpful to differentiate between the broad historical framework of civilization and historical cycles, and the more modern concept of "the system". "The system" is at once a major rigorous and flexible analytical concept that can be applied to various aspects of a political, social, or economic process (and, of course, to the physical and technical processes from which the concept stems as well).[3] For example, the production and/or distribution of goods or the decision-making process can be treated as a system or as a subsystem of an entire process or system — the national political system. Of course, the decision-making process can also be broken down into subsystems, etc., and the broader, more general analytical terms just as civilization or cycle can also be treated as systems. For our purposes here the broader and perhaps less precise analytical concept is more useful. The study of the development of the basic idea over constantly changing ethnic and social basis requires an element of intellectual breadth and generalization. This is especially so since the flow of political social organizations and leadership elites resulting from the historical processes cited above is asymmetrically cyclical. These cycles have been postulated by many and will be discussed later in this chapter.

The patterns of establishment, growth, and modification over varying times and places, and the patterns of dissolution have only been guessed. The patterns do not seem symmetrical either historically on the basis of macrosocial analysis or even in more systematic microsocial studies of various social groups. Nor have completely accurate factor analysis techniques been developed for rigorous collerative study — especially over significant time spans. The resiliency of integrative social myths does however emerge as a central factor for these cycles. In addition as political social and economic life increase in complexity, so do the thought patterns, that are both outgrowth and an ideological cement. Competitive ideologies or integrative myths arise and reflect the social conflicts and the power struggles within political social organizations and between them. They also reflect this asymmetry of development and this factor as well leads to volatile ideological clash.

Ideology historian I. L. Talmon attempted to come to grips with the modern socio-political mystiques. His histories of ideological development illustrate clearly the processes of myth growth. In his book Political Messianism he so describes the development of both socialism and nationalism in the 19th century.[4] In the 19th century vast new regions needed organization. Population growth was enormous. Industrialisation and consequent urbanisation were new and mighty dislocation factors. Rootless new social groups had to be digested and controlled. Politically the French Revolution and Napoleon had proved the handmaidens of the acceleration of social and political decay. The new organisational, integrative ideas had to be at once heady and realistic in goal-setting and goal-prosecution as well. Realisable and chiliastic, functional and utopian, simple and complexly manipulative — these were exactly the native components of the competing ideologies of the post-Napoleonic European nation-state system Socialism and Nationalism. The early messianism and chiliastic aspects of nationalism made it the obvious ally of the revolution. Classical early 19th century nationalist thinkers like Michelet in France, Mazzini in Italy, Mackiewitz in Poland were all convinced that there was an inordinate tie between nationalism, the development of the nation state (but particularly their own) and the betterment of social conditions in Europe. Talmon writes here:

> "It is no mean paradox that nationalist ideology became rooted in highly elaborate conceptions of universal history and that nationalist greeds appeared at first as universal gospels to humanity and messages of imminent universal fulfilment. They found themselves on common ground with the socialist movements, for the two sprang from the same motives. The question of whether they be allies or foes became in time a matter of decisive importance."[5]

By the middle of the 19th century it became clear that these two messianic movements, the one a logical theoretical attempt at constant reform, the other a diffuse, pseudoreligious set of theories would not be allies. De Tocqueville pointed to the insane fear of socialism within nationalist ruling circles and E.H. Carr has written:

> "The ruling middle classes who were the bearers of the 19th century nationalism entertained almost everywhere throughout the middle years of the century a lively fear of revolution from below."[6]

The French historian Eli Halévy, calls the nineteenth century a century of conflct between these two conceptions and credits nationalism

with a victory resulting in World War I. But not only socialism was combated and defeated in this century by messianic nationalism. The jealous
dreams of the national communities could be and were turned against
any and all competitors. Various nationalisms competed against each
other, and the reformist prophets either fell by the wayside after 1848
or they could echo the words of the French poet patriot Alphonse de
Lamartine, "We love Poland, we love Italy, we love all the oppressed
peoples, but we love France before all." As Hans Kohn, one of the century's most profound contemporary writer on nationalism, pointed out in
his book *The Mind of Germany* it was the Polish question which robbed
the Frankfurt National Assembly of 1848 of most of its moral legitimacy. The German delegates to the ostensibly revolutionary assembly
rebuffed the Poles emancipatory nationalism, and in so doing helped
to scuttle their own.[7] German nationalism was, of course, much
more virulent than that of Lamartine or Michelet or Mazzini or even
Mackiewitz. It is important to bear in mind, however, that out of the
universal religion of nationalism, various sects developed, aided and
abetted by the nationalist emphasis in the ideas of these emancipators.
The sects maintained their religiosity, one that reflected the heat of
religious revival that was part of the French Revolution. The French
nationalist Charles Maurras said that, "L'humanité avait alors pour ga-
rantie la chrétienté. Depuis que la Réforme a coupe en deux notre
Europe, la chrétienté n'existe plus. Où est le genre humain, pour
chaque homme? Dans sa patrie."[*]

[*]"Humanity had then to guaranty christianity. Since the Reformation cut
our Europe in two, christianity exists no more. Where is the human genre,
for each man? In his country."

Immortality, as Fichte pointed out, was "promised (to the citizen) . . . by the continuous and independent existence of his nation."[8]
Nationalism maintained the "joy and ecstasy" of a religion with "social
rites", with the "customs and usages of historic Christianity", with
"admission to salvation" and "an ideal of immortality", with "faith in
mission and destiny."[9] Nationalism was also, as Kohn and Hayes and
Rosecrance have pointed out, the ideology of the soldier. Rosecrance
has argued that the technological ability to field large numbers of
troops plus the natural desire of elites to maintain their power pre-
determined the growth of an ideology like nationalism. Its militant

aspects simply reflected the trends of the nineteenth century ideas which attempted to replace the shattered myth of previous eras with new regulatory mythological systems. The result was a very heady type of West European nationalism, made all the more so by the early encroachments of the nationalistic French troops in other areas. A kind of syndrome developed from West to East with regard to nationalism, a syndrome which by the way is as evident today as it was then. Nationalism developed relatively functionally in the European nations west of the Rhine.

Here it is necessary to return to the earlier discussion of change in social organization.[10] The *Ancien Régime* of the seventeenth and eighteenth centuries provided a political structure replete with organizational processes and myths: the dynastic despotic principles, the established churches and nobilities, etc. But it carried within it the seeds of its own social destruction. In the lands west of the Rhine it was unable to integrate the rising bourgeois class that was necessary for the financing of the essentially national political entities that had been juridicially sanctified by the Treaty of Westphalia. Regardless of when we date the final emergence of the present modern historical cycle (if such a dating is indeed possible), it must include such factors as the rise of a bourgeois class, urbanization, industrialization, capitalism (entrepreneurism), etc. The rising bourgeoisie brought its new myth systems into its struggle to reorganize the Westphalian political entities. The new political systems for the Western areas would revolve around the bourgeois moral ethic and nationalism; and bourgeois-controlled parliaments would provide the manipulative means to filter the assimilation process of the expanding society ideologically, economically, and martially into the needs of the nation-state. West of the Rhine (and in the United States) this process of modification and growth had an inner logic, and its chiliastic cement — nationalism — retained much of its early messianic humanism. The breaking out of functional boundaries, which occurred during the French Revolution, and the chaotic situation of Europe between 1800 and 1815, restructured these ideas as they moved further East. The universality of the nationalist principle could not remain intact in a world in varying stages of development. The result was the aforementioned syndrome. Western nationalism appears in Eastern areas, incurs resentment from the feeling of inferiority that the Easterners feel.

The initial feeling of inferiority in turn leads to nationalist upsurge, to feelings of superiority and headiness. One can speak almost in exponential terms then of the development of nationalist ideology in its movement from West to East.

It was thus possible east of the Rhine to channel released social energies inherent in the Industrial Revolution into an indigenous leadership-supporting pattern of nationalist activity. True, a man like Disraeli would attempt to use nationalism and Empire, and with some success, to conservative advantage in Great Britain and in France as well, would come assaults on the Republican form of government from extreme nationalist groups. But as Gilbert Ziebura, one of Germany's foremost students of French history, has pointed out, essential differences existed between France and Germany and the uses of nationalism in these nations,[11] differences which held true for most of Eastern Europe. Talmon has written:

> Unlike the tradition bound and class-ridden reactionary and timid conservatism of the old Right, nationalism was bent upon giving an outlet to the dynamic quality of modern man. It supplied at the same time, in the nation a centre of loyalty and a framework of a more concrete and tangible nature than the airy heavenly cities of the world proletariat or liberated humanity. The national brotherhood makes class differences irrelevant (or we might say seem irrelevant). We all fulfill ourselves in the nation. The original ideology of political messianism wandered eastwards and away from its homeland, spread as the creed of alien and distant civilizations sharing thus the fate of other great religions. . . . Within the self-sufficient national state there developed a vaster type of messianism, the mass movement of the right. By checking the course of political messianism as a universalist movement nationalism did not put an end to the messianic cravings of the European peoples, it rather stifled what was noble in messianism and diverted the salvationist impulse into channels of perverse neuroses which in moments of crises was to break out into murderous madness.[12]

It is this excessive intemperance of chiliastic nineteenth-century European nationalism that called forth some of these definitions, e.g. John Stuart Mill writing in 1849: "European nationalism makes one indifferent to the rights and interests of any portion of the human species save that which is called by the same name and speaks the same language as themselves. . . . . In the backward parts of Europe and even, where better things might have been expected, in Germany, the sentiment of nationality far outweighs the love of liberty, that the people are willing to abet their rulers in crushing the liberty and independence of any people not of their race and language"[13]; or Lord Acton writing in 1862: "Nationality does not aim either at liberty or prosperity, both of which it sacrifices to the imperative necessity of making the nation a mould and measure of the state. Its course will be marked with material as well as moral ruin."[14]

The list could be extended ad infinitum.[15] The important point here is that this nineteenth-century nationalism was the driving force of human events, an all-encompassing nationalism that swept everything before it. As we have seen, nationalism began as a universalist type of movement, one with functional roots in modern political systems. In the twentieth century, outside Europe, outside the old European nationstate system, nationalism was able to combine with social revolutionary movements. In the alliance of Communism and nationalism leaders of these movements seem usually "to turn out more nationalists than Marxists."[16] It is, however, an undeniable fact that the quality of nationalism changes in relation to historical development, to sociological groups which identify with accepted nationalist truisms, and to the technological structure of a given state at any given time. We have indulged in a historical, somewhat philosophical analysis of nineteenth-century European nationalism because this method will concern us in our discussion of Germany and also because the quality and intensity of inherited ideas are reflected in the internal national social conflicts and within the nation-state system. We can speak of a kind of vast historical matrix where the quality and intensity of an idea relate to social form, and to the method and degree of social conflict. The results of these relationships spill out upon the international system and react upon the national political culture. So far we have touched primarily on the history of ideas and ideology. This can give us only one aspect of the political phenomenon of nationalism. We must now try to define nationalism politically and to look for the sociological groups most attracted to and manipulated by nationalism and the elites and would-be elites who do the manipulating.

Nationalism was of course more than merely a religion or a messianic movement. It had to be more than that because it provided and still provides the integrative myths for much of our modern political system. It had to satisfy some functional purpose in the development of European society, and it had to satisfy these functions in more ways than simply the ideological-philosophical. It had to be part and parcel of the real development of European life. It had to reflect the need for the interchange of goods and for the creation of secure living areas of political cultures, which are the flux of historical development. Karl Deutsch has done more than any other political scientist in tracing this functional development, showing how it led to nationalism. Much as a cultural anthropologist would trace the development of tribal societies into the city-state, into the slave empire, etc., in various cyclical ways at various times in human history, Deutsch traces the growth of nationalism and the nation-state as indeed part of a cyclical process. He observes cyclical processes that reflect the constant, almost Hegelian functions of integrative and dissolutionist trends, and claims a certain universalism in nation-building, "A general and uniform process of development" of what has come to be the nation-state.[17] The nation-state implies a vertical development of human life as opposed to the horizontalism of the feudal cycle and indeed, one might add to the horizontalism of the international political structure of the incipient national dynastic period. The verticalism was a process in which the nation-state developed as a reflection of the "'dynamic processes of social mobilization and cultural assimilation or at least of political integration, even with continuing linguistic and cultural diversities," which had been taking place in Western Europe for at least a 200-year period while dynasties were still making the horizontal international politics of that period.[18] Verticalism implies that the organization of goals and the variables of decision-making and the social mobility of individuals and social groups rest upon the closed political system with various levels of social goal satisfaction and power. The atttainment of rewards can only be achieved through relations and movements between levels along a vertical social axis. The nation-state developed an almost tribal-like organization for inner mobility and the distribution of reward and punishment along vertical lines from the highest decision-makers to the lowest peasant. The great national tribe was able to organize and insulate itself in a pattern which made it highly independent of outside systems (church, international class structures, and even to a degree multi-national markets.). Culture patterns (national character, national religion, national art forms), communication lines and symbols (language), economic structure (national economy — here lay the biggest exception, explaining perhaps the strenuous protective policies and closed market colonial systems of the national elites), and of course security (huge multi-

self-awareness in and communicated through the national group; (7) ethnic awareness as represented by the acceptance of national symbols; and (8) political compulsion as represented by developed elite grouping manipulating communication grids and national symbols.[20] This pure development varies from place to place and the unique features of each country can only be understood through comparative study. What this comparative study shows is that the cycles in history (we can speak of the nationalist nation-state cycle, which includes the period we are now discussing), are to a great degree asymmetrical cycles i.e., that in the same time spans social groups, political cultures and hence nation-states develop at different levels of social mobilization. Within the states we get social stress through what Deutsch would call the asymmetry of social mobilization and assimilation i.e., more people coming into the society than can be assimilated into the society at any given time. In addition, while the ideology of nationalism may have had an absolute functional antecedent in some Western states, its fullblown spread into Eastern Europe and Germany with their very different political developments and their very different levels of social mobilization led to distortion of actual developing models. (It is significant here that critics of nationalism of the intellectual power of the Anglo-Saxons Mills and Acton are missing in nineteenth-century Central and East European thought). These developments are what the classical social historians like Bendix, Veblen, and Schumpeter would call atavisms in historical processes. In his comparative study on the pre-conditions of development in Japan and Germany, Reinhard Bendix illustrated how these atavisms played a role in the establishment and type of nation-state in both these Empires. The fact that the functional processes were not completed, the fact that various political and sociological processes were co-opted by elites of a dynastic pre-industrial, pre-nationstate character led to the manipulative elitist nationalism of these two Empires.[21] It is not that an elite is not necessary. Compulsion and coercion are part of any national construct, and Deutsch has written that an existing distribution of governments is therefore necessary for a nation-state's development. He adds, however, that patterns of nationalism may well be arbitrary in their accents depending on existent elite groups.[22] Here he agrees with Bendix and moreover with Schumpeter. Perhaps the only case of a pure functional development of a nation-state and of nationalism is that of Switzerland. Here clear economic and security interests of a basic socio-political nature were made without elite-manipulated ritualistic elements of nationalism as was the case in so many other areas of Europe.[23]

The point remains, however, that nationalism and the nation-state, despite distortions, did perform a necessary function in the cyclical development of our modern political systems. Daniel Katz in his article "Nationalism and Strategies of International Conflict Resolution" assigns three major political functions to the nation-state in our era: (1) It provides internal integration (we will have more to say about the integrative effects of nationalism later); (2) It assures the maximalization of favorable input/output ratio to the society; Katz calls this maximization of the "dynamic" of modern industrialized nations "maximization of the operations of the system." This also means maximization of whatever is to be won by the development of the nation-state.[24] Deutsch writes: "Ony if nationality is valued, if it seems as a winning card in the social game for prestige, wealth or whatever else may be the thing culturally valued at that time and place, or if it fulfils a need on the personality structure which individuals have developed is that in that particular culture, or if it is at least valued for lack of any more promising opportunities, only then does it seem probable that consciousness of nationality will strengthen its development."[25] Nationality then is also a means of maximizing the goods and services of national standards of living. (3) Nationalism contributes to survival and to the protection against external enemies. This may seem obvious, but then again it is perhaps not so obvious because the question of whether nations come together as a form of internal consensus or as a reflection of the fear of an enemy has not been satisfactorily analysed. In considering German nationalism we will see that the element of fear of an enemy and the choice of enemies play a significant role. In any event, whether as a result of a rational consensus to maximize functional efficiency and the distribution of what is to be won, or through fear of others, the nations satisfy security-orientated psychic necessities and nationalism provides an important outlet for the aggressive resultant aspects of those remaining insecurities. Or in the words of Deutsch: (1) the nation-state keeps order; (2) the nation-state maintains its limited capacity for enforcement of its command and rules based on widespread habits of popular compliance; (3) the modern nation-state accepts a general role of responsibility for responding to many diverse needs of its people; (4)

the nation-state protects because it reduces the transmission of any national shocks; (5) the nation-state preserves group privileges; (6) within its secluded territory and economy the nation-state enhances upward social mobility; (7) the nation-state offers psychic reassurance through these processes.[26] However, as we have seen, these functions can easily be distorted.

Two major distortive or manipulative elements inherent in the nation-state are its communication grids and symbols and its elitist activity. These seem to be two major aspects of the nation's political life. Obviously national consciousness and the choice of certain national symbols are determined by the information that can be perceived by the sociological groups opting for this particular set of national symbols or group of symbols. It can be argued that control over communications was a salient function of the development of nationalism in the nineteenth century, and indeed the level of national and international contacts provides an indication of the relative strength of nationalism in Europe and in Asia today.[27] It is this complex of communicatory symbols rather than simply language which is the important feature of nationalism. It stands to reason, as the English conservative political theoretician Edmund Burke pointed out long ago. "Let us only suffer any person to tell us his story morning and evening but for one twelfth month and he will become our master." Communication is undoubtedly a more subtle matter than mere propaganda. It pertains to the whole body of coded symbols that is perceived by an individual in society and, indeed, that he interprets and evaluates. As Deutsch and Merritt pointed out, there is a difference between evaluative relationships to political and social events and cognitive relationships to these events.[28] The evaluative relationships maintain a very strong hold on large elements of the population despite all intrusive political events. This phenomenon is all the more marked in less sophisticated social groupings or groupings which are at the threshold of their entry into a modern information market. The same holds true for the ability of elites to manipulate these less sophisticated sociological groups. Levels of political sophistication are important here, but nationalism has proved to be the tailormade lever for elite manipulation under any conditions. The national unit lends itself to elite dominance. Deutsch has written that: "Even the narrowest kind of power over men requires two things, first the assembly of an effective inner structure, an effective past within the individual or group, and second the assembly of means to carry into effect the implications of this inner structure, to impose them on institutions in the outside world."[29]

The identification of sociological groups with the leadership elites carrying out familiar traditional roles and executing familiar and positively evaluated political tasks has proved to be a persistent aspect of national political life. The psychological satisfaction elements of the nation-state can only be achieved through the activity of an evaluatively acceptable elite grouping. The fact is, however, that these elite groups are not always representative of the various sociological groupings within their society. The mobilization of the nationalist ideology has been a successful means to overcome these uneven relationships, which are the natural result of the asymmetric historical developments that mark internal political structures as well as the international political structure. Katz has characterized four types of states with four different kinds of nationalist expression: (1) The revolutionary (or emancipatory) society, characterized by the development of a nation as the expression of new institutions; (2) The empire building society, characterized by the extension of national power on an exploitative basis; (3) The bureaucratic technical society, either of a capitalist or of a socialist type, with the declining nationalist ethos; (4) The declining society in which the state or its sub-systems are blocked, threatened, or losing power.[30]

It is conceivable that elite groups may also remain in power after one phase of state development has been crossed, i.e., a revolutionary elite might be in control of a bureaucratic technological society as some observers maintain is the case in the Soviet Union (others would disagree). Far more likely is that elements of elites whose political education took place in an empire building society remain in power in the third phase and attempt to maintain their authority through a recasting of the nationalism that was part of that previous society. German nationalism was the integrating force of the second of the above described states, and Germany's elitist nationalism was not only integral but also needed exploitative outlets. Up to the end of World War II there was only the empire building society in Germany. The social conflict between an elite with norms developed in one phase of national development, and sociological groups (in Germany let us say Weimar intellectuals or industrial workers) who are driving society into the third type of state is a natural development. This is true as well of conflict between various sociological groups within a given society. For instance, certain groups with a pre-industrial ethos are still within the process of being mobilized into the modern society, i.e. farmers, self-employed artisans and possibly small businessmen as well. The same may be true of certain regions within a national area. These regions may have remained apart from the overall national development, perhaps they have assumed a different economic role or have evolved a different set of sociological verities than the national group as a whole. Here it is interesting to note that such groups may hold very firmly to an older pattern of nationalist development. These social or socio-regional groups may, especially in twentieth-century Europe and the United States, cherish a nineteenth-century view of what the nation is all about. As Reinhard Bendix has pointed out, social conflicts extend themselves very easily into national conflicts.[31] M. Rainer Lepsius, in his booklet *Extreme Nationalism*, takes off from Bendix's analysis and postulates a moral imperative for certain groups in the nationalist experience.[32] He singles out the middle class as being particularly prone to this moralization of nationalism. The conception of the nation becomes a reflection of the middle class's own perception of what that nation should be, both politically and morally. Lepsius deals primarily with Germany, but he bases a good deal of his analysis on the works of the American sociologists Talcot Parsons, Martin Trow, Seymour Martin Lipset, and the Swede Sven Ranulf.[33] Using the German farmer, Lepsius indicates that a sociological group can be thrust into an extreme nationalistic position through the weakening of its group leadership and through the attacks of macroscial system development upon its micropolitical culture and social forms. The same is true of certain regional groupings, especially when within this region one certain sociological group determines life patterns – e.g., the farmer in Schleswig-Holstein. Using the work of the German sociologist Rudolf Haeberle, Lepsius charts the pattern of farmer regionalism, its destruction, and its eventual embracing of a substitutive extremist nationalism as an illustration of this phenomenon.[34] We will deal with this typically German problem later. It is important for us now, however, to recognize the existing relationships between social conflict and the development and support of extreme nationalism within certain social groups. It is through this social conflict that the romantic messianic ethos of the nineteenth century can be carried on into the twentieth and into states that are not or that, sociologically speaking, should no longer be essentially bound by the same kind of historical determinants. Lepsius writes:

> Nationalist mass movements break out suddenly but they are founded upon complex and relatively heterogeneous social and cultural conflicts that can be limited and controlled. It is the coincidental coming together of these conflicts that make them dangerous, because then they become unbounded and uncontrolled. The lack of manifest large nationalist movement parties and groups does not guarantee any kind of security in the face of extreme nationalism. Only steady control of latent nationalist structural phenomena that exists in the society can protect against the sudden coincidence of their breaking out.[35]

Complementary to this social conflict is the psychological conflict inherent in the constant flow of change in society. The asymmetries that were talked about above are still evident. The personalized, or what the sociologists Erwin Scheuch, Hans Klingemann, and Paige in their joint study of current right-wing radicalism and industrial society call the primary system of life does not necessarily square with the new technologically dominated public or secondary system. The set of social norms arising out of middle-class or working-class family structure does not prepare the individual for the kind of psychological social decisions that have to be made in a modern kind of technological society.

These conflicts are postulated by Scheuch, Klingemann, and Paige for all Western industrial societies (and undoubtedly take place in Eastern industrial societies as well), and they result in political mass movements that arise in times of rapid industrialization and new economic and social organization. These movements, generally but not exclusively rightist, are reactions against the disturbance of these primary relationships. These political movements are attractive because they promise a resuscitation of these primary kinds of relationships which in their essence reflect certain nineteenth-century moral codes and social forms. The attraction of totalitarian movements is based on the fact that the primary moral system is promised with the efficiency of the secondary industrial system i.e., the moral code will be retained, as will the efficiency of the technological society. Obviously, then, for large portions of the society there is a looking back toward an earlier period, a mythical period of psychological calm and absolute moral verities.

The political movements that result in Western society include the following characteristics: a rigid orientation and value system in private life (often apostrophized as the so-called authoritarian personality, and so analysed by Adorno and Lipsett) and political philosophies with romantic views of a stable pre-industrial society. Groups which are psychologically attracted to this kind of political movement will be at least conservative, and perhaps radical right wing. Remembering the chameleonlike character of nationalism, we can postulate for nationalists in the twentieth century in Western Europe and the United States – i.e., in those states crossing the threshold or having crossed the threshold into Katz's third grouping – a direct relationship to certain sociological groups that maintain a conservative and/or right-radical position in domestic conflicts. Groups that have an imminent tie to the nationalism of the nineteenth century through a continued identification with the historical past of the nation-state or through certain social, or regional moral imperatives that they see as the moral imperative of the nation will be political groups tending towards nationalist solutions for essentially internal problems. These groups need the protection of the vertical national axis, for they are the most threatened by a realignment of value and upward mobility systems inherent in a new historical cycle. For nation-states today, the United States and those of Western Europe and indeed of Eastern Europe and Japan, tend to preserve a privileged economic situation, looked at comparatively on an international scale.[36] This privileged economic position relative to the rest of the world, a world in the throes of unstable chiliastic emancipatory if not expansionist nationalism, is most cherished by those elements of society that are psychologically and economically endangered by the modernity of the new cycle. For in terms of broad historical processes, our modern cycle may have passed the stage of possible modification. The exigiencies of twentieth-century life have called into question many old verities, e.g., the family, especially in its paternalistic patterns; national religious (hypocritical carry-overs from the feudal pre-nationstate cycle); the entrepreneurial principle of economic organization; and indeed the nation-state and nationalism itself (one might even go so far as to label the two great wars of this century both symptomatic and accelerative of deep structural change that marks the end of historical epochs). The identification of certain social groups with some or all of these verities (clusters of belief patterns are the rule) is apparently of elemental

necessity for the groups in question. These groups may be characterized, according to Klingemann, by three types of sociological definition. The already mentioned Adorno-Lipset authoritarian personality,
it is assumed, congregates in these groups. A second type of analysis,
developed by a number of political scientists, defines these groups as
status-endangered groups or of 'skill-mismatched groups' i.e., groups
that are being pressed by political and sociological developments of
their state and feel their position weakened by this type of new development.[37] The described sociological groups are very much susceptible to the international political events which have a great impact
upon their political creed. Talcott Parsons stresses this susceptibility
in his analysis of the right and postulates a further strengthening of
traditionalist ascription. Lepsius enlarges on the identification of
middle-class groups with the glory of the nation: "The self-employed
middle class is particularly susceptible to nationalist tides. . . Its ex-
pectation of social prestige is tied up with the definiton of the nation. . . The middle classes' self-respect is based on its definition of its
own role within the nation and the nation's position among other
nations."[38]

But not only national "glory" is important here. International developments that may restructure domestic, indeed regional, relationships will drive sociological groups with this preordained disposition
towards nationalist solutions into extreme rightist and conservative
political movements into nationalist excess. In this connection Lipset
writes of authoritarian working-class groups. Authoritarian personalities, as Lipset points out, are not necessarily confined to right-wing
parties. They will, however, tend towards the same absolute solutions
for their social group as for their "personal" sector, and satisfaction
will be offered by political movements tending towards "closed" ingroup satisfying solutions. These must maintain the element of "preservation" necessary for "primary sector" appeasement. In both cases
the political movement is "right radical" or "conservative" penchant. The intensity of social stress will probably determine whether
the political movement is "right radical" or "conservative".

In any event, the definition of the political character of the movement depends on regional or national criteria. The integral ideological
force of nationalism, however, and the psychological attraction of the
process of identification with "national" goals is an essential aspect of
this political process. In this sense the "authoritarian" personality

really complements the susceptibilities of status-endangered groups and indeed serves as a positive filter for group nationalist perceptions of internal and external events.[39] Scheuch, Klingemann, and Paige have developed these four characteristics of right-wing groups: (1) they reject existing political institutions and tend not to accept the rule of the game of democracy; (2) they show extreme nationalism marked especially by hatred of outgroups within their own society, which are very often identified with foreign states; (3) they develop conspiratorial theories and a paranoic conception of politics; (4) they are usually orientated towards conservative economic and political ideologies of a nineteenth-century nature.[40] This strengthens our theory that in dealing with nationalism in Western Europe, and particularly in Germany, we are going to be dealing with the types of social group mentioned before i.e., for the most part pre-industrial groups which feel their status position in danger; groups with a strong tendency towards a moral imperative; and perhaps regional groups which also tend towards particularistic nationalism. In all these groups we will encounter a strong element of dogmatism. It is no accident that the *Deutsche Stimme,* the newspaper of the Deutsche Partei (German Party), a regionally strong national grouping centered in Lower Saxony in the 1950s, could state: "The true nationalist idea can really only arise out of a truly understood conservative thought pattern. The one is not possible without the other, anyway not in its true and real meaning."[41] It is not that nationalism a priori is a conservative or right-wing development, but (and this fact seems true of all Western industrial nations) sociological groupings within a nation which would normally support conservative parties and in times of increased social stress radical right parties are also attracted to nationalism. This becomes significant if we postulate the theory that nationalism and the nation-state are losing their functional role within society. Not only is what John Hertz has called the "soft shell of modern states" i.e., their inability to protect the population that lives within them, due to this weakening in the functional role of the nation-state and nationalism. The necessity of economic interdependence and the perpetuation of international wealth differences, characteristic of the nation-state, which many feel is a disaster for the development of the future, calls the national vertical into question.[42] Johann Galtung has postulated, in an interesting theoretical analysis, that the world is already confronted with four growing sociological trends that are in

At least, it toppled this pillar for certain large numbers, albeit probably minorities. Generational and certain intellectual group codes of communication function better over international grids than through the traditional nationalist verticals. The important quantitative questions of percentages of sociological groups involved in these trends has, of course, as yet to be answered. Indeed, Deutsch has shown in a series of studies that quantitatively the nationalist vertical has not as yet decreased in absolute terms in relation to the regional or international.[44] But these analyses based on mail flow, newspaper content, and overall economic transactions do not necessarily contradict Galtung's elite or avant-garde group-orientated theory. Probably, some contacts are qualitatively more important than others; and qualitative intensities of expression, participation, and committment have yet to be assessed in relation to quantity. Deutsch himself would certainly consider nationalist orientations as atavistic.[45]

The second important pillar of nationalism, the manipulative abilities of the elite, are in jeopardy as a result of the development of cross- and transnational trends. It is very difficult to maintain control over technological expertise when this technological expertise has the ability to move outside elite purview, that is, outside the narrow boundaries of the nation-state, and when symbol perception becomes international. Other integrating elements outside of those of pure national goals will have to be developed by nation-states in Katz's third developmental state if they wish to hold the modernist groups. These groups are leaving the national vertical; they clearly belong to the new development cycle, to the non-nation-state cycle, to the forces that are weakening the position of the nation-state and associated sociopolitical verities within twentieth-century Europe and North America. This development is particularly strong among certain European states. The fact is that the Western European states have really not got the power to act as nation-states in the nineteenth-century sense of European development. The fact of lack of power is also an influential variable for the devaluation of nationalism. Without power, obviously, the security satisfying element of nationalism cannot function. Most states in question have obviously become too small a unit for either protection or even the satisfaction of nationally orientated economic goals. And nationalism in its aggressive form seems to depend on the ability to be aggressive; the reality of power is heady, but the deadeningly realistic fear of failure certainly works as an inhibiting factor. Nevertheless, nationalism certainly is not dead. We have seen that as an ideology it has a flexible resiliency and a chameleonlike character. The groups that support it vary, as do in a sense the elites who manipulate it, as does the course of its development. Nationalism was always a chiliastic type of ideological movement. Its problem at the present time, and this is true of German nationalism in particular, is that it is messianic but past-orientated. It is in a sense a historic backflow of pre-industrial nature, into a millenium that never was. It depends for its support nowadays on sociological groupings that are in their essence either pre-industrial, or the protectors of a pre-industrial moral tradition, or aggressive and authoritarian in their psychological make-up. It must place the national vertical in a defensive, protective posture, especially vis-à-vis the emancipatory strivings of the new states and the reformist elements within the internationalist or modernist social groups. It is the ideology of those whose status is under attack and of those who are inflexible as regards the future. It is, as it was in the latter part of the nineteenth century, the ideology of those who wish to hinder the accelerating reform of society, but it is by no means certain that it can command the respect that it did in the nineteenth century. Those who utilize it, however, as the central point of their political spectrum must realize that they are depending on elements within the society which, whatever their numerical strength may be, are not those elements which will strengthen the society in the functional way nineteenth-century nationalist ideology and nationalist groups did, for all the disasters of hyperbole. In addition, if we refer to the matrix of ideas and social groups there is another problem for nationalist political movements: They are hoist with the petard of their integrative ideology. Its past excesses, still impregnated on susceptible social groups, force potential nationalist which, in the European sense that means "rightist" political leaders (in Communist parties as well), to find ostensibly past orientated, ideologically and historically suspect political formulas, that will hold together the disparate conservative, regional, and economic social groups in a political mass movement, and still be functionally adequate for the rapidly developing new social and political structures. Indeed this is the essential problem for German nationalists.[46]

Notes

1. Richard Rosecrance, *Action and Reaction in World Politics*, Boston, 1962.
2. R. M. MacIver, *The Web of Government*, New York, 1947, *passim*. Charlton J. Hayes, *Nationalism – A Religion*, New York, 1960, p. 14.
3. For an introductory explanatory analysis J. D. Singer, "The Global System and its Subsystems", in James N. Rosenau (ed.) *Linkage Politics*, New York, pp. 21–43.
   J. G. Miller, "Living Systems: Basic Concepts", in *Behavioural Science*, Vol. 10 (1965), pp. 193–237 and pp. 337–379.
   A. D. Hall and R. E. Fagen, "Definition of a System", in W. Buckley (ed.), *Modern Systems Research for the Behavioural Scientist*, Chicago, 1969. Indeed for the particularly interested: Buckley, op.cit., *passim* as well as W. Buckley, *Sociology and Modern Systems Theory*, Englewood Cliffs, 1967.
4. J. L. Talmon, *Political Messianism*, London, 1960, p. 25.
5. Talmon, op.cit., p. 242.
6. Cf. Hans Kohn, *The Age of Nationalism*, New York, 1962, For de Tocqueville, p. 41.
   H. R. Carr, *Nationalism and After*, London, 1946, pp. 9 and 10.
   Compare for the role of anti-Communism in Germany's contemporary nationalism:
   K. P. Wallraven, "Nationalismus und Rechtsradikalismus", in *Neue Politische Literatur*, H. 3, 1969, pp. 321–343, especially p. 323.
7. Hans Kohn, *The Mind of Germany*, New York, 1960, pp. 128–143. Talmon, op.cit., p. 478.
8. Kohn, *The Idea of Nationalism*, New York 1943, p. 136 Boyd, C. Schaefer, *Nationalism, Myth and Reality*, London, 1955, pp. 84 and 261.
9. Hayes, op.cit., pp. 154–180.
10. For a German analysis of social change cf. W. Zapf, (ed.), *Theorien des Sozialen Wandels*, Cologne 1970, especially the introduction dealing with the work of Martindale, Lockwood, Dahrendorf, and Parsons. Parsons' considerations of normative cultural changes have been more intellectually inspirational for much of our theoretical discussion here than the more institutionally or even elite bound analysis.
11. Gilbert Ziebura, "Die Legende der Erbfeindschaft", unpubl. ms., Otto-Suhr-Institut, Berlin, *passim*.
12. Talmon, op.cit., pp. 513–514.
13. Kohn, *The Age of Nationalism*, New York, 1962, pp. 11–12.
14. Quoted by E. H. Carr, op.cit., p. 3
15. The ubiquity of the phenomenon is illustrated by the Indian philosopher R. Tagor's repetition of much the same definition. Sir Tagor writing in 1917: "The idea of the nation is one of the most powerful anaesthetics that man has invented. Under the influence of its fumes the whole people can carry out its systematic

programme of the most virulent self-seeking without being in the least aware of its moral perversion, in fact feeling dangerously resentful if it is pointed out."

16. Hugh Seton Watson, *Nationalism Old and New*, Sydney, 1965, p. 13.

17. K. W. Deutsch, "Nation Building and National Development — Some Issue for Political Research", in: K. Deutsch and William J. Foltz, *Nation Building*, New York, 1966.

Deutsch, "The Growth of Nations. Some recurrent patterns of political and social integration," in *World Politics*, Vol. V, January 1953, pp. 171 and 172.

Deutsch, "Social Mobilisation and Political Development", "*Yale Papers on Political Science*, No. 2, September 1961, pp. 443 and 444.

Others of course have presented cyclical theories of historical development: Polybius, Machiavelli, Pareto, Sorokin, Toynbee, etc. Deutsch however attempts rigorous quantification of these long-term historical processes and with some measure of success.

18. Deutsch, "Nation Building", op.cit., p. 6.

19. Deutsch, "Nation and World", *American Political Association Paper*, New York, February, September 9th, 1966, unpubl. ms., p. 7 and footnote 14.

20. Deutsch, "The Growth", op.cit., pp. 169–172. For a study of communication codes and grids cf. Deutsch, *The Nerves of Government, New York*, 1959 and Deutsch, "Communication Codes for Organizing Information", *Behavioural Science*, Vol. 11, No. 1, January 1966, *passim*.

21. Cf. Reinhard Bendix, "Pre-conditions of Development. A Comparison of Japan and Germany", in: *Aspects of Change in Modern Japan*, edited by R. P. Door, Princeton, 1967, p. 31.

Cf. as well Karl Deutsch, *Nationalism and Social Communications*, New York, 1953, p. 52.

22. Deutsch, *Nationalism and Social Communications*, pp. 18–22 and p. 49.

23. Deutsch and H. Weilenmann, "The Social Roots of Swiss National Identity", *Yale German Review*, Spring 1966 and "The Swiss City Canton — a Political Adventure", *Comparative Studies in Society and History*, Vol. VII, No. 4, July 1965, The Hague.

24. D. Katz, "Nationalism and Strategies of International Conflict Resolution",

25. Deutsch, *Nationalism and Social Communications*, p. 152.

in: Herbert C. Kelman, *International Behaviour*, New York 1966, pp. 358–359.

26. Deutsch, "Nation and World", p. 18.

27. Cf. Deutsch, *Symbols and Society. Conference on Science, Philosophy and Religion*, New York 1955. Deutsch, "International Communication — the Media and Flows", *Public Opinion Quarterly*, Spring 1956.

28. Deutsch and Richard L. Merritt, "Effects of Events on National and International Images", in: Kelman, op.cit., *passim*, especially conclusions, pp. 182–184.

29. Deutsch, *Nationalism and Social Communications*, p. 49.

30. Katz, op.cit., pp. 362 and 363.

31. Reinhard Bendix, *Nation Building and Citizenship*, New York, 1964.

32. M. Rainer Lepsius, *Extremer Nationalismus*, Stuttgart, 1966.

33. Cf. Martin Trow, "Small businessmen, political tolerance and support for McCarthy," *American Journal of Sociology*, Vol. 64, 1958, p. 270 ff.

Cf. Talcot Parsons, *Structure and Process in Modern Society,* Glencoe, 1960, p. 226.

Sven Ranulf, *Moral indignation and middle-class psychology,* New York, 1964.

Seymour Martin Lipset, *Political Man,* New York, 1960.

34. Rudolf Haeberle, *Landbevoelkerung und Nationalsozialismus,* Stuttgart, 1963.

35. Lepsius, op.cit., p. 40.

36. Deutsch, "Nation and World", op.cit., p. 24.

37. Cf. Scheuch, Klingemann and Paige, "Theorie des Rechtsradikalismus in westlichen Industriegesellschaften," in: *Materialien zum Phaenomen des Rechtsradikalismus in der Bundesrepublik,* 1966.

Erwin K. Scheuch, Hans D. Klingemann, p. 93.

The political scientists primarily referred to are Richard Hofstatter, S. Stoufer, M. Chesler, and R. Schmuck.

Cf. as well T. Parsons, "Certain Primary Sources of Aggression in the Social Structure of the Western World," in: *Essays in sociological theory,* Glencoe 1958, Chap. XIV. For a German analysis of psychological predeliction to nationalism and authoritarianism cf. U. Beckmann and H. E. Richter, "Studie ueber das Selbstbild der NPD-Anhaenger," unpubl. ms., and references to it in *Spiegel* 152/68, pp. 32 and 33.

38. Lepsius, op.cit., p. 17.

39. S. M. Lipset, op.cit., particularly Chapter IV. For a different interpretation of authoritarian personalities leading to a study of dogmatism M. Rokeach, *The Open and Closed Mind,* New York, 1960.

40. Scheuch, Klingemann and Paige, op.cit., p. 92.

41. H. Meyn, *Die Deutsche Partei,* Duesseldorf, 1965, p. 130.

42. Deutsch, "Nation and World," pp. 23–28.

43. Johann Galtung, "On the future of the international system," in: *Journal of Peace Research,* 1967, Vol. 4 Robert Jungk and Johann Galtung, eds. *Mankind 2000,* New York, 1968.

44. K. W. Deutsch, C. I. Bliss, A. Eckstein, "Population sovereignty and the share of foreign trade." *Economic Development and Cultural Change,* Vol. X, No. 4, July 1962.

K. W. Deutsch, A. Eckstein, "National industrialization and the declining share of the international economic sector, 1890–1959." *World Politics,* Vol. XIII, No. 2, January 1961.

K. W. Deutsch, "The Propensity to International Transactions." *Political Studies,* Vol. VIII, No. 2, 1960. Cf. as well for another rigorous interpretation of regional integration.

J. Nye, "Patterns and Catalysts in Regional Integration," in: *International Organization,* 1965, p. 870, and following.

J. Nye, "Comparative Regional Integration: Concept and Measurement." *International Organization,* 1968, p. 855 and following.

45. Deutsch, "Nation and World," op.cit., p. 23.

Deutsch has written "people cannot live, it seems to most of them, without the nation-state, but in a world of proliferating nuclear weapons, they are unlikely to survive long within it," and Deutsch, *Nationalism and its Alternatives*, New York, 1970.

46. For a complete bibliography on "Nationalism and National Development," cf. Merritt and Deutsch, *Nationalism and National Development*, New York, 1970. For a complete analysis of the many ideas developed by Deutsch and elaborated here Cf. A. Ashkenasi ed., Karl W. Deutsch, Nationbildung Nationalstaat—Integration, Düsseldorf, 1972.

II
German Nationalism: Its Historical and Sociological Context

Chapter I showed that nationalism has taken on the same general forms throughout the modern period. Nevertheless, the diffuse character of nationalism has made it differ significantly from region to region. One may argue that this was true because of the asymmetrical relationships in social development, the resulting differences in levels of social conflicts and the relationships of these levels of social conflict to philosophical and historical antecedents. Furthermore the entire process is complicated not only by atavistic thought patterns on the part of jeopardized social groups but by normatively atavistic elite groups. These elite groups may be primarily responsible for the perpetuation of older thought patterns that contribute to the social conflict within one area. Past-orientated political symbols often have, as in the case of diffuse nationalism, an integrative effect. Conflicts, insoluble within existing political and social structures, are defused by functionally irrelevant identification processes. Conflicting groups are superficially united under emotionalist banners. All of these phenomena, when added together, contribute to the intensity of nationalism within the national vertical. In the case of Germany there seems to be no doubt that the national principle was developed to its most intense form and that its integrative effect on German society was paramount. No matter how nationalism is defined, the German example of the phenomenon must be treated as a most volatile and/or extreme element of a universal philosophical and social phenomenon. Fritz Stern defines excessive nationalism as a function of Western cultural pessimism. He writes: "The success of National Socialism in Germany should not obscure the fact that the nationalist attack on modern culture is a general Western phenomenon that preceded and has outlived National Socialism."[1] But Stern is also forced to write: "Although the conservative revolution was a European phenomenon, only in Germany did it become a decisive intellectual and political force. I believe that this particular reaction to modernity was deeply embedded in German thought and society and that this curiously idealistic unpolitical discontent constitutes the main link between all that is venerable and great in the German past and the triumph of National Socialism."[2] Hans Kohn also draws certain invidious comparisons between German nationalism and other nationalisms.[3] Karl Deutsch ascribes to the German pattern a certain universality; however, Deutsch maintains that Germany more rigorously closed its channels of communication to outside thought patterns. This was particularly true, according to Deutsch, in the period of extreme nationalism under National Socialism. Deutsch writes: "Social scientists could point out or predict what has perhaps been least often described, the cumulative impact of all the changes in social communication over time up to the loss of the ability to assimilate experience i.e., up to collective insanity careening to national destruction. Germany in the 1930s and 1940s followed this path farther and with more bitter consequences than any other nation has done thus far, and so in their own way did most of the German minorities in Eastern Europe, but neither the path nor the results were peculiarly German."[4] What we have in German nationalism, which is certainly central to the development in Germany in the period from 1800 to the present, is an exaggeration of a dominant universal trend. This exaggeration is apparent whether one deals with cultural intellectual patterns of thinking, whether one follows broad historical trends, or whether one rigorously investigates certain sociological patterns. We will try to do all three.

One most important series of historical facts about Germany seems to involve the imminent vitality of the German speaking peoples which allowed them to spread over Central Europe and penetrate Western and Eastern Europe. Huge colonies developed especially in the East. The Germans were never able to consolidate their central European position and their population dominance there into a firm political control; furthermore the political control by others over German speaking colonies exacerbated a sense of historical injustice.[5]

The Germans as a language group and to a large degree as a cultural group were divided historically in two ways. Firstly, the obvious religious division inherent in the Reformation divided Germany very much along north/south lines. Secondly, and this is important for the sociological development of the country as well, Germany was divided along an east/west socio-economic axis. The elements of developing capitalism and bourgeois society that one found along the Rhine and the concurrent bourgeois emancipatory movements were not reflected in the sociological construction of Eastern Germany. Prussia remained feudal well into the nineteenth century. The religious conflict within Germany (Protestant/Catholic) and the conflict between the more authoritarian feudal structures, exemplified by Prussia or the Prussian system, and the more modernly attuned sociological structures of the Rhineland and Wurtemberg made for divisive socio-political conflicts of a relatively unique nature. In addition, as Deutsch and Edinger stress, Germany's economy declined as world trade routes shifted to the Atlantic Ocean and away from the Hansa cities and the other German trading centres. "These unfavourable developments left the German middle class economically and culturally backward as well as politically weak and lacking in self-reliance, at a time when the middle classes in the West were becoming more prosperous and self-reliant."[6] Perhaps the Pietist Protestant acceptance of order devolved from this lack of middle class quality. The prediposition to established order helped to torpedo indigenous emancipatory German nationalism and helped the acceptance of Protestant German nationalist elites.[7] These basic divisions were complemented by the many minor duchies and more or less middle-sized German states that had been established after the Treaty of Westphalia and which often mirrored the basic dichtomies of Germany's development. Moreover, the formal political divisions left Germany, especially along the Rhine, at the mercy of a hegemonial France right at the formative stage of Germany's emancipatory nationalist cycle. The two great divisions, the economic particularism and the political splintering of Germany, hindered a unity of nationalist emancipatory revolt against indigenous elites, right from the start. The nationalist revolt became by and large an anti-French or anti-Western emancipatory movement. This emancipatory movement had everything that these movements have today, even a guerilla army — General Luetzow's famous "Wilde Jagd" or "Schwarze Schar". The fact that this group was practically decimated by German troops made no impression on the legend of free-wheeling emancipatory Germanism. The nationalist movement directed against the Western social and cultural usurper was immune to facts.[8]

It is perhaps an historical accident that the German troops who fought against this nineteenth-century Freecorps were Catholic, whereas the Freebooters were in their majority Protestants. But the Protestant/Catholic break had, according to most historians, fateful results for enhancing the anti-Western tendency within the German nationalist philosophical development. The liberal, contemporary German historian H. Pross writes: "The fact that not the Renaissance of Petrarch or of Erasmus from Rotterdam but the Reformation marked German history led in the sixteenth and deep into the seventeenth century to a sharpening of the internal German conflict between cosmopolitanism and the national swarm and to the removal of Germany from the general European development."[9] However much the Protestants reacted against a European cosmopolitanism that was more strongly developed among Southwestern and Western Catholic Germans, they were not above seizing a conception which was a basic part of German nationalism and of Catholic thought as well. That is the conception of the *Reich* or Empire. Another contemporary German historian, Werner Conze, has written of a strongly marked self-awareness and a differentiation from other nations among the Germans as early as the thirteenth century; this differentiation was part of the conception of Empire in Central Europe.[10] This Empire, of course, was centered in Swabia in Southern Germany. It was essentially an expansionist Empire, especially in the thirteenth century, which attempted to consolidate Europe under the Hohenstaufen. Kohn writes: "These overreaching ambitions of the thirteenth century left their mark upon German history. They prevented the consolidation of a rationally circumscribed German political order. When in the age of nationalism the attempt was made to create German nationalist unity in a modern state, the heritage of the middle ages was revived, and nationalism fused with the consciousness of the imperial mission and with the feeling superiority of the imperial people, the Reich."[11] Kohn maintains (citing the writings of nineteenth-century German historians Karl Christian Planck and Franz Schnabel) that this conception imbued the ethos of the establishment of the German nation in 1870. "As the new Prussian imperial crown had no roots in history, a scholarly legend had to provide them. Sober Germans, among them King William of Prussia, did not welcome the imperial dignity but historians, poets, and publicists provided a halo to the new crown by proclaiming Bismarck's Empire . . . as a legitimate heir of the Holy Roman Empire, the second Reich."[12]

Earlier conceptions of the Reich had to a great extent been developed as a romantic reference to Germany's role in, if certainly not a cosmopolitan Europe, at least a Europa Cattolica. Typical of this poeticized history was the work of Schlegel. Kohn cites Schlegel's poem "The Vow" and writes: "For all his nationalism, Schlegel longed for the days when the concept of the Reich — which he thought the Germans alone could appreciate — and the universalism of the church maintained the appearance of unity among the nations of Western Christendom."[13] This expansionist and ethnocentric conception outlived Bismarck; in fact its virulence helped to push this essentially Prussian politician out of power. With the passage of time the myth of Empire grew to a pseudo-intellectual shibboleth, an *idée fixe* for a whole generation. Kurt Sontheimer, an important contemporary student of German nationalism, has sketched the Empire idea in its various intellectual forms in the Weimar period. Its metaphysical content and its powerful appeal for a people in a central position on the European Continent, a position which could be conceived as either defensive or expansionistic or both at the same time, culminated in Moeller van den Bruck's idea of the Third Reich. Van den Bruck's effusive Germanic idealism had little in common with Hitler's Third Reich but it nevertheless provided part of the eventual mystique of National Socialism. The Empire idea formed one of the basic myth components of German cultural and significantly Germanic political nationalism. This leads us to another element of German nationalistic thought, its *Romanticism*.[14] The same Schlegel who talks about Empire feels compelled to resuscitate the values of the pre-enlightenment age. Especially when the enlightenment is associated with the French, and later in the minds of many German historians of the late nineteenth century with Great Britain, this critique of nationalism takes on political vitality.

A pattern of special liberty has to be found in a pre-enlightenment period. For Schlegel, and for many others, Germanic liberty was of necessity communal The seeming unity and harmonic structure of the middle ages provided a nonrational model. As the contemporary German historian Helga Grebing points out: "The idea of Freedom in

Germany was Christian Germanic, old German, romantic and not part of the Western enlightenment. This is brought out clearly in the works of Ernst Moritz Arndt and Friedrich Ludwig Jahn, who determined the conception of their time more eminently than did such a differentiating patriot and humanist like Wilhelm von Humbolt."[15] Kohn also stresses this attachment to romantic conceptions.[16] This romanticism, as we have seen, influenced nationalism everywhere and contributed to its chiliastic components and its excessive religiosity. In Germany it took a far more volatile and self-isolating turn. What began as a perhaps essential part of a common European intellectual experience of the romantic movement, became in Germany a predisposition towards the irrational and the utilization of a mystique in political affairs. Fritz Stern has indicated how a certain romantic predisposition turns into nationalist excess over the road of cultural despair and anti-modernist pessimism. Stern has written of the cultural pessimists: "They were disinherited conservatives who had nothing to conserve, because the spiritual values of the past had largely been buried and the material remnants of conservative power did not interest them. They sought for a breakthrough to the past and they longed for a new community in which old ideas and institutions would once again command universal allegiance."[17] In addition, as Stern points out, the conservative revolution in its nationalistic garb strove to remedy the social conflicts which were everywhere apparent in Europe in the late nineteenth century and which were especially prominent in the rapidly industrializing Germany. The romantic conservative revolution embraced the philosophical traditions of Germany and the communal myths of the German political culture. The conservative revolution was a rebellion against the modernity and change that lies latent in Western society. Similar thought patterns of conservative idealistic discontent were flourishing elsewhere, but their force was especially prominent and powerful in Germany. Stern's studies of Lagarde, Langbein and Moeller indicated how this essentially irrational nationalist romanticism could span the period from 1850 to 1933.[18] These three examples of the conservative revolution, based on the romantic tradition of what Stern calls a "metaphysical moralistic and thoroughly unempiracal manner of dealing with political questions", reflected "the galling cultural discontent which inspired nationalist phantasies" and elite nationalist phantasies at that.[19] Sontheimer stresses this romantic, perhaps even apolitical, cultural, and intellectual current in German history in his book *Anti-demokratisches Denken in der Weimarer Republik.* It is central, he feels, for the virile nationalistic mystique of this period. Romantic sentimentalism, unyielding opposition to liberalism and socialism, indeed to the rationalism that spawned them both, was basic to the development of German nationalism. It could be used for any attack on rationalist reform or even rationalist analysis, because, as Stern has pointed out, the conservative romanticist revolutionaries "often mistook change for decline."[20] Any recommendation for change, any critical analysis of conflict was unacceptable to the meta-physical romantic conceptions of community. But romantic idealism was political, for as the conservative German political theorist Karl Schmidt ironically pointed out, "everything romantic performs in the service of other non-romantic energies." And as Thomas Mann wrote: "In any spiritual position the political is latent."[21]

The vitality of nationalism and its utilization by governmental elites and by anti-modernists and exclusivist German political movements was to a large part a result of the ethnocentricity and anti-alienism of political conceptions. This romanticized *ethnocentricity* (what Kohn calls "germanophilism") had an enormous influence for the German nationalist process. The extremist nationalism, which is associated with the Nazi period by most of the sociologists, is considered by many of the philosophical historians to be latently existent and certainly in the maturing throughout the period of the nineteenth century. Stern (among many others) cites Fichtes' famous speech to the Germans attributing to it the same romantic ethos that he does to the cultural pessimists. Fichte wrote: "You are of all modern people the one in whom the seed of human perfection most unmistakably lies and to whom the lead in its development is committed. If you perish in this your essential nature then there perishes together with you every hope of the whole human race for salvation from the depths of its miseries."[22] Certainly, the blend of romanticism and ethnocentricity is no better illustrated than by Arndt. Arndt wrote of the Germans' original purity: "The Germans have not been bastardized."[23] Elements of *voelkisch* i.e., racist conceptions, increasingly found their way into the romantic ethic. This element combined with a strong anti-French prejudice, and this too became a component of German nationalism. This anti-alienism was reflected in the German minorities' policy, especially after 1870, towards the Alsatians, the Danes, and especially the Poles. A relatively liberal German historian like Hans Delbruck commented on this anti-Polish policy: "In reality we would like to exterminate all the Poles, but actually we limit ourselves to expropriating several hundred Polish estates and paying the highest compensation. We annoy them with some language regulations, we do not appoint Poles to the better civil service posts and we teach Polish children the German language in an unintelligent rather than an intelligent way."[24] The intensification of this spirit of anti-alienism in the twentieth century would have shocked Delbruck as indeed it probably would have appalled the most virulent nationalists of this age. But the ethnocentrism of the period was a direct precursor to the more abandoned and volatile excesses of the National Socialist period. This germanophilism did not simply permeate the philosophical tradition but was an essential element in the integration of the German nation. Gilbert Ziebura has written that the conflict with France was an essential element of the Bismarckian system. "It arose," he writes, "out of the nature of the Empire. It had to be absolutely irreparable and definitive. The annexation of Alsace and Lorraine was carried out in order to abet this essential conflict with an enemy. In order to justify the annexation the entire arsenal of francophobia was elevated into the position of a national fundamental belief." In addition, the annexation of Alsace and Lorraine made imperative that the *voelkisch* component in the German national conception dominated. In addition, the anti-French policy fitted perfectly into Bismarck's internal and social political concept. The fear of France and its embodiment of the Republican principle could lend justification to the established leadership of the pre-industrial conservative autocratic elite and consolidate the power of the elite already united with the heavy industry and intellectual leadership.[25] This is what Ziebura and other German observers labelled the "domestic primacy of foreign policy." Foreign policy from the so-called middle geographic position meant a foreign policy that was essentially anti-alien, aggressive, and a justification for conservative elites.

The viciously anti-Polish attitudes of the Weimar period were simply an extended expression of this nineteenth-century component of German nationalism. The anti-Semitism of the Nazis was a combination of ethnocentric alienism and irrationalist romantic anti-emancipatory illiberalism. The Jews were emancipated through the Napoleonic movement and the French Revolution. Jewish history in modern Europe was closely associated with that of rationalist liberal principles. If rationalistic principles and especially liberalism were harmful to society, if critical analysis representing the rationalist point of view was alien to society, and if socialism as well as liberalism was an expression of this rationalist critique, then obviously ethnocentrism and anti-alienism were not simply a reflection of the primacy of foreign policy and nationalism gone wild, but also essential elements of the domestic political conflict. Three mystiques, Empire, romantic irrationalism, and ethnocentrism, merged to give the nationalist principle an extreme vitality; this irrationalism influenced the development of a pseudorealistic posture. This is a fourth element of German nationalism, its adherence to statism and to a mystique of power, specious realism and militarism.

It is historically commonplace to show how liberalism in Germany succumbed to the "blood and iron" of Prussian unification. It is important here to illustrate that this did not simply come about as an abject submission to the unification movement but reflected an intellectual predilection for the utilization of power and its romantic glorification by the great minds of German history and literature. Fichte's call for a *Zwingherrn* and Hegel's authoritarian conception of the state were typical. Kohn writes: "But beginning with their greatest nineteenth-century philosopher Hegel and their greatest modern historian Ranke, the Germans have often refused to recognize the demonic character of power. On the contrary, they have surrounded power with a halo of a philosophy which they extolled for its alleged understanding of history and human nature. An understanding, as they claimed, deeper than the superficial Western moralism which, to them, only masked the power drive. In the modern West, people distrusted power and feared its abuse; modern Germans felt an almost religious reverence for power. Ranke regarded it as the manifestation of the spiritual essence and its embodiment in the authority of the state. State and power found in the late nineteenth-century Germany their most popular symbol in the army and the uniform."[26] Prussian discipline received its passport to the less martial areas of Germany through this philosophical relationship to power. Power worship and the idealization of force grew in the same exponential fashion as other elements of German nationalism expanded, along the time line of the nineteenth and twentieth centuries and within the philosophical framework of German cultural history. Although often eventually disappointed by the resultant real domestic power system, many great German minds were responsible for the perpetuation of the myth. Kohn associates Mommsen and Dahlmann with writers like Sybel, Treitschke and Droysen. All of them contributed to this mystification of the power element within the state. All of them considered themselves realistic in their analysis: "Now [after 1848] the intellectuals seized upon the revelation of power, from the *exercise of which they remained excluded* — with typical German thoroughness, and with the enthusiasm of converts to a new faith they overestimated and idealized power and the state. . ."[27]

From the acceptance of a moral imperative of power in politics it is a short step to the writings of Ernst Juenger. Sontheimer stresses this militaristic and heroic nationalist element in the Weimar period. He quotes Jünger: "The war is our father, it created us in the glowing womb of the trenches as a new race, and we recognize with pride our antecedents. That is why our values should also be heroic, they should be the conceptions of warriors and not those of shopkeepers who would like to measure the world with their rulers."[28] Sontheimer writes that national self-expression and national success seemed for many Weimar romantics a direct function of the militant qualities of the society. He quotes Jonas Lesser: "Much of the youth supports war as a basic principle and an ideology and supports it with romantic joy in high and higher tones as something holy, almost a religion."[29] This cross-breed of the so called realism of the German nineteenth-century historical school and nineteenth-century romanticism was particularly evident in the many youth groups of the Weimar period. The paramilitary nature of much of German society in Weimar was surely a reflection of the increased social conflict of that period, but is also mirrored a historical continuance of the philosophical acceptance of violence in politics.[30] There are three historical features that heightened these philosophical tendencies in nineteenth-century Germany and expedited their virulent growth in the twentieth.

Firstly, after 1870 nationalism in an extreme form was a politically viable conception. Germany was obviously powerful enough to encourage and maintain this kind of nationalistic pattern. A certain headiness develops as a result of the feeling of ability. Nations and their citizens feel their oats, as it were, and the elements of anti-British world power conceptions, that appear in Germany, in the late 1890s, reflect the expansion of national hybris.

Secondly, as Conze points out and stresses, Germany was confronted with the constant problem of strong Germanic pockets outside of the Reich. This was true for the entire historical period after the fourteenth century. But it was in coordination with the anti-Polish and generally anti-Slavic nature of much of German nineteenth-century nationalism that these Germanic pockets were remembered and nationalistically re-idealized. This gave to German nationalism in the East a particularly virulent character, and it also gave it a spurious *raison d'être* which Western nationalist states never had. The Easternism that one finds in Lagarde, for example, coordinates well with this relationship to the pockets of Eastern German minorities. Here too it was left to the National Socialists to extend this historical feature of German life into one of brutal population substitution. The principle of conquest was inherent though in Wilhelmine policies; World War I bears that out. The 500-year old phenomenon of large German colonies in Eastern Europe was an historical feature that contributed to the overall German nationalist ethos and galvanized it into concrete expansion.

Thirdly, defeat in World War I shocked the German nationalist ethos and released upon Weimar the conceptions of the nineteenth century in an infinitely more virulent pattern than would have been the case had history not taken a combative path. Paul Valéry, the French philosopher, wrote: "All the fundamentals of our world have been affected by the war [World War I], more than that the mind has indeed been cruelly wounded. It passes a mournful judgement on itself; it doubts itself profoundly."[31] The intellectuals of the victor states certainly doubted themselves and their society — one can see that not only in the writings of Valéry but in the United States in the relative nihilism of Hemingway's *The Sun Also Rises* and *A Farewell to Arms*, and in the lost souls of John dos Passos' postwar novels. But the victors had won. For the losers, saddled as they were with a conception of their own invincibility and the psychologically destructive aspect of the trenches, any self-doubt had to be wiped away by an irrational, hyperthyroid emphasis on all the national principles of the nineteenth century. Psychological instability joined with a shocked but still intact historical cultural pattern to produce an excessive virulence. The Versaille Treaty with its supposed favoring of the Poles simply reinforced the older sentiments. If nationalism had been the major integrating ideological component of the pre-World War I period, was it not that much more of a psychological necessity after the cultural shocks of defeat?

A young German historian, Lutz Niethammer, has described the integrative function of nationalism as the process of removing ideological nationalism from the plurality of particularistic conceptions of order and then manipulating it to integrate the various competing social conceptions within the nation. "The political management of this nationalism is the major integrative aspect for a society with multiple social and ideological conflicts."[32] According to Niethammer, World War I did not really bring a common concept of what the German nation was. The non-accepted defeat and the manifestations of the Versaille Treaty and the inflation following strengthened the emotional factor of German nationalism. In addition, the October Revolution in Germany and the anti-middle class terror in Russia strengthened middle class tendencies to accept this emotionalized nationalism. The old conflict between nationalism and Marxist socialism received a new and volatile impetus in Germany; in addition, the social Democratic Party, which according to Niethammer had given pre-World War I German society a precarious anti-extremist balance, was split by the October Revolution.[33]

Obviously this analysis overreaches the realm of cultural history and the historical imperative (if such a thing exists). The heuristic matrix of the first chapter indicates that the philosophical writing and that the historical events of a century do not simply reflect the accidents of a given set of ideo-political positions, but that the sociological make-up of the state in question acts as a filter for these ideas. Social conflicts and structure help determine the reaction to historical events and the further prosecution of the state's history; they also determine the life and death and intensity of certain philosophical tendencies. For many sociologists the over concern with the philosophical history has seemed to create a mystification of the German national character. Lepsius writes: "These waves of German national feeling can obviously not be explained away through an authoritarian German *Volkscharakter* or by a certain tragic development in German philosophic history, as both are stable factors that are not changeable in the short run."[34] Lepsius feels that it is the structural elements in the society that will answer the question of nationalist excess in Germany.

Lepsius' work *Extremer Nationalismus* is primarily concerned with explaining the rise of National Socialism. During the periods before National Socialism, Lepsius sees German society as if not nonnationalist certainly not extreme in the sense that National Socialism was extreme. The difference between preaching and practice is the essential problem. In order to back up his claim of the relative stability of German society, Lepsius presents charts of election returns for *Reichstagswahlen* (parliamentary elections) between 1903 and 1912 and between 1920 and 1928 which show a relatively constant political split in Germany. Returns of 29–40% for leftist parties, of 41–50% for so-called centrist parties and 12–26% for right-wing parties are

TABLE I[35]

Results of *Reichstagselections* 1903–1912 in % of Votes Cast.

	1903	1907	1912
Right (Conservative)	14	14	12
Nationalliberals Freisinn, small parties	27	31	29
Center	20	10	16
Middle	47	50	45
Left (SPD)	32	29	35
other, especially protest- parties of ethnic minorities	7	7	8

Results of *Reichstagselections* 1920–1928 in % of Votes Cast.

	1920	1924	1924	1928
DNVP	15	20	21	14
NSDAP (National Socialists)	—	6	3	3
Right	15	26	24	17
DVP, DDP Small parties	25	24	24	28
Center, BVP	18	17	17	15
Middle	45	41	41	43
SPD, USPD	40	20	26	30
KPD	2	13	9	10
Left	42	33	35	40

recorded. It is interesting in this regard to make the distinction between conservative parties and either conservative revolutionary or right-wing radical parties. This dichotomy between traditionalist and/or conservative rightist politics and rightwing radicalism will be of even greater concern to us in the post-World War II period.[36] Kurt P. Tauber has made it a basic element in his analysis of German nationalism in the postwar period as the title of his voluminous and definitive book *Beyond Eagle and Swastica* would indicate.[37] Whichever way we define rightist politics in Germany during Weimar, the National Socialist period, and indeed in our post-World War II period, the Germanic ideology was one of the traditions that the conservative German elite and the cultural revolutionaries who prepared the way for National Socialism share.[38] This Germanic ideology was a constant philosophical noise impregnating all elements of German society. It could maintain this constant impregnation because of Germany's closed communication system during this period and through the manipulative ministrations of an atavistic elite. Nationalism made the Hartzburger Front possible and provided the cement for the alliance of idealistic, anti-plutocratic, ethnocentric social revolutionaries with the majority, the traditionalist elements of German society and the still intact Wilhelmine elite. Essentially one group always gobbles up the other, and at Hartzburg the traditional Nationalists lent their respectability to the whirlwind. During the Wilhelmine period nationalist susceptibilities helped a traditionalist elite to dominate society. This seems to be the basic element that set Germany off from other modern nations: The susceptibility of the middle class to integrative nationalism, the middle class's acceptance of an elite grouping which did not really represent the middle-class interests. Early in the century Ekkehard Kerr, in his book *The Primacy of Domestic Politics*, stressed the conception of the primacy of foreign policy we mentioned earlier, and maintained that this primacy of foreign policy was simply an extension of domestic social and political goals.[39] The young German historian Heinrich August Winkler in his book, *The German Middle Class between Liberalism and National Socialism*, points out that the social basis of liberalism was simply not strong enough in Germany to penetrate the psychology of the bourgeoisie. This situation was enhanced by the social conflicts arising in certain key historical situations. For example, the depression of 1873–1878 coincided with the development of Bismarcks' nation-state. The middle class or bourgeoisie — the terms seem to be interchangeable in this period — did not have the self-confidence to ride this depression out by itself. The middle class demanded the protection of the new government, and they got this protection in the form of tariffs and the establishment of the bourgeois form of life as the moral imperative for German society, that is for everyone below the birth line of a Junker. They also achieved upward mobility, improvement of their economic situation and prestige which provided a strong cultural and economic barrier against the rising proletariat. Winkler maintains that this fear of being majorized by the working class dominated the German bourgeoisie and many skilled artisans as well, far into the Weimar period.[40]

One of the major reasons for the acceptance of National Socialism by the German middle class was the continued need for a clear security line between middle class and proletariat. Actually this is not a strikingly new concept. Harold Laswell wrote in 1933: "Insofar as Hitlerism is a desperation reaction of the lower middle classes it constitutes a movement which began during the closing years of the nineteenth century. Materially speaking, it is not necessary to assume that the small shopkeepers, teachers, preachers, lawyers, doctors, farmers, and craftsmen were worse off at the end than they had been in the middle of the century. Psychologically speaking however, the lower middle class was increasingly over-shadowed by the workers and upper bourgeoisie whose unions, cartels, and parties took the centre of the stage. The psychological impoverishment of the lower middle class precipitated emotional insecurity within the personality of its members, thus fertilizing the ground for the various movements of mass protest through which the middle classes might revenge themselves."[41] Both Lipset, and the German political scientist Karl D. Bracher have definatively analysed the election returns of the last years of the Weimar Republic. Lipset's table of percentages of total vote received by various German parties, when compared with that of Lepsius, shows the striking break-up of the 'liberal' middle class parties and indicates as well that a considerable percentage of conservatives also moved to the Nazi party.[42]

The conservatives remained right wing. In co-opting middle-class parties National Socialism simply expropriated the so-called middle ground. Whether or not these middle-class parties were ever truly liberal is another question. Certainly some doubts persist as to the Small Business Party and the German People's Party. In this regard it is interesting to study the paramilitary youth group that was associated with the German People's Party, the Jungdeutsche Orden. It was made up for the most part of individuals born around 1890. Many of its members had voted for conservative parties and then switched to the 'national liberal' German People's Party. It was an organization whose membership varied from 35,000 to 150,000, and its members came out of the self-employed middle-class group which we are considering. It is interesting to note that in a group supposedly representing a significant portion of German liberal thought, no Jews were allowed entry. Although its concept of foreign policy was far less virulent than either that of the Nazis or the conservatives — it was after all a paramilitary organization of the Stresemann party — it considered Poland to be nothing but a Versaille upstart and not an equal partner to a German state. This anti-alienism grew out of the ethnocentrism of this organization, which could not conceive of a state's foreign policy but spoke of a people's foreign policy. In other words the *voelkisch* idea had certainly impregnated this middle-class group

TABLE II[43]

Percentages of Total Vote Received by Various German Parties, 1928–1933, and the Percentage of the 1928 Vote Retained in the Last free Elections 1932

| Party | Percentage of Total Vote | | | | | Ratio of 1928 to Second 1932 Election Expressed as Percentage |
Conservative Party	1928	1930	1932	1932	1933	
DNVP	14.2	7.0	5.9	8.5	8.0	60
Middle-class Parties						
DVP (right liberals)	8.7	4.85	1.2	1.8	1.1	21
DDP (left liberals)	4.8	3.45	1.0	.95	.8	20
Wirtschaftspartei						
(small business)	4.5	3.9	0.4	0.3	—	7
Others	9.5	10.1	2.6	2.8	.6	29
Total proportion of middle-class vote maintained:						21
Center (Catholic)	15.4	17.6	16.7	16.2	15.0	105
Workers' Parties						
SPD (Socialist)	29.8	24.5	21.6	20.4	18.3	69
KPD (Communist)	10.6	13.1	14.3	16.85	12.3	159
Total proportion of working-class vote maintained:						92
Fascist Party						
NSDAP	2.6	18.3	37.3	33.1	43.9	1277
Total proportion of increase in Fascist party vote:						1277

and strong Eastern expansionist tendencies were strikingly evident. In addition, hegemonial ambitions were cultivated in this group and others associated with German 'liberalism' as well: the power-orientated attitudes of the Empire League of German Industry (Reichsverband der Deutschen Industrie). Eastern economic expansionism and tough internal anti-Marxism characterized this highly influential, money giving interest group in the 'liberal' DVP.[44] Grebing explains this as the amalgamation of feudal militarism and bureaucratic authoritarianism with the expansionist tendencies inherent in capitalism. She quotes Theodor Schneider: "The conception of state power of Prussian conservative antecedents and the bourgeois economic expansionist drive joined in an indissolvable marriage."[45] The actual groups which waved the flag for this marriage, according to Grebing, were the steel, coal, and iron industries; the ship builders, and owners of shipping firms, businessmen, functionaries, but most avidly the so-called *Bildungsbuergertum* — the academicians and teachers. It is these academicians, of course, that Kohn has examined, and this may be the reason that there is such an anti-German edge to his book. It was certainly the academicians and teachers who led into what Deutsch called the "nationalist whirlpool". They are probably not completely typical of the great mass of the middle class, but this mass could be activated and cooled by Weimar's rising and falling curves of social conflict and through the crushing psychological effects of World War I, a war whose loss was not brought home in a convincing fashion. The importance of the nation for the moral well-being of the middle class and the national identification process of this group was if anything strengthened. The shock of the war may have been stronger for the 'liberal' middle class, than for the conservatives, but no real changes were established in the German social order, and all groups maintained a healthy identification with the nation and an expansionist, nationalist preference. This can be seen in the attitudes of all parties including the Social Democrats to the military establishment. The military was allowed to re-arm through secret budgetary manipulation and was allowed a position of relative independence in the state. None of the parties, with the exception of the Communists, seriously questioned this situation.[46]

A second important point, and this seems especially important for the middle class, was the continued regionalism in Germany throughout the period between 1870 and 1933 (a regionalism which has persisted, however, into the present). At this time Germany, outside key urban centers, consisted of regional particularist societies which identified with the nation. The identification process filtered through the prism of regional social structure. Regional hierarchies and moral verities were left pretty much intact by both the conservative Prussians and later the Weimar State: The social pecking order of the town and countryside was not disturbed, and the mentality of the nineteenth century and its social mores received a secondary defensive social wall through this continual regionalism. The effects of modernization and industrialization were buffered and weakened within the regional grouping. The threats involved were dull, constant, and real, but the order survived and defended itself. The sense of moral, cultural, and status insecurity and the "anticity" complex buttressed this sense of regionalist national psychological imperative. Increased social ferment led to quick extremist reaction.[47]

Regionalism also gave the regional social groupings, through a regional hierarchy, a vehicle with which to identify with the state. When this regional hierarchy was threatened or when, as Lepsius points out in a pre-World War II study of German farmers based on the German sociologist Haeberle, the regional hierarchy loses the confidence of a major regional economic group, an excessive identification with the nation and with extreme nationalism develops. Lipset also has pointed out this factor in reference to Hesse, Saxony, and Bavaria.[48] These regional considerations are an important aspect of the middle-class political construction in Germany, and we find this situation not only in Germany but in other European nations and in the United States. The strength of this nationalist ethos within German society is illustrated by the degree to which it penetrated the German working class. Conze has pointed out how the working class, or in any event the organized working class within the Social Democratic Party as opposed to working-class groupings that remained unorganized, was driven into a kind of anti-nationalist ghetto after 1870. This, however, did not mean that the workers and/or their leadership did not maintain a consistent nationalism.[49] Again this nationalism was part of a certain sociological ethos. It would be interesting in this regard to see just how the German apprentice, journeyman, and master system influenced the acceptance of a bourgeois mentality on the part of much of the German working class. This acceptance was — and is — true for the working class outside of the organized plant workers, and many of the

Social Democratic leaders came up through this craft guild system and many of the so-called leftist voters were impregnated with this nineteenth-century nationalist ethos. It has always been assumed that the SPD lost many of its voters to the Communists during the economic crisis of 1929/33. It would be interesting to see just what percentage of SPD voters may have moved into the ranks of the National Socialists. This does, however, weaken the main argument: It was the middle class, be it established or newly developing in Weimar that was most vulnerable socially and philosophically to extreme nationalism and to the perpetuation of the nationalist ethos in Germany. The point is that although organized workers were inhibited towards supporting this type of nationalism, the social structure of Germany with its regional attitudes and its pervasive nineteenth-century morality made it possible to split off elements of this potentially oppositional force.[50]

This was perhaps more true of the workers than it was of the second group that was inhibited in its acceptance of National Socialism, the Catholics. The inhibited groups, as Lepsius calls them, were the groups that did not identify with the Prussian state as it was conceived in 1870, or were susceptible to the National Socialist blandishments from 1929–33. It is interesting for our study of social groups to understand that some of the same sociological nationalist pre-dispositions were inhibited by milieu-orientated anti- or a-national identification processes. For example, the Catholic middle class was reserved towards extremist nationalism, although subject to much the same influences and pressures as the Protestants. In the case of National-Socialism this inhibition held true as well for some conservative elements of the population, although it is interesting to note that in a rule-of-thumb antalysis one could suppose that the further East one went, the more conservatives followed the drummers of the conservative revolution and National Socialism.[51]

Certainly both the regionalism and the conservative nineteenth-century ethos of the German middle class were heightened by the fact that Germany as a state did not develop functionally as was the case in England and the United States, but that the state was superimposed by Prussia. This point is stressed by Bendix as predicating a completely different development.[52] The atavisms referred to in Chapter I were dominant in the case of Germany. The political superstructure of the Prussian aristocracy and the maintenance of a neo-feudal Prussian social structure immunized the militarism, the primacy of foreign policy considerations, and the attitude towards the East from political dislodgement. Furthermore, the oligarchic conceptions of Prussia, and the traditional and social political privileges of class dominance at the head of the army and bureaucracy were carried over into the institutions of the Empire and Weimar.[53] A strong functional component was thus added to the anti-liberalism inherent in romantic anti-nationalism. The Junkers whose power in the German nation state was thus established were, according to Rosenberg, "experts in local tyranny." They were no longer a colonizing group but retained the same dynamism, and, as Bendix points out, in the Prussian garrison state there was little room for cultivation of civilian manners. This helps account for the militarization of civilian life that exacerbated the heirarchical class and status distinctions of German society well into the twentieth century. (There are still elements of the German military who value a military ethos in the organization of civilian life.)[54] This factor played a pseudo-functional role in the buttressing of nationalism because of the supposed need to defend the established German society and Germany's borders.[55] Although its strength waned in the Weimar period, it was possible for the conservative German elite to maintain its social position in the Nazi period.

The conservative elite made their peace with Nazism through the Harzburg Front, but German conservationism was never as susceptible to National Socialism as was the middle class. This is not surprising in that the conservative elite conceived of itself as a national elite. It was National Socialism which provided the middle class with the ability to share in this atavistic elitism which had foisted itself upon the German state after 1870. Militarism, elitism, anti-Eastern thinking, not so much politically here as in terms of the superiority mystique, all were partly a heritage of the atavistic Prussian control of the German state, as was the acceptance of hierarchical authoritarian control patterns and the primacy of power-orientated foreign-policy thinking. The social crisis of the Weimar period, both psychological and economic, captured the majority of the susceptible German middle class for an extreme nationalist position. The philosophical conceptions of the past provided the essential psychological buttress for the nationalist paliation of the social conflict. The conflict was marked, as the contemporary German sociologist Ralf Dahrendorf has pointed out, by a highly industrial society with low social mobility and a pre-industrial ethos. In addition, the atavist social structure maintained unbridgeable Wilhelmine gulfs between elites and masses in the Weimar period.[56] Conze also points out the insecurity of the most numerous generational segment, the age group born from 1910–13 (the years of the largest population growth). The enormous potentially active age group (15–30 years) provided an additional conflict variable for the troubled society. Three million new voters, between 1928 and 1932, reached adulthood during a period of economic crisis and internal upheaval.[57]

The integrative need for nationalism was strengthened by the historical inconsistencies of German social development and the consequent enormous insecurities these generated. Its volatile nature was a reflection of these inconsistencies and the hyperbole of the nineteenth century. National Socialism profited from all these factors. Nationalism was the feature of German life that the Nazis could manage without actually developing a real social program of their own. Niethammer writes: "The more historians analyse the inner structure of the National Socialist ruling system the more important integral nationalism becomes, not so much because of its ideological content but because of its function for this short-lived regime. Integral nationalism was easily utilizable as a fictitious leadership-orientated political belief system that at least temporarily was able to integrate the different various bourgeois groups and to cover up the failure in solving the social problems that caused these differences."[58]

The key question for Germany after WW II is this: After the crushing defeat which brought home cogently enough the demons lurking in extreme nationalism, can this integral nationalism still function in a similar manner? Correlatively, will Germany once more have to deal with the extremist types of nationalism which have been analyzed? Are past political structures and thought patterns still viable? Niethammer writes that "that experiment in integral nationtalism in Germany left a smashed state, a ruined countryside and an egalitzed social thought pattern; the traditional was torn but not completely broken."[59] However a restoration of sorts marked post-war German political and social culture. Not only the possible but improbable resuscitation of neo-National Socialism will concern us in the following chapters. The possibility of using the integrative aspects of nationalism and so bending this diffuse ideology as to make it again a viable component in postwar German political affairs, will be central to our study. The same social groups that existed in Weimar present us with the conservative middle-class political coalitions in Germany today. It was argued in Chapter I that in the post-war Western political culture it is past-orientated groupings that are most susceptible to nationalism. There is no doubt that nationalism plays its role in post-war Germany. Its integrative strength depends not only on its appeal but on the possibility of its translation into concrete political movements. How intact is historical German nationalism, which social groups are most susceptible, which political movements utilize and profit from this susceptibility? These are questions for further analysis.

Notes

1. F. Stern, *The Politics of Cultural Despair*, Berkeley and Los Angeles, 1961, p. XV;
Cf. G. L. Mosse, *The Crisis of German Ideology*, Intellectual Origins of the Third Reich, London 1966.
2. Stern, op.cit., p. XXIII.
3. Hans Kohn, *The Age of Nationalism*, op.cit., pp. 13 and 14 and *The Mind of Germany*, op.cit., pp. 224–48.
In addition H. Pross, *Dialektik der Restoration*, Olten und Freiburg, 1965, p. 22.
We have already cited John Stuart Mill's deprecatory references in the opening chapter. Kohn goes on to compare Germany with the United States and calls as his witness Goethe, whom he considers the last great representative of cosmopolitan German thought pattern including Lessing, Herder, Kant, Schiller, and Humbolt. Kohn felt that Goethe in the nineteenth century clearly perceived the different patterns of nationalistic thought and of nationalism developing within both nations.
4. Karl Deutsch, *Nationalism and Social Communications*, op.cit., p. 158.
5. Werner Conze, *Die Deutsche Nation*, Goettingen 1963, stresses this feature of German history, p. 22 ff and p. 103 ff.
6. K. Deutsch and L. Edinger, *Germany rejoins the powers*, Stanford 1959, p. 12.
7. K. Pinson, *Pietism as a factor in the rise of German nationalism*, New York 1934;
Cf. as well E. Fromm, *Escape from Freedom*, New York 1964.
8. Kohn, *Mind of*, op.cit., pp. 83 and 84.
9. Pross, op.cit., p. 200.
10. Conze, op.cit., p. 19.
11. Kohn, op.cit., p. 14.
12. Kohn, op.cit., p. 175.
13. Kohn, op.cit., p. 61.
14. Kurt Sontheimer, *Antidemokratisches Denken in der Weimarer Republik*, Munich 1968, pp. 222–244.
Kohn, op.cit., pp. 332–340.

For Moeller van der Bruck see Stern, op.cit., pp. 183–266.
For romanticism and youth movements Tauber, *Beyond Eagle and Swastika,* Middletown, Conn. 1967, pp. 5–7.

15. Helga Grebing, "Nationalismus und Demokratie in Deutschland", in: Iring Fetscher, Helga Grebing, *Rechtsradikalismus*, Frankfurt a.M. 1967, p. 34.

16. Kohn, op.cit., pp. 49–68. The three writers stressed by Kohn are Schlegel, Novalis, and Johannes Mueller.

17. Stern, op.cit., p. XVI.

18. Ibid, pp. XVI–XXVII and *passim*, and Tauber, op.cit., especially pp. 6–12, Footnote 6, p. 1001.

19. Stern, op.cit., pp. 280 and 292.

20. Sontheimer, op.cit., pp. 41–63; and Stern p. XXVIII.

21. Sontheimer, op.cit., pp. 20 and 44.

22. Stern among others, p. 279.

23. Kohn, op.cit., p. 76 and pp. 75–84.

24. Kohn, op.cit., p. 292.

25. G. Ziebura, "Die Legende der Erbfeindschaft", unpubl.ms., Otto.Suhr-Institute, Berlin, pp. 10 and 11.
Cf. as well Conze, op.cit., pp. 32, 33, 79, 80.

26. Kohn, op.cit., pp. 10, 71, 72, 172 and 264.
Cf. as well in this regard the interesting book by Gerhard Ritter, *Daemonie der Macht,* Munich 1948, written under the influence of the destruction of Germany in World War II, and intimate contact with German histiography, Ritter contrasts the continental attitude towards power, which he calls realistic and derived from Machiavelli, to those of the Anglo-Saxon states which he calls insular and derived from Thomas Moore. The German experience, according to Ritter, was the logical conclusion of an extremist extension of continentalism without recognition of the character of power.

27. Kohn, op.cit., pp. 140, 152, 153, 183, 188, and Grebing, op.cit., p. 42.

28. Sontheimer, op.cit., p. 103, quoting Preface to "Juenger" in *Der Aufmarsch,* ed. von F. G. Junge, Leipzig 1926, p. XI.

29. Sontheimer, op.cit., p. 109, Citing J. Lesser, *Von Deutscher Jugend,* Berlin, 1932, p. 143.

30. Tauber, op.cit., Ch. I, footnotes 9, 10, 11.

31. Kohn, *Age of Nationalism,* p. 62 and pp. 61–67.

32. L. Niethammer, *Angepasster Faschismus,* Frankfurt a.M., 1969, pp. 18 and 19.

33. Niethammer, op.cit., pp. 17–21.

34. Lepsius, op.cit., p. 7.

35. Lepsius, op.cit., p. 7.

36. For an attempt at a theoretical delineation between right-wing conservatism and right-wing radicalism see H. Kneutter, "Ideologien des Rechtsradikalismus in Nachkriegsdeutschland," *Bonner Historische Forschungen,* Bd. 19, Bonn 1961, pp. 15 ff.
For a study of German conservatism
K. L. Klemperer, *Germany's new conservatism,* Princeton 1957, *passim;*
for Fascism, Ernst Nolte, *Der Faschismus in seiner Epoche,* Munich 1963.

37. Tauber, op.cit., p. 63, pp. 91 and 93 especially and *passim*.

38. Cf. Stern, op.cit., p. 289.

39. E. Kerr, "Der Primat der Innenpolitik," *Gesammelte Aufsaetze zur preussisch – deutschen Sozialgeschichte im 19. und 20. Jahrhundert*, Hans Ulrich Wehler, ed., Berlin 1965.

40. Heinrich August Winkler, "Mittelschicht zwischen Liberalismus und Nationalsozialismus," here especially the Chapter "Der Rueckversicherte Mittelstand", unpubl. ms., Otto-Suhr-Institute, Berlin.
Cf. as well H. W. Wehler, *Bismarck und der Imperialismus*, Berlin 1959.
H. Rosenberg, *Grossdepression und die Bismarck – Zeit*, Berlin 1967.

41. Harold Laswell, *The Political Quarterly*, No. 4, 1933, p. 374 quoted by Lipset, op.cit., p. 135.

42. Cf. K. D. Bracher, *Die Aufloesung der Weimarer Republik*, Dusseldorf, 2. Auflage 1957, and E. Matthias and R. Morsey, ed., *Das Ende der Parteien, 1933*, Dusseldorf 1960.

43. Lipset. op.cit., p. 141.

44. Cf. B. Johannes, "Aussenpolitische Vorstellungen des jungdeutschen Ordens," unpubl. seminar paper, Otto-Suhr-Institut.
"Gesellschaft und Aussenpolitik in der Weimarer Republik," G. Ziebura, quoting K. Hornung, *Der Jungdeutsche Orden*, Dusseldorf 1958 and A. Mahraun, *Gegen getarnte Gewalten*, Berlin 1928.
Cf. G. Schindler, "Die Aussenpolitischen Wert- und Zielvorstellungen des Reichsverbandes der deutschen Industrie, RDI, im Hinblick auf die zukuenftige Stellung Deutschlands und die Friedensvertragserfuellungen," unpubl. seminar paper.
"Gesellschaft und Aussenpolitik in der Weimarer Republik," G. Ziebura, Otto-Suhr-Institut, based on Walter Lambach hrsg., *Politische Praxis*, Hamburg and Berlin 1926, and Hans Dreger hrsg., *Arbeitsausschuss Deutscher Verbaende 1921–31*.
The papers in the Ziebura Seminar "Gesellschaft und Aussenpolitik in der Weimarer Republik" give an excellent view of the various attitudes towards foreign policy maintained by the political groupings in the Weimar Republic. These papers are available in unpublished form at the Otto-Suhr-Institut in Berlin. They have the publication date 1969/70 Wintersemester.

45. Grebing, op.cit., p. 46 and pp. 43–48.

46. Cf. R. R. Lasicki, "Reichshaushalter und Geheime Aufruestung," in: "Gesellschaft und Aussenpolitik, op.cit., and
Cf. Gordon Craig, *The Politics of the Prussian Army*, New York, 1956, especially the chapters on Weimar for a criticism of the SPD.
A. Rosenberg, *Geschichte der Weimarer Republik*, *passim* and especially in reference to the independent military, p. 102.
For SPD nationalism, E. Matthias, *Sozialdemokratie und Nation*, Stuttgart 1952.

47. Sontheimer, op.cit., pp. 44–53.

48. Lepsius, pp. 18–25, Haeberle, op.cit., *passim* Lipset, op.cit., p. 144 and footnote 16. Lipset's words of caution as to Protestant and Catholic concentrations and to their differing political patterns despite similar social structures are well taken. Lepsius tries to explain this away by claiming that the natonalist principle

was more virulent for Protestants, and indeed this is born out through the last 60 years of German history, but Catholic regional groupings could also suffer the fate of the farmers if they lost faith in their regional Catholic leadership or should the church accept some form of nationalist conservative German government. For a primarily economic interpretation of the agricultural-class support for National Socialists see W. Kaltefleiter, *Wirtschaft und Politik in Deutschland*, Cologne, Opladen 1966, especially p. 42 ff. Undoubtedly this economic insecurity played a role in all the other aspects of heightened farmer insecurity and support for National Socialism.

49. Werner Conze and Dieter Groh, *Die Arbeiterbewegung in der nationalen Bewegung*, Stuttgart 1966, especially pp. 61, 62 and 122–126.

Grebing, op.cit., pp. 40, 49, and 51.

P. Gay, *The Dilemma of Democratic Socialism*, New York 1952.

C. Schorske, *German Social Democracy 1905–1917*.

50. For organized working-class and Catholic inhibitions Lepsius, *passim*, and K. Liepelt, "Anhaenger der neuen Rechtspartei," in *PVS*, 8. Jg., 2. Heft, June 1967, *passim*.

White collar workers, members of the so-called new middle class remained highly susceptible to nationalist blandishments throughout Weimar.

51. Lipset, op.cit., p. 142.

52. Bendix, *Nation Building*, op.cit., *passim*,

and *Preconditions of Development*, op.cit., pp. 48–52.

53. Grebing, op.cit., pp. 44 and 45.

54. Bendix, *Preconditions*, op.cit., pp. 51–61, especially his analysis of the German legal philosopher Otto Hinze and cf. Chapter V.

55. Cf. Kohn's analysis of Weber and Naumann on p. 284, in *The Mind of Germany*, op.cit.

The conception of border defense – a synonym perhaps for Eastern expansion and the so-called middle position of Germany inspired a whole generation of geo-politicians, the most intelligent of whom was perhaps Prof. F. Ratzel, cf. *Erdmacht and Voelkerschicksal*, Stuttgart 1940.

56. Cf. R. Dahrendorf, *Society and Democracy in Germany*, New York 1967 (*Gesellschaft und Freiheit*, Munich 1963) particularly p. 275.

57. Conze, op.cit., p. 129.

58. Niethammer, op.cit., p. 22.

59. Niethammer, op.cit., p. 23.

its continued dependance on the United States for its security, the technological restructuring of German industry and the German economy and a continuing change in the German social structure (a change that began in Weimar) have not been able to eradicate past psychological evaluations and identifications or adherence to a pre-World War II value system from large portions of the German population.

In postwar Germany substantial governmental efforts were made to eradicate at least the most overt and extremely nationalistic elements of the pre-World War II political culture. At first this was done with some vigour by the American and British occupation forces, after 1949 with less aplomb by the Federal German Government. It is questionable if these governmental efforts, and especially those of the Allies, abetted or hindered the establishment of a new set of "value images" within the German population. The important point here is that we have in Germany a combination of spectacular events, the cumulative events, and the governmental efforts. One could then expect over two or three decades, or at least towards the end of the period of major influence by the pre-war generations, a significant shift of some opinion within Germany. This kind of a shift is not definitively reflected through demoscopic investigations of public opinion. Perhaps this is true because, despite some significant social changes in Germany, certain basic mores in certain social groups still remain evaluatively intact. "Men cling to their earlier memories and character. They call upon the support of their social groups to defend their images and beliefs, they distort many of their perceptions and deny much of reality in order to call their prejudiced souls their own."[2] The spectacular defeat in World War II may have had the effect of a kind of stubborn reaction, a re-strengthening of certain older prejudices, especially in the smaller communities and within intact geographical social regions where the association and strong identification with the mores and value images of a region left individuals relatively immune: Immune to the evaluative aspects of the spectacular defeat in World War II, resistent to the cumulative events of the postwar period, and indifferent to and/or resentful of any governmental effects from the national level to change these evaluative viewpoints. Members and sympathizers of various European political movements belong to relatively stable human networks (systems of social contact and information), both formal and informal that resisted the images of change and encouraged the restoration of favourable political images.[3] This is true as well of most stable human social networks. Those networks that were not completely crushed in Germany by World War II quickly discovered their pre-World War II ideological predisposition. This does not necessarily mean that the Germans retained a love for National Socialism. It does mean that all social groups will retain and resuscitate past philosophical or ideological elements of a value system as long as they remain internally socially acceptable. This is particularly true since a repressive suppression function can also be operative in the relation of the perception of events to the value systems. "If messages or memories of our past events do not directly reinforce a strongly held image they may be selectively screened or distorted until they do so."[4] Over a period of time certain, perhaps half-discredited, past conceptions may be resuscitated through the repression of events or their distortion within the perception system. In addition, within the context of a postwar period, events may be filtered so that past conceptions may be reinforced. "Messages about events and policies often reinforce images that people already hold whether by long tradition or from recent experience."[5] The obvious situation in postwar Germany was that the re-establishment of the Soviet Union as an enemy to be feared and the establishment of Communism as an ideological principle to be combatted allowed for certain elements of ideological stability within the German society. These elements of ideological stability reinforced public opinion patterns over a long period of postwar era. The Cold War, the re-establishment of a social structure similar in its hierarchic organizational precepts and economic philosophy to that of the Weimar period, and (for all the incursions of large groups of refugees) the persistent intact nature of regional areas and their continuing particularism (for example Bavaria, Lower Saxony, Northern Hesse, and Schleswig-Holstein) enhanced this trend. Essentially it would be necessary to distinguish between levels and forms of past patterns and reactions to postwar influences. This is difficult, because no real means have been discovered for measuring atavistic ideological principles within certain social and regional groups, let alone developing their relationship to a national political culture. On the other hand, by sacrificing the intellectual rigour of a true system of factor analysis one can arrive at some broad statement about the levels of intensity involved in the reception of nationalist values by the postwar German society and analyze their possible re-interpretation by elements of that society. In addition, while considering the distinctions between conservative national elements and right-wing and extreme nationalist elements, one can also attempt to determine if the national potential within Germany brings with it a special predeliction for the development of an extreme nationalist party. Recalling the diffuse nature of nationalism it is possible to postulate a broad scale of nationalist attitudes, indeed of competing national conceptions. These factors have made the measuring of both nationalist potential and organized nationalist party potential (NPD, etc.) rather difficult. Post-World War II Germany confronts the observer with a society which may very well have been seeking its ideological self-satisfaction in the pre-Nazi, pre-Weimar, Wilhelmine political culture. On the other hand, elements of Nazi thought did live on in the immediate postwar period. This chapter will attempt, on the basis of various public opinion polls, to indicate some trends in the relation of German thought to various complexes of attitude that relate, historically and socially, to German nationalism. These complexes are: (1) attitudes towards National Socialism and its history. (2) attitudes towards foreign policy. (3) attitudes towards foreigners or alien groups which may very well include ersatz alien groups within one's own society. (The Jews in the National Socialist period are a typical example. Some observers feel that protesting students in the latter part of the 60s and early 70s are being placed in this role. This feeling is especially widespread among students themselves. Other observers feel that the guest (foreign) workers in Germany fulfill this function.[7]) (4) attitudes towards democracy of political and social tolerance. (5) attitudes towards the military. In addition to establishing certain trends relating to these five concepts over a chronological period, one can attempt to show the relationship between nationalist potential and the NPD and attempt to show which social groups and which regional areas seem to be most susceptible to this party. A separate section will deal with the rapidly changing attitudes of German youth, especially academic youth, towards these problems.

In addition, three broad chronological periods will be analysed. The isolation of periods is justifiable when one attempts to describe trends. In postwar Germany three distinct periods can be determined: (1) The period of 1945–1950, the immediate shellshock period of social dislocation and economic and ideological insecurity. (2) The period of 1950–1963/4, the reconstruction period of the 'march together' (Gleichschritt) generation. This is the Adenauer era of political, economic, and social restoration. (3) From the middle sixties to the present, with the sudden incursion of 'new' competing ideas and the inherent struggle over the future course of Germany. Needless to say the boundaries between these periods are quite fluid.

A study of German public opinion in the American Zone of Occupation from the period 1945 to 1949 indicated that German national feeling survived the Armageddon that had been visited upon it. In March 1946 residents of the American Zone (which had not been hit as hard in the War) were aware — in their majority — that the problem of expellees from the East would be difficult to solve, but they were more than ready to accept these expellees as Germans and to give them full rights and economic equality within the American Zone. Of the Baden-Wurtemberg population, 71% did not feel that ready solutions would be found to the food crisis, and 78% felt that the refugees from the East would create an economic burden for the American Zone. Yet 81% felt that expellees from the East should be given economic equality, and complete political rights was favored by 74%. In November of 1946, i.e., at a time pessimistic economic opinions were being sampled, 83% of the Baden-Wurtembergers concurred that the refugees should be able to participate fully in political affairs. And in late 1947, 67% of the indigenous residents of the American Zone saw the refugees as full German citizens. This is all the more interesting since these expelees came from areas in Eastern Europe, Czechoslovakia, Poland as well as from German provinces. A feeling of national togetherness and national identification with the East survived the war and indeed was perhaps heightened by the common suffering incurred at the war's end.[6]

The same report shows the percentage spread in the immediate postwar period between those answering samples in a National Socialist fashion, i.e., those responses indicating support for the National Socialist regime per se or revealing an empathy for this regime, and those expressing nationalist sentiments per se or expressions of national justifiation for the twelve years between 1933 and 1945. The study's admittedly impressionistic judgement is that "roughly 15-18% of the adult population were unreconstructed Nazis in the immediate postwar period."[7] This is especially interesting as the figure 15% seems to keep popping up from 1945 to 1968 for potentially extreme nationalists. In specific attitudes toward National Socialism an average of about 7-12% of the population admitted to direct support for Hitler. For example, 12% recalled trusting Hitler as a leader up to the end of the War. As a matter of fact 12% of the respondents would have wished to spare Hitler the humiliation of having to appear before the Nuremberg Trials Commission; 7% admitted to having read *Mein Kampf* in its entirety, and another 16% claimed to have read parts of it. The study shows attitudes towards Hitler notwithstanding that large numbers of postwar Germans in the areas under American control continued to express opinions characteristic of National Socialist and/or extreme nationalist ideology. Nine percent agreed that "a civilian is an unworthy person compared to a member of the army"; 10% agreed "that in all probability foreign nations and races are enemies, therefore one should be prepared at all times to attack them first"; and "if a pure German marries a non-Aryan wife he should be condemned"; 12% agreed that "the horrors committed by the Germans are an invention of the propaganda of our enemies"; 15% "the Communists and Social Democrats should be suppressed"; 18% "only a government with a dictator is able to create a strong nation"; and "this war was caused by a conspiracy between the international bankers and the Communists"; 19% "the German people were the victims of a conspiracy by other nations" 20% "it would have been much better for the Allies to have had a war with Russia instead of with Germany"; 29% "the publication of any book which criticizes a government or recommends any changes in government should be prohibited"; 30% "Negroes are members of an unworthy race"; 33% "Jews should not have the same rights as those belonging to the Aryan race"; 37% denied that "extermination of the Jews and Poles and other non-Aryans was not necessary for the security of Germans"; 52% agreed that territories such as Danzig, Sudetenland and Austria should be part of Germany proper.[8] In addition, in eleven separate surveys between November 1945 and December 1946 an average of 47% felt that National Socialism was a good idea badly carried out. In August 1947 this figure rose to 55% and remained constant, throughout the remainder of the occupation. The percentage of respondents thinking that National Socialism was a bad idea dropped from 41% to about 30%. An ominously high percentage of people under the age of 30, 58%, felt that National Socialism was a good idea badly carried out. Interestingly enough, these people tended to be more critical of the postwar news media with their liberal tendencies, and more likely to find fault with democracy. The respondents were, politically speaking, at least authoritarian-type persons and security-seeking people i.e., people who favor government structures offering a maximum of order and a minimum of tolerance and liberty. In addition, between November 1945 and February 1949, when asked to choose between National Socialism and Communism, on the former date 19% of another group of respondents chose National Socialism, 35% chose Communism. However, by February 1949 over 40% chose National Socialism whereas only 3% chose Communism. A year and a half after the war the opinion survey section of the United States Government classified 21% of American Zone residents as anti-Semites and another 18% as intense anti-Semites, a total of 39% anti-Semites in the American Zone of Germany in December 1946.

In addition to anti-alien and obviously nationalistic sentiments, a strong inclination towards security consciousness was also prevalent and there remained an ambiguous relationship towards democratic principles and democratic structures in immediate postwar Germany. In June 1947, 31% of all respondents chose commercial freedom as the most important freedom, 22% chose religious freedom, only 19% chose free elections and 14%, not even half of those who wished to maintain the right to economic preference, chose free speech. Corollary to this, one third were willing to give up political rights "if the state would thereby promise economic security," and half of those willing to give up these rights would have been willing to give up the right to vote for a political party of their choice. Another third of this third i.e., 11% of all respondents, would have given up the right to read all the books and magazines that they would have wished to read. Interestingly enough, 55% of the respondents agreed that free speech should be applicable to Communists.[9] In their relations to political affairs and to the association with the Federal Republic governmental institutions an ambivalent attitude was discovered, and this ambivalent attitude continues into the present time. Germans are relatively well-informed about political affairs but tend not to participate in the democratic political processes of their country except to vote at elections. This is considered by many citizens as an obligation rather than an exercise of democratic rights. A 1963 analysis stated: "Awareness of politics and political activity, though substantial, tends to be passive and formal. Voting is frequent, but more informal means of political involvement particularly political discussion and the forming of political groups are more limited, and norms favouring active political partcipation are not well developed. Many Germans assume that the act of voting is all that required of a citizen." Interestingly enough, this analysis was stressed in a later study of German youth in the late 60s.[10] In this latter study this lack of emotional support for governmental legitimacy and for the West German institutional political structure is verified again, the same holds true for a study of youth a year later by the Ministry of Youth & Family Affairs.[11] These two studies will be considered later in this chapter. Here it is important to sum up that as of 1949 the German population was riddled with nationalist conceptions, a significant minority still openly adhered to the National Socialist experiment, and a large percentage (undoubtedly the majority) was ambivalent in its relationship to the democratic political process. In addition a large majority was virulently anti-Communist and for many this anti-Communism satisfied a need for social rehabilitation after the war, latent national Easternism, and the virulent anti-alien complex that had come down to them through German history.

Unfortunately the in depth polling of the American occupation authorities ceased after 1949 so that consistent spot checks of trends within the German society had to be left to the various young polling insitutions and to the developing German sociology in the formative period of the 1950s. The best compilation of German attitudes until 1957 is found in Deutsch and Edinger's book, *Germany Rejoins the Powers*. Deutsch and Edinger report that although one could have expected a general concept of postwar trauma in Germany, most Germans did not feel that the war itself was the worst period in German history. When asked in 1951 to identify the worst period of Germany in the twentieth century seven Germans out of ten named the first three postwar years, 1945–48, and only one out of ten named the war years 1939–45.[12] In addition, nationalist attitudes continued to be strong, perhaps stronger than the 1945–49 period, throughout the early 50s. In June of 1954, 38% of all Germans felt that Germany would become once again one of the most powerful nations in the world. In September 1955 though, this percentage dropped to 25% and expressions of pessimism rose from 41–48%. Four-fifths of the West Germans polled in March 1951 declared that Germany should not be content with the present Polish/German frontier, although much smaller percentages were willing to risk either a conflagration or were interested in moving back into these Eastern areas. In April 1952 three-quarters of all respondents maintained that the German claim on the Oder-

Neisse areas i.e., the areas taken by Poland after the war, should not be abandoned juridically, even if earlier reunification could be bought through this renunciation. And 70% reaffirmed this view in polls in June and August of 1955. In addition, respondents between the ages of 15 and 24 years polled in November of 1954 saw "the most urgent future task for us Germans in the foreign policy field as reunification," and reunification was ranked first by 47% in a listing of specific foreign policy desiderata, followed by 22% responding that making sure of peace was most important. European understanding managed to garner only 7% of the responses, as first choice. Interestingly enough, only 1% named rearmament. As a matter of fact the war and its crushing aftermath weakened one major element of the German nationalist construct, the militaristic component. No high percentages are found in any returns, in any groups of the population for either rearmament or utilization of war as a means of foreign policy.

Cognitive evaluations of the Soviet Union indicated a healthy respect for its power on the part of the German population; evaluative responses showed a continuing distrust for the Soviet Union and antipathy for Communism. "German public opinion seemed thus largely united in disliking and distrusting Communism and Communist governments, in fearing and rejecting war, in seeking at least economic and political equality with such other Western powers as France, the United Kingdom, and desiring to remain friends with the United States. Subject to these overriding beliefs large majorities wished for eventual national reunification and less urgently for the recovery of former German territories in the East.[13] Certainly the Germans may have had reason for mistrusting the Soviet Union, and certainly it was easy for the Germans to associate Soviet policy with domestic Communists. Even passionate Socialists like Kurt Schumacher were willing to make this association forcefully and without much qualification.[14] But the important fact was that it was the Communist Party with which many associated the nefarious practices of dictatorship and lack of freedom. The association of unpleasant characteristics of authoritarian political life with neo-nationalist or neo-Nazi parties was watered down and/or repressed. In 1952 the Socialist Reichspartei (SRP) was banned in Germany. This party was obviously a successor party to the National Socialists.[15] A public opinion poll in January 1952 indicated that only 23% of all respondents favored banning the SRP, whereas 43% favored banning the Communists; 32% were against banning the SRP, whereas 35% were against banning the Communists. By November 1952, after the British authorities had given the SRP its share of notoriety, 37% of all Germans were willing to ban the SRP, but by June of 1954 even 55% wanted to ban the Communists. It is interesting in this regard that women were less willing to ban the SRP than were men; the figures were 19% for banning in January of 1952 and 31% for banning in November of 1952. Female respondents were more likely to accept a ban of the Communist Party with 48% in January of 1952, increasing to 62% in June of 1954.[16] These figures are the more interesting since various studies throughout the 50s and 60s have shown that neo-Nazi parties have a predominance of masculine members and are favored primarily by male voters. Women, it would seem, will tolerate neo-Nazi parties, but vote more conservatively. Deutsch and Edinger report that the polls for the period of 1949 to 1956 indicate a steady group of 25% "all-weather democrats" i.e., individuals who reported that they would do all they could to keep a new Nazi party from coming to power, asserted that men who had worked in Germany in the resistance movement against Hitler should be eligible for high government positions, and endorsed democracy in terms implying awareness of shared responsibilities and duties as well as rights. However, Deutsch and Edinger also report that approximately 25% of all Germans during this period were emotional supporters of the Nazis or extreme nationalists, professing predominantly favorable opinions of Hitler or Rudolf Hess or the Nazi youth leader von Schirach. They felt that Germany had lost the war because of the *Dolchstoss*, a new stab-in-the-back legend of domestic sabotage and treason, and they wished to bar from high government positions any man who took part in wartime resistance against Hitler.[17] In addition, anti-Semitism remained persistent within Germany during this 50s period; about 33% of Germans polled in 1952 retained anti-Semitic views. Two fifths opposed legal punishment for anti-Semitic propaganda; 37% said, in December 1952 and again in April 1956, that it was better for Germany not to have any Jews within the country; 30% polled gave unequivocally anti-Semitic responses in 1957. The same upper 30% figure that we have encountered since 1945 called the total of Jews dead through Nazi persecution (in this instance a low estimate of 5 million) "too high."[18]

Germans giving above-average nationalistic and anti-democratic responses were, in general, men, persons with just grade school education, individuals with two to six years of military service, and those between the ages of 35 and 50. Those most inclined to be intensely nationalistic were farmers, men with more than six years of military service, persons with university degrees, in that order. If we contrast this analysis to the Merritts' earlier study, we do not get an absolute correlation. The Merritts' study claims that "the more democratic individuals were those living in large cities, respondents with 12 or more years of schooling, professionals rather than workers or employees, adherents to the Social Democratic Party and middle-income groups."[19] On the other hand, it seems clear that urbanized members of society and those open to cosmopolitan thought patterns and communication grids are less likely to tend towards extreme nationalist views and are probably more likely to support democratic forms or at least to maintain a certain tolerance towards social and cultural pluralism. This analysis is further verified by the later study of Deutsch and Edinger, who found Nazi ideologies to have survived most strongly in smaller social units, villages and towns in Bavaria and Lower Saxony. One could probably add Schleswig-Holstein and Northern and Middle Hesse to these regional areas. Both studies point to a "dualism" in Germany's political culture. It is questionable if, especially in executive and juridical elites, this dualism existed in this form during Weimar. Certainly new is the penetration of some elites by determined democrats. The so-called 45er who came into government thanks to the destruction of National Socialism was ever wary, and the journalists of the allied licensed press maintained strongly anti-authoritarian attitudes. None of the pre-war elites (outside of the military, the church, and to a lesser extent big business) survived intact. And although a pragmatic conservatism was a feature of the postwar restoration, the elite quality and ideological baggage of the 19th century was diluted. Urbanization has continued its steady growth.[20] New as well was Germany's international situation and the organizational intactness of the SPD. New too, as we shall see, was the first postwar generation's political orientation. But before looking at post-45 generation of babies let us look at the Nazi-formed generation.

Important for any analysis of public opinion in the early 60s is a consideration of the views of the German youth of the 50s. Deutsch and Edinger report polls among young people between 15 and 25 in November of 1953, 54, and 55, showing about 10% professing favorable opinions of Hitler and of National Socialism, in other words no astonishing change since the period of the late 40s.[21] In a June 1956 poll of men and women between the ages of 18 and 29, 16% declared that they would "welcome the efforts of a new Nazi party to come to power." One month later in a separate poll of young males, the same percentage declared without qualification that National Socialism had been a good idea.[22] Tauber, writing on postwar youth in Germany, has tried to come to grips with the multiple polling done during the 1950s and into the 1960s. Tauber, basing part of his analysis of the 50s on an elaborate 1956 DIVO poll, reports that 41% of respondents, youths between the ages of 16 and 24, approved of the statement that "we should again have a single strong national party which really represents the interests of all classes of our people"; 42% disapproved. Thirteen percent agreed that taking everything into consideration there was more good than bad in the ideas of National Socialism; 22% felt that there was more bad, and 21% believed that there were equal amounts of good and bad, while a tremendous 44% indicated that they had no opinion. On the other hand the relation of these respondents to a democratic versus authoritarian political structure was not as ambivalent: 62% disapproved of the statement that "we should again have as before a national leader who rules Germany with a strong hand for the welfare of all," 21% approved. Seventy-three percent favored "the pluralistic parliament" while only 13% took an authoritarian option with the chancellor, as opposed to the Bundestag, as the last source of decision between important political questions. To add to the confusion of these polling procedures Tauber cites a report by the German sociologist Helmut Schelsky. Schelsky found that 23% of the male youths he interviewed were authoritarian and 20% pluralistically inclined. Interestingly enough, of the authoritarian youths 34% rejected Hitler, whereas 39% approved of him. Of those who were pluralistically inclined a larger percentage, 48%, rejected Hitler, but 22% still approved of him. Schelsky found an overall 40% preference for a single party state.[23] This result contrasts with a full 56% that a confidential US High Commissioners' poll of German youths between 18 and 24 found, approving the proposition that a strong national one-party state was desirable. Schelsky, at the end of his investigation, writes: "If one selects from the various political expressions of opinion those which answer relatively uniformly, but by no means totally uniformly, in a National Socialist or totalitarian sense we come to approximately 4% of the male youth." Schelsky arrives at this figure by establishing a series of correlations between the various question groups. He further writes: "To suspect that they would form themselves an ideological neo-Fascist opposition to multi-party democracy is a politically and socially absurd judgment."[24] This was written by Schelsky in 1957. Tauber quite intelligently questions the scientific rigor and any definitive results of the various polls. Indeed, no absolute conclusions can be drawn. To complicate the matter even more, Tauber cites a study of values, motives, and orientations of German youth by Walter Jaide in which three separate types of youth are posited: the conservatives with their variant, the naive, forming one type, accounting for 27% and 12%; the disinterested with their variant, the aloof, 26% and 8%; and the searchers with a small number of committed, 24% and 2%.[25] This report, made in the early 60s, holds that the conservatives combine "restorative tendencies with a credulous glorifying way of judging the German past." Although rejecting the excesses of National Socialism, the conservatives generally admire in Hitler "the idealist who wanted the best for his people," with the failure of Naziism being ascribed to "inexorable fate". The real hero of these conservative youths, however, is Bismarck and the favorite period is the Wilhelmine Empire.

The second type, the disinterested, refers to the indifferent group which is too sceptical to accept any kind of political engagement. These people have nationalist elements and do not necessarily adhere to established political parties, but they are democrats in the sense of wishing to participate in the democratic process without being enmeshed in bureaucratized political organizations. Unfortunately no attempt was made to relate these three attitudinal patterns to political activity or political preference and the plethora of polls and polling practices still leave us with impressionistic and qualitative assessment of German opinion in the Reconstruction Period. However, it is fair to maintain that in the population as such, strong nationalist conservative tendencies were maintained, and that these nationalist conceptions were passed on to the younger generation, although in all probability not in the firm, resuscitory fashion in which they were used by the established society to repress the Nazi experience and justify pre-National Socialist living patterns. In the 1950s assessment we again encounter this familiar percentage of between 8-15% of German youth mobilizable for extremist nationalist political activity.

Throughout the '50s survey researchers try to relate anti-democratic attitudes to nationalist attitudes (probably reflecting the influence of Adorno and his concept of the authoritarian personality on the re-established German sociology). Tauber's criticism of the polls and of their lack of true correlations can be accepted. These criticisms can be overcome: a) if polls are used to measure trends over a long pe-riod of time, where the same type of question is asked to the same type of social group; or b) if comparative attitudes are measured with-in one time spectrum in different political cultures; or c) if accurate methods of establishing correlates between different factors being measured by pollsters can be established; or d) if separate social groups within political cultures are compared in relation to their po-litical attitudes and political activity. More sophisticated demographic techniques were utilized in the '60s to satisfy some of these criteria. If we compare these later results with those of the '50s and the late '40s we can perhaps verify the results of the previous period. The In-stitute for Demoscopy in Allensbach combined some of these methods. One question that the Institute asked over a period of ten years from 1954 to 1965 was "do you believe that Germany will again become one of the most powerful states in the world?" Negative respondents in 1954 were 35%, in 1955: 48%, in 1962: 52% Positive respondents in 1954 were 39%, in 1955: 25% (you will recall Deutsch and Edinger reported these figures), in 1962: 19% and in 1965: 17%[26] Here we see quite clearly a drop in the attitude of Germans in their assessment of the eventual power ability of the state. We hypothesized before that a drop in one's conception of the state as an independent and power-ful factor will cause a drop in nationalist sentiment. It is interesting to see that there was no essential difference between the age groups from 16 to 29, from 30 to 44, and from 45 to 59 in the negative re-sponse (53–51%). But it is also interesting to note that the highest percentage of those who felt that Germany could again become a powerful state was found in the group from 16–29 (20%). In addi-tion, the most optimistic response, 20%, was made by the so-called new middle class, employees and civil servants.

In a second question Allensbach asked: "Do you think that we are more talented and more proficient than other peoples?" Negative re-sponse was ellicited in 1955 from 39%, in 1956: 42%, in 1959: 50%, in 1960: 55% and in 1965, interestingly enough, again 50%, a slight drop in the negative response. Positive answers were: 60% in 1955, 56% in 1956, 48% in 1959, 42% in 1960, and a slight rise to 45% in

1965. These positive answers were divided into exceptionally positive and qualified positive, with the qualified positive having a relationship of approximately 2:1 to the exceptionally positive answer. Again Allensbach broke the answers down by age groups and found that here the 16–29 group entertained a considerably less nationalistic viewpoint than the other groups — with 56% for the highest group answering negatively and 30% positively the lowest group by far. The same correlate however could not be completely established for the middle class: the old middle class, the self-employed, answered least negatively with 46%, with 21% the most exceptionally positive, and 47% as the overall positive figure was the only group that surpassed its negative responses with positive responses. This time, however, the other portion of the middle-class group, functionaires and employees, was less nationalistic in its response. Essentially these responses seem to bear out a trend that the new and growing middle class is less open to conservative and nationalist blandishments than the slowly shrinking pre-industrial old middle class. Interestingly enough, regional proclitivites seemed to be non-existent. This may be true because the 'regions' here are far too great a geo-sociological area to reflect wide differences. Within the States: North Hesse, Franconia, and others, more positive correlations would probably be found. The same overall trend towards a decrease in nationalist sentiment was discovered in the question "In which country of the world would you most like to live?" Germany was mentioned by 66% in 1950, and again by 66% in 1954, indicating the pattern of responses from the '40s into the '50s that we discovered earlier in our investigation. In 1966 only 54% responded affirmatively, and here only 39% of the age group from 16 to 29 have affirmative responses for Germany, trailing the other elements of German society. In this answer grouping it was the farmers, with 69% positive, who gave the most nationalist answers.

In 1955, and then again in 1969, Allensbach asked "One hears often that the Germans are not well liked in the world. Why do you think that that is so?" In 1955, 25% felt that it was so because the others in essence envied the positive aspects of German life, for example honesty, courage, diligence, proficiency. In 1969 20% mentioned the positive aspects of German national character as being responsible for German unpopularity. In 1955, 14% denied that Germans were unpopular, 9% denied this in 1969. In 1955, 45% were willing to ascribe German unpopularity to negative aspects of the German national character: arrogance, bad manners, excessive ambition, plus the experiences of the Third Reich. In 1969, 60% were willing to ascribe German unpopularity to Germans' negative characteristics, and interestingly enough the Third Reich jumped from 13% to 38% i.e., the Nationalist Socialist experience was mentioned by almost two-fifths of the respondents as being the cause for German unpopularity. Here again the group between 16 and 29 gave the least nationalistic answers in 1969 with 16% claiming positive national characteristics as being at fault and 63% negative characteristics and only 7% saying that Germans are not unpopular. It is true that of the 30 to 44 year old group, 64% of the respondents mentioned the negative characteristics, but 19% mentioned positive characteristics, and 11% claimed that Germans were not unloved. Here again it was the middle class who gave the most nationalistic answers, especially the self-employed. Admittedly these are not conclusive patterns of responses, but they do indicate a slight decrease of perhaps 5–10% in overall nationalism into the '60s, and they do indicate that the population group between 16 and 29 years of age tends in the '60s to be less nationalistic than the rest of society. As we shall see, the results from polling questions, analogous to these and made over a period of years, will reveal the same pattern when compared with results from the '50s. In addition the old middle class and farmers consistently respond more nationalistically than other segments of society.

A second means of establishing a certain amount of validity for demoscopic analysis is the comparative means, comparing certain social groups in two or three or more countries. This was essentially Verba and Almond's method in coming to their conclusions about legitimacy of political institutions and political participation in Germany. Deutsch, Edinger, McCridis, and Merritt attempted the same thing in comparing elite attitudes in France and Germany. On the basis of a whole series of answers it could be ascertained that West German elites were less overtly nationalist and more overtly interested in questions like European integration. West German elites were also more optimistic regarding this question. In the early '60s, 42% of German elites felt that Europe would be united in ten years.[27] Only 19% in France felt that this would be at all possible. Of course these questionnaires were made out during the height of the Gaullist period in France. Nevertheless it is conceivable that the French elites and the German elites simply reflected certain deep seated attitudes within their own country. On the basis of a table on "friendliness and trust attitudes" in French and West German relations towards four countries, prepared by Richard L. Merritt and Donald J. Puchala, a good case can be made for a stronger popular attachment to Western nations and alliances in Germany than in France. The only country towards which higher French percentages of good feelings are found is, significantly, Italy. In addition, since 1955 German 'attitudes of good feelings' have increased proportionately to French 'attitudes of good feelings'. The period measured here is between 1955 and 1961.[28]

Undoubtedly this German attitude reflects a higher level of mistrust towards the Soviet Union, but interestingly enough, while this high level of mistrust may engage the domestic aspects of German opinion, lead them along nationalist lines and into the arms of conservative political groupings, it tends to counteract active nationalism by making German elites and the German public aware of the relative weakness of the German international position. (Although resentments do help a small minority of the public to an extremist position). Despite polls that clearly show a recession in nationalist sentiment in Germany, extending into the 1960s and, as election returns verified, a decreasing disposition to support extreme nationalist parties, a "new nationalism" seemed to burst upon the German scene around 1965.[29] According to Kurt Sontheimer, its ideological content was a new issue of the same diffuse conglomerative ideas that the rightist Weimar opposition used against the Republic; these were simply refitted to the political needs of the Federal Republic. The only difference was, "Now you call yourself a democrat whereas during the Weimar period you didn't."[30] Sontheimer cites Erhardt's government message of November 10, 1965. As Chancellor of the Federal Republic he declared the postwar era to be at an end. Erhardt's speech was full of allusions to a new role for Germany. Franz Josef Strauss, always on the national conservative wing of German politics, picked up these attitudes and maintained that Germany was being criminally discriminated against. Erich Mende, at that time Vice-Chancellor and leader of the Free Democrats, felt it was time that Germany stopped running round in the hair-shirt of history; and Eugen Gerstenmaier, the President of the Bundestag, brought out a small book under the title *New Nationalism*, in which he appealed to the national awareness of the Germans. This national awareness was couched in national conservative terms, self-sacrifice, obedience, honor, etc. Gerstenmaier included most of the shibboleths of the national conservative movement in his nationalist concept; he was seconded by the CDU Minister for Family and Youth and later General Secretary of the CDU, Bruno Heck, and more ominously by the Secretary of the Interior, Lücke. This sudden burst of nationalism was definitely conservative in its nature; it was probably a reaction to Gaullism, to the détente developing between the United States and the Soviet Union, and to the decrease in national sentiment especially among the German youth, which may have been dully perceived by all of these neo-Wilhelmine non- or anti-Nazi members of the German postwar political elite.

Yet it was not this attempt at rejuvenation of old ideas which caused international and national analysis of German nationalism. Rather it was the sudden emergence of the National Democratic Party as a vote getting factor in German elections. Latent German nationalism, had not frightened anyone until the successor party to the National Socialists appeared to be in a position to enter the German Bundestag. Actually, some of the same people in a similar predecessor extreme nationalist party had already been in the first German Bundestag from 1949–53.[31] Most observers, however, had assumed that this type of national renaissance would not come to Germany, and that if it did come, it would come only at times of serious economic or international dislocation. Immediately a new rash of public opinion polls and studies were made to determine the German potential for an extreme nationalist party.

The first of these and the one which received the most publicity was the assessment by Erwin K. Scheuch and Hans D. Klingemann. On the basis of their series of questions and correlations the NPD could eventually expect support from 15% of the population in 1966.[32] Scheuch's survey showed that 9% of the population desired an increase in the strength of the NPD while 72% declared to be against the party. He allocated from the 19% that were undecided, 7% to the NPD on the basis of correlates and ascertained through affirmative responses to these concepts: (1) efficient leadership is more important than freedom; (2) pluralism in cultural and moral questions is to be rejected; (3) the wellbeing of the entire people is more important than that of the individual; (4) economic nationalism is desirable; (5) the alliance policy as a sort of appeasement policy is to be rejected. (The Weimar term *Erfuellungspolitik* was used here.) The assessment 15% was questioned by the young sociologist Armin Meyer in a report prepared for the Institute of Political Science in Berlin. Using another set of statistical correlates he did not reach a percentage above 9% in his analyses.[33] This academic dispute very well indicates the difficulty — even when rather rigorous scientific methods are applied by the best sociologists in the field — in developing firm indicators of potentially organizable extreme nationalist support in any given period. Nevertheless the attitudes determined by Scheuch and Klingemann are well founded in all instances pro-NPD people i.e., the 9% that wished a strengthening of the NPD, had higher percentages of positive answers to the concepts described above than the 72% who were anti-NPD. This at least verifies the hypothesis that criteria used by Klingemann and Scheuch in determining tendencies towards nationalism and extreme nationalism are relatively valid. Scheuch and Klingemann found that 25% of all their respondents considered current German foreign policy (i.e., German foreign policy in the year 1966) not to represent real German national interests, whereas 59% felt that this statement was not true. Those who felt that whether the form of government were democratic or a dictatorship, the important thing was that a real statesman was sitting at the head numbered 17%; 77% preferred democracy under any conditions. Twenty-nine percent felt that Germans should buy German goods; 68% felt that it made no difference where these goods came from as long as they were good and cheap. Fourteen percent were opposed to pluralism in basic questions of religion, culture and morals; 71% accepted this pluralism. Thirty-one percent accepted independence and the development of a will to freedom as values for the education of children, whereas 19% desired obedience and the acceptance of authority.[34] Interestingly enough, in a later questionnaire made by the Cologne Institute under Klingemann's leadership, more positive nationalist reactions were assessed when relative scales of acceptance and disapproval for these questions were established. On the average, 23% of all respondents agreed strongly with the statement that "The Germans as a conquered people were appeasing the victors." Twenty percent agreed to the statement moderately, whereas 13% agreed weakly. As a whole, then, 56% agreed with the statement. Thirty percent agreed strongly with the statement that "It is bad for Germany that our economy is falling more and more into American hands." Twenty-two percent agreed to the statement moderately; 18% weakly.

Twenty-one percent agreed strongly with the statement "We have nothing against a strong leader like the ones we had before if he is fair and really cares for everyone"; 23% agreed moderately and 14% weakly.[35] In all these instances the majorities spoke out for anti-democratic and nationalist principles. Here again the pro-NPD people had higher positive percentages and much higher percentages when strongly agreeing. What these two demoscopic investigations show is that a steady buzz of latent nationalism is still evident in German society well into our third chronological period; however, any extreme articulation of these feelings will be made only by small minorities, and smaller minorities still are willing to support political parties which proclaim a nationalism associated with the Nazi period. Probably this is true because of the fact that many Germans vote economically and not ideologically in the postwar political spectrum, and because potentially nationalist voters are also likely to be highly security-conscious. This was not necessarily true of the Weimar period.

An interesting analysis that bears out some of the foregoing theories about right-wing radicalism and the population is one prepared by Vigo Graf Bluecher.[36] Bleucher in the fall of 1968 established a group of 4% of the population that would vote for the NPD in a national election. Approximately 10% of his respondent group were friendly towards the NPD. Again we seem to be reaching that disputed 15%. Bluecher arrived at his figure of 10% through the following method: He established that 24% would like to see a party that would be more nationalistic in its attitudes. He established that 6% would rather have a strong NPD than a strong FDP, and that 9% of his respondents wanted a party like the NPD to be much stronger. But this 9% did not belong to the first group that would have voted for the NPD. He also established a group of 15%, in addition, who were nationalists but not potential NPD sympathizers. He found 58% to be absolute opponents of the NPD, and 13% who did not make a clear statement of position. He established the figure of 15% nationalists on the basis of answers to this series of six foreign policy questions: 15% of his respondents agreed that divided Germany is just a playball of the world powers; 16% answered that if war came we (Germany) would be fighting for foreign interests; 16% stated that an alliance of strong European states would bring about Germany's unity. (This is an interesting question since the nationalist element in Germany is becoming more and more interested in a strong European military defensive union.) Eleven percent agreed that as long as the German people meekly accept their division, and the Federal Republic undertakes nothing to change this division, Germany will continue to be faced with its current difficulties; 13% maintained that what is absolutely necessary is a strong reunited Germany and then the unification of Europe; 14% agreed that we (Germany) need an independent German policy free of foreign interests. Bleucher also came up with the interesting information that of his respondents, when asked to comment about the NPD, 83% gave negative appraisals of the party; 12% positive appraisals of the party. Of those who appraised negatively i.e., of the 83% group, 25% mentioned the NPD's association with Nazis, Fascists, and Hitler's policies as the negative factor about the NPD. Only 3% mentioned authoritarian and reactionary policies or German conservative nationalism, and only 3% mentioned cultural intolerance. However, 10% mentioned totalitarian dictatorship, and another 11% fixed upon the overstressing of nationalist goals and big power policies in the NPD program. Bleucher also compared reactions over a time period. He used Emnid (a polling organization) statistics from the period 1953 to 1968 (August). In 1953, 12% of the respondents would have supported a man like Hitler; in 1958: 10%; in 1963: 5%; in 1965: 4%; and in 1967: 4%. By 1968 the positive figure had climbed again to 6% of the respondents. However, the negative group grew steadily into 1968. In 1953, 67% were opposed to any support for a Hitler type leader; in 1958: 81%; in 1963: 77%; in 1965: 80%; in 1967: 83%, and in 1968 again 83%. Interestingly enough, and one finds these correlations as well in the study that Scheuch has made, 42% of the NPD supporters opposed a man like Hitler in 1967, whereas 36% were still in favour of having such a man as a German leader. Of the group sympathizing with the NPD but not supporting it, only 11% would be for a man like Hitler, 62% against him. In the nationalist group the average was lower than the overall national average. Only 3% would have supported a man like Hitler, whereas 83% would be against him.

These demoscopic investigations and many others in the period from 1965–67 indicated a continuing significant percentage of Germans (a good guess would be approximately 40%), still acceding to many nationalist precepts. However, the virility of this nationalism was in no way comparable to that of the pre-World War II period, and acceptance of National Socialism had decreased since the 1950's.[37]

In addition, a significant break in the generations became apparent in the period after 1965.

German Youth and Nationalism

There are two important reasons for isolating the under-thirty group in a society for special analysis. Firstly, as the above in this chapter seems to indicate, political and social attitudes, once accepted, tend to live long. In Germany the warped romantic idealism of the WW I generation maintained a political impetus into the post WW II years. The trend studies analysed here previously, indicated that changes in attitudes of society do occur, but relatively less within age groups than in following generations. In coming chapters the importance of age groups and their pre-formed steady opinions for assessing political movements will become even more evident.

Secondly, the age group 18–30 is certainly the most dynamic within a society. Social change seems unthinkable without the thrust of the newly engaged. Indeed Deutsch's process of social mobilization is one that constantly applies to youth. An analysis of the youth and its leadership and/or academic elite seems indispensable for an assessment of future social trends and stability. Certainly the *Sturm and Drang* of German youth has been a major historical factor in German development. The nationalist excesses of the past depended in no small measure on the elitist romanticism of the young.

Tauber, in his analysis of postwar German youth, points to a decline in the membership of overtly nationalist and *voelkisch* (folk centered, quasi racist) German youth groups in the '60s.[38] Here again, trends seem to be more important than the amount of members that can be established for nationalist youth groups. Tauber calls attempts to assess membership "the numbers' game", and indeed it seems to be just as difficult to establish membership statistics for nationalist youth groups as it was to establish percentages of the amount of Germans who are truly nationalist, or for a degree to which they are nationalist. Tauber cites the German sociologist Ryschkowski's figure that approximately 25,000 to 30,000 young Germans were organized in overtly nationalist groupings during the '50s. These groups were considered extremely nationalist, of residual authoritarian character and characterized by *voelkisch*, anti-Semitic ideas. Other figures vary from the 30,000 established by the Ministry of the Interior to higher estimates of about 200,000 in the British press. Perhaps the number of youth organized in these groups is less important than their influence on the society at large. There were approximately 56,000 to 91,000 youths organized in *voelkisch* and martially nationalist groups during the Weimar Republic. On the other hand, it is obvious that nationalist and *voelkisch* ideas permeated most of the other youth groups of the Weimar Republic at the same time. This is certainly not true of non-nationalist youth groups in the postwar period. It was established above that there was not a great distinction between young people in the '50s and the German population at large. The relatively large number of nationalist, organized youths during this period should not come as a great surprise. In addition, the level of nationalist agitation in refugee youth groups was certainly an important factor. (If the extremist nationalist newspapers of these organizations are any indication, the relationship between these homeland-stressing organizations and youthful German nationalism is probably a positive one.)[39] The question is, of course, how much the youth of these organizations has been permanently influenced. No complete studies have been made on this problem. None of the foregoing changes the fact that membership figures of national youth organizations have declined rapidly in the 1960s. Tauber estimates approximate 6,000 youngsters still in overtly nationalist youth groups.[40]

Scheuch's study, however, provided an exception to the trend that we have observed. Scheuch maintains that the NPD was particularly attractive for young people between the ages of 18 and 21: "Until this time no radical party had been as attractive to young people between the ages of 18 and 21. Here symptoms of a weakness in our [Germany's] current party political constellation are apparent. Disapproving young people see no real alternative to voice disenchantment. The parties that are represented in parliament are inadequate for that purpose."[41] Scheuch, then, does not attribute excessive nationalism to these young people. He sees their reaction as one of dissociation and protest. As we shall see, the question of the legitimacy of the German government for young people, something already mentioned in relation to Almond and Verba, may be more important than excessive feelings of nationalism in determining young people's attitudes towards organized nationalism. Scheuch reported the group between 18 and 21 as having the highest percentage of pro-NPD respondents, 14%, and the lowest percentage of contra-NPD respondents, 58%. It is hard to see, however, why the 18–21 group should have a percentage so much higher than either the 16–18 group or the 21–25 group, who reported 5–6% pro-NPD respectively.[42] If we look at a series of later studies, this pro-NPD or nationalistic or authoritarian attitude on the part of the young people can be called into question; not, however, the sense of disaffection that enervates them politically. Indeed it may also be that between 1966, when Scheuch's report came out, and 1967, significant changes in the opinion of young people were taking place; Allensbach reports that in the summer of 1966, 57% of the students questioned felt that the Federal Republic had the right to speak for all of Germany (including the East) in international affairs. The report makes a distinction between students and young people in general. Students tend to be far less nationalistic, and far more democratic, in fact radically democratic. Generally they respond in a pattern distinct from (or non-conforming to) the rest of the society to a far larger extent than do non-students. In the summer of 1967 the percentage had dropped to 41%,[43] in 1967 37% were opposed to the statement, in 1966 52%; in 1966 34% of the students were ready to recognize the German Democratic Republic, 56% opposed. Here too a change is in process. In the summer of 1967, 38% gave positive responses, 53% negative responses. Only 46% were ready in 1966 to recognize the Oder-Neisse Line, whereas 47% would not have recognized it. In 1967, 57% were ready to recognize, 32% negative in their response. In the summer of 1966, 41% were not willing to fight against East German soldiers, 39% were willing. In the summer of 1967, 46% were not willing and 37% willing. In the summer of 1966, 54% were ready actively to combat the idea of Communism, and 37% were not ready to carry out an ideological battle against Communist ideas. By the summer of 1967 we notice another reversal with 39% combatants and 54% non-combatants. Interestingly enough, the number of negative responses to the question "Does our parliamentary system function, generally seen, well or not well?" grew from 41% to 48% during this period. Fully 81% of the students tend towards a kind of neutralism in world politics, especially in regard to freeing Germany from Western wardship. These results probably are more indicative of the young people's desire to get on with the new type of society, or at least reform the old society, and an unwillingness to accept the firm reference criteria of the postwar era. This trend as well as the thrust of opinion change analyzed above has been strengthened in the 70s. Certainly the most in-depth study made of the students and youths in Germany in the postwar period is Wildenmann and Kaase's analysis. In this report, made in 1968, democracy scales were set up, similar to the dogmatism scales, although absolutely reversed in content.[44]

Without commenting on the scientific validity of these scales we can say the percentages acquired provide us with excellent comparative material between students, youthful respondents in general, and the society as a whole. (As Youth here is considered everybody between the ages of 17 and 24, the society as a whole includes all citizens of the Federal Republic over 14.) Of the three groups analysed certainly the student group was given the most attention and the student sample (3,000 respondents) was the largest. Interestingly enough, Wildenmann and Kaase's percentages in relation to recognition of the German Democratic Republic display some variance from those of Allensbach, although interviewing for both surveys was done in the summer of 1967. Forty-six percent of the students were willing to recognize the German Democratic Republic unconditionally, with another 36% willing to recognize it under certain conditions. Only 17% were opposed to recognition. Of the non-academic youngsters, 29% were willing to recognize unconditionally, 34% conditionally, and 36% were unconditionally opposed. The figures for the society in general were: 22% unconditional recognition, 36% conditional, and 40% unequivocally opposed.[45] The differences here between Allensbach, and Wildenmann and Kaase are typical of percentage differences that arise in polling practices. One must insist, however, that trends are definable and important, as are the differences that are developing between the generations regarding these problems. Wildenmann and Kaase cross-tabulated their dogmatism scale with answers to the question on recognition and found the most positive reactions to the recognition of the German Democratic Republic under the most democratic or least dogmatic of their groups. This was true as well for the recognition of the Oder-Neisse Line. Of all the students, 58% were for absolute recognition of the Oder-Neisse Line, 38% opposed. Here, apparently, there is no great difference in Allensbach's figures. Among the non-academic youths, 46% were opposed to recognizing the Oder-Neisse Line, 36% for recognition.

On this question, then, as on many others, there are significant differences between youths and students. A brace of attitudes dealing with relative levels of nationalism was tested. The general tendency of youths to be more nationalist than students was apparent here. This was especially apparent when answers were rated extremely positive, moderately positive, or slightly positive and slightly to extremely negative. Youths always were more positive in their nationalism when giving positive responses and students more definitely negative; however, the problem of nationalism probably became mixed up with the problem of independence from the West and independence from the United States. These answers then probably need more investigation; nevertheless the tendencies are relatively clear and there is a residue of nationalist feeling in both groups.[46]

The responses on anti-Semitism are even more interesting in that they clearly show that students are less anti-Semitic than those young people who have not gone to university. In a survey of all youth, 42% answered affirmatively that "The difficulties that arise among peoples in living in cooperation with the Jews are a result of inborn Jewish Characteristics." The positive student response was 19%. That 42% of Germany's youth may still have residues of anti-Semitic doubts seems significant enough since most of these young people have never ever encountered a Jew. This may be a reaction to the excessive philo-Semitism that smothers the German press and TV; thus people feel that where there is smoke there is fire.[47] The brace of questions on National Socialism indicate a major differentiation between students and young people in general (differences of 15–40% in the responses), and a beginning break between young people and the rest of society in their relationship to National Socialism. Nevertheless young people in general seem closer in their views to society at large than they are to the students.[48] A major question for further analysis must be: "How deeply and how fast are student attitudes penetrating the non-academic youth?" As yet no trends are observable. And indeed in the 70s we are witnessing a perceptible increase in political conservatism at the high school level. It is interesting enough, however, to notice that nationalist or indeed any tendencies towards the acceptance of the National Socialistic past do not flow into an acceptance of militarism, or the military. Of Germany's non-academic youths, 46% absolutely refuse to damn a conscientious objector, and this is the highest percentage of responses. Fully 80% accept conscientious objection, whereas only 18% would look down a conscientious objector.[49]

Generally a certain tolerance towards those social matters that pertain to their lives is developing among German youth. In a brace of questions on sexual relationships youths in general gave almost as tolerant responses as students. There are no comparable respondents from the population in general but judging from impression one can imagine that attitudes would not be this tolerant. The only exception is the question of homosexuality where youths in general, probably because they did not feel affected and are not as abstractly tolerant as students, maintain a far less generous attitude.[50] One thing seems apparent: the more one is placed in a minority position within the society, the more democratic and undogmatic one seems to be come. As the youthful subcultures develop, and as identification processes are strengthened between youth in general and those adhering to aspects of these subcultures, one can expect a rise in tolerance levels among young Germans. This attitude is apparent in the assessment of the controversial National Emergency Laws by the youths: 35% felt that they were not necessary, 33% felt that they were necessary. Of the students, 50% felt they were not necessary, 42% felt they were necessary. Nevertheless, the non-academic youth in Germany has still not accepted completely the legitimacy of the democratic process. This is probably true because of the feeling of dissociation from the political process, that a majority still has a feeling of helplessness in the face of political events.

Majorities in every instance are found for feelings of helplessness in the face of the government. These majorities are not as large as those of the whole society, but nevertheless they seem significant. This attitude of dissociation from the democratic process is verified by another study made by the Ministry for Family Affairs.[51] It is also interesting to report the verification of the unpopularity that the military has among young boys. Especially interesting here is the drop-off between 18 and 19 year olds in the number who would be glad to serve in the armed forces, a drop of 22.6% to 4.9%. In addition 30.9% of the 18 year olds and 51.3% of the 19 year olds would serve unhappily; 3.6% and 2.4% respectively would refuse to serve.[52] Generally, the report of the Family Ministry goes into deep psychological detail about German youth and establishes an attentist attitude for youth in its relationships to the government; a mistrustful waiting attitude, especially vis-à-vis political ideologies and opinions. This generation, then, despite the ideological engagement of many of the students, is remaining sceptical. The study maintains that young people adopt an attitude towards the government as an administration dispensing material security, but they do not accept its legitimacy. These youngsters as citizens may develop a childish, regressive attitude if the government is not able to satisfy many of their material claims in the future. Here again we see the verification of trends that we have been able to follow all along: No strong attachment to nationalism or National Socialism, but mistrust vis-à-vis the governmental processes as they have developed in Germany over the last 25 years. For the time being, however, a majority of both the students and the non-academic youth are willing to support parties within the political system despite dissociation from this system.

TABLE I[53]

Party Preference from 1–5 in %

	Students	Youth	Population
NPD			
1	1	3	2
2	1	1	3
3	2	2	5
4	20	30	32
5	71	55	45
No answer	5	5	13
	100%	100%	100%
DFU (now DKP) (Communist & Leftist Socialist)			
1	4	1	1
2	5	2	0
3	10	4	4
4	53	52	44
5	23	36	38
No answer	5	5	13
	100%	100%	100%

Table I indicates high preferences for a Social Democratic Party on the part of young people in general and very low preferences for the NPD. However again in regard to the NPD, students are more engaged in their opposition than the non-academic youth and more engaged than the public at large. The difference between students and non-academic youth is greater than that between non-academic

TABLE I (Continued)

	Students	Youth	Population
SPD			
1	41	45	41
2	36	36	34
3	18	14	15
4	2	2	2
5	0	0	1
No answer	3	3	7
	100%	100%	100%

	Students	Youth	Population
CDU/CSU			
1	26	40	43
2	22	35	36
3	31	16	10
4	17	4	3
5	1	2	1
No answer	3	3	7
	100%	100%	100%

	Students	Youth	Population
FDP			
1	25	8	6
2	33	23	20
3	36	58	57
4	4	7	6
5	0	1	2
No answer	2	3	9
	100%	100%	100%

youth and the population at large. It is interesting, however, to note the strength that the CDU and the CSU have with the non-academic youth. Here a very strong difference develops between non-academic youth and the students, and this is interesting since most of the politicians we cited at the beginning of our analysis of public opinion, who beat the nationalist drum in 1965 and 1966, belong to the CDU/CSU. (The only exception was FDP member Mende who has since been cast from party grace and ended his career as a failure in the CDU.) The strength of the FDP among students reflects this turn in the party's course from a national "liberal" party to a party that is attempting to be really liberal. These attitudes are verified by a similar poll taken for the Ministry of Families, although in this poll the beginning age of questioning is ten so that a very high percentage of "don't knows" was registered.[54] For the time being, however, it does not seem that the NPD has made a great inroad into German youth, and it does appear that this German generation and especially its intellectual elite is less susceptible to the blandishments of National Socialist thinking or extreme nationalism than any previous generation since 1848. This does not mean that eventual social conflict could not affect this generation much as it has others. Economic crises such as faced the non-academic youth of the Weimar period in the extended social conflicts of

TABLE   II[55]

Guest Workers
"Many Guest Workers are employed in Germany now. What do you think of them. Here are some opinions. Which are correct?"

	Youths 10–19 Total n=1699 %	Girls n=832 %	Boys n=867 %
Indifferent to them	44	39	50
Hard working, diligent	24	26	21
Forward	21	17	24
Bother German girls	20	19	21
Take work away from Germans	19	23	15
Vivacious	19	22	16
Poor	17	19	15
Friendly	17	16	17
Primitive	16	18	14
Easy going (light derogatory overtones)	14	13	15
Ignorant	12	13	11
Dirty	12	13	12
Decent	10	12	8
Religious	9	9	9
Easy to like	6	6	6
Modest	6	8	4
Hospitable	6	5	7
Proud	5	5	4
Dependable	4	4	5
Good lovers	3	2	4
No Answer/don't know	1	1	1

the late '20s, and the closing of social mobility, now open in West Germany, might cause a return toward nationalist thinking. The National Democrats have tried to establish the guest labourer as a kind of bogey man for German society. Over two million guest workers from Italy, Turkey, Yugoslavia, Spain, and Greece are employed in German industry. The attitudes of young people towards these guest workers are highly ambivalent as one can see in Table II, a survey of the Ministry of Family and Youth.

The majority of these young people are indifferent to guest workers. Negative responses are slightly higher than positive responses and it would seem that enough resentment can be encountered among the respondents that this particular issue may well be the one in times of social crisis to turn German youth to extremist parties. On the other hand, the same investigation shows that 57% of German youths felt that if a German was in love with a guest worker he or she should marry that guest worker, 38% were opposed. Whether or not this indicates a general attitude to sexual tolerance among German youth, it is certainly a more tolerant position than one would have found during the Weimar period towards non-Germans.

Attitudes towards guest labourers by the general public, again unfortunately based on a separate survey, are less ambivalent. In 1967 a slight recession may have helped 62% of the respondents decide that guest workers would have to be fired; 32% felt the question was one of the level of proficiency of the individual worker.[56] This generational differentiation has not been without a certain amount of conflict for the German political scene. The ideological engagement, especially of a minority of the students, and its expression in street demonstrations has caused trouble. As of late 1968, a cleavage was developing between the society and a significant portion of the students which continues into the 70s. In 1968 Emnid did a study of public attitudes towards student demonstrations. Of those asked, 32% felt that student demonstrations and demonstrations of youth in general (since some demonstrators were concerned about higher prices of street cars, etc., and were not necessarily ideologically motivated) were a distinct danger to the Federal Republic, 33% felt that the demonstrations were a fresh breeze in German politics and should be greeted positively,[57] Interestingly enough, the figures for those under 21 were thus: 17% saw the danger, 52% saw the fresh breeze. As age groups were differentiated the percentage fearing danger rose in proportion to age group. It must be pointed out here, however, that fully 35% of all respondents gave no answer at all, and that this undecided group is probably maintaining a wait-and-see attitude towards the entire problem. Perhaps more important than these figures were the responses to the question of whether or not the government should interfere more energetically with youth in general, or let the young people have their head. 52% were in favour of energetic interference, 26% for more tolerance. Again one notices the same pattern of increased concern with youth demonstrations with age progression. Some observers feel that continued street demonstrations will aid the National Democrats; on the other hand, many of the last major student demonstrations were a direct protest against the National Democrats during the election of 1969. These student demonstrations served to expose the potentially violent character of the NPD, and they seem to have damaged the NPD image among those elements of the German social structure who are interested in a nationalist party, but who do not want anything to do with those more violent aspects of extreme nationalism practised by the Nazis. Therefore these demonstrations alone probably will not add to authoritarian or nationalist popularity in Germany, and certainly not to the strength of extreme nationalist parties. Of course, much depends on the demonstrations themselves, how they are carried out, and what their goals are. It is also too early to say anything about youthful unrest generally. The engaged minority of the students are campaigning under symbols not acceptable to the society at large. The question remains: What are these symbols more than simply accoutrements of protest? How much of the intellectual ferment among today's German students and their obviously tolerant position is simply a reflection of dissociation from the current establishment? Are the protests a kind of mirror image of the Cultural Revolution and pessimism of the past, where everything seems to be happening backwards and where right hands are now left hands? These are questions that — perhaps due to the still rather primitive correlations and the excessive positivism of opinion polls — demoscopic anaysis alone cannot answer. Certainly, however, the nationalist conservative revolutionary element does not play the role today that it played during Weimar, and nationalism does not play the role today in the thinking of German youth that it did in the 1940s and 1950s. But do people have to be active nationalists in order to eventually support a national party or a party of national opposition? If we consider that things other than sentiments or references to past ideas are important as well then we can reject the notion that constant adherence to a body of nationalist thought is absolutely necessary for the success of the nationalist party. If political nationalism is an extension of social conflict, it is still a possibility in Germany, and to a lesser extent a possibility among German youth.

The trends indicate that the tarnished images of nationalism will certainly have to be refurbished if they are to have the impetus in German society in the next ten years that they had in the last 25, to say nothing of the period before that. Our trends indicate that in all our five categories (attitudes towards National Socialism authoritarianism, attitudes towards foreign policy, attitudes towards foreigners, attitudes towards democracy, and attitudes towards the military) the German population in this third post WW II period is less inclined towards nationalist political constructions and/or authoritarian political constructions than they have been at any time since 1849. Furthermore, Germans are no more nationalistic now than people in other Western societies, and possibly less so. In addition, the powerful philosophical conceptions of nationalism do not seem to have taken hold of the postwar generation. This is important if we remember the broad matrix that we posited in earlier chapters. The ideological frame of reference should not be the same as it was even 15 years ago. The intellectual elite of the country should be less nationalistic still. All of this, however, does not mean that there are not powerful national conservative elements in Germany and would-be 'modernizers' of right-wing ideologies, including nationalism, who will try to reverse this trend. Rear-guard actions can be bitter and costly.

Notes

1. Deutsch and Merritt, op.cit., p. 183.
2. Ibid., p. 182.
3. Ibid., paraphrased, p. 153. The authors refer here to the Communist Party, but the same holds true for others.
4. Ibid., p. 145.
5. Ibid., p. 144.
6. All the following statistics are taken from Merritt and Merritt's highly informative study "Public Opinion in Occupied Germany", unpubl. ms., 1969/70, *passim*.
7. Ibid., p. 38.
8. Most of these responses are from OMGUS report No. 19, August 19th, 1946,

"Basic Attitudes Explored by the German Attitude Scale." Perhaps the high percentages are influenced by the fact that 10% of the respondents were political prisoners but one notices many of the same results later in the 40s.

9. Ibid., p. 45.

10. Quoting G. Almond and S. Verba, *The Civic Culture*. Political Attitudes and democracy in five nations. Princeton 1963.

Wildenmann and Kaase, "Die unruhige Generation," Mannheim 1968, unpubl. ms., Lehrstuhl fuer politische Wissenschaft.

11. Der Bundesminister fuer Familie und Jugend, "Aufbereitung und Analyse von Ergebnissen aus der Studie zur Situation der Jugend in Deutschland," unpubl. ms., Bad Godesberg 1968.

12. Deutsch and Edinger, op.cit., pp. 16–27.

13. Ibid., p. 27.

14. Cf. Ashkenasi, *Reform, Partei und Aussenpolitik*, Cologne, Opladen 1968, pp. 14–25 and for SPD anti-Communism, *passim*.

15. Cf. below, Chapter IV.

16. Deutsch and Edinger, op.cit., p. 63.

17. Ibid., pp. 38–43.

18. Ibid., p. 41.

19. Merritt and Merritt, p. 42.

For a more detailed analysis of postwar nationalism see Chapter IV.

20. Cf. W. Zapf, *Die Wandlungen der Deutschen Elite*, Munich 1965, p. 138 ff. and W. Zapf, "Die Verwalter der Macht," in: Zapf ed., *Beitraege zu einer Loesung der deutschen Oberschicht*, Tubingen 1964, p. 105 ff.

21. Deutsch and Edinger, op.cit., p. 40 ff.

22. Tauber, op.cit., pp. 373–386 and pp. 1127–1176 for all cited percentages.

23. H. Schelsky, *Die skeptische Gerneration*. Eine Soziologie der deutschen Jugend, Dusseldorf 1957, pp. 439–440 (cited by Tauber).

24. Tauber, p. 376, ff., citing Schelsky, pp. 434–444.

25. Ibid., p. 383 ff.

26. Institut fuer Demoskopie Allensbach, Sonderdrucke. "Deutschland Unter Alles." Tables 1–4, as well as all following Allensbach information.

27. Deutsch, Edinger, McCridis and Merritt, *France, Germany and the Western Alliance*, New York 1967, p. 245. Cf. as well pp. 213–251.

28. Ibid., p. 248.

29. Cf. below, Chapter IV.

30. K. Sontheimer, *Sehnsucht nach der Nation*, Munich 1966. pp. 7–33, especially p. 23, and Sontheimer, *Antidemokratisches Denken*, op.cit., pp. 317–347.

31. Cf. below, Chapter IV.

32. Scheuch, op. cit., p. 5 for the ominous 15% assessment. Cf. generally pp. 3–28.

33. Armin Meyer, Bericht ueber ein Zweitauszaehlung der Studie "Anfaelligkeit gegen Rechtsradikalismus," December 16th, 1966, unpubl. ms., Institut fuer politische Wissenschaften, Berlin 1967.

34. Scheuch, op.cit., p. 77.

35. R. Kuehnl, D. Sager, R. Rilling, *Die NPD, Struktur, Ideologie und Funktion*, Frankfurt a.M. 1969, pp. 326–328.

36. Vigo Graf Bleucher, "Die Rechtsradikalen und die Bevoelkerung," unpublished address to the Kuratorium Unteilbares Deutschland in Berlin, September 9th, 1968, pp. A 13–A 18.

37. Cf. for a series of responses for the years 1965–1967, that vary between 15 and 58 on nationalist questions and a frightening 58–75% positive responses on questions of anti-establishment attitudes and mistrust of a petit bourgeois nature that are lanced by the NPD:
The report *Die offentliche Meinumg, herausgegeben* v. Elisabeth Moeller und Peter Neumann, Institut fuer Demoskopie, Allensbach, Bd. IV, 1965–67, p. 204.

38. Tauber, op.cit., pp. 366–437, and footnotes 7 and 8.

39. Cf. E. Weick, "Gibt es einen Rechtsradikalismus in der Vertriebenen-Presse?" in: Fetscher ed., *Rechtsradikalismus*, op.cit., pp. 95–124.

40. Tauber, op.cit., p. 37.

41. Scheuch, op.cit., p. 11.

42. Ibid., p. 14.

43. Institut fuer Domoskopic Allensbach, "Student und Politik," Summer 1967, unpub.ms., pp. 56–59.

44. Wildenmann and Kaase, op.cit., *passim*
Cf. for dogmatism scales M. Rokeach, *The Open and Closed Mind*, New York 1960, and
M. Rokeach and F. Kerlinger, "The Factorial Nature of F and D Scales," *Journal of Personality and Psychology*, April 4th, 1966, and
K. Roghmann, *Dogmatismus und Autoritarismus*, Meisenheim 1966.

45. Ibid., pp. 61–63.

46. Ibid., Tables 925–930.

47. Ibid., Table 935.

48. Ibid., Tables 931–934 and 937.

49. Ibid., Table 938.

50. Ibid., Tables 801–884.

51. Ibid., Table 201, and
Der Bundesminister fuer Familie und Jugend, "Aufbereitung und Analyse von Ergebnissen aus der Studie zur Situation der Jugend in Deutschland," June 30th, 1968, unpubl., Bad Godesberg, Tables 22 and 22a.

52. Der Bundesminister, op.cit., Tables 24 and 24a.

53. Wildenmann, op.cit., Table 42–43.

54. Wildenmann, op.cit., Table 405;
Der Bundesminister, op.cit., Table 23.

55. Der Bundesminister, op.cit., Table 26.

56. Jahrbuch der oeffentlichen Meinung, op.cit., p. 265.

57. Emnid, prepared by Siegfried H. Drescher, for Kuratorium Unteilbares Deutschland, pp. A 1–A 13 1968;
Emnid, *Information Paper No. 34*, 1968, pp. 3–5.

IV

Organized Nationalists and Their Struggle For Power in Postwar Germany

One of the major mistakes in the analysis of German nationalism has always been the inability to recognize the varied types of German nationalism and the multifaceted ideological and organizational struggles within nationalist movements. In postwar Germany three distinct types of German nationalists were active in organized political movements. Within these three groups various subgroups could also be distinguished. The first active group was the old-fashioned conservative nationalists. These were mostly political figures who had been members of the DNVP and the DVP, the conservative German Party and the national liberal German Party of the pre-Hitler era. Inevitably these political figures emerged from the right wings of these parties. They represented the traditional Wilhelmine and Weimar German conservative. But the conservative nationalists harboured not only traditionalists, although these certainly were the majority. A second group of conservative nationalists included the conservative revolutionaries of the '20s who had broken with the National Socialist movement and who were able to immediately carry on in the postwar era because of their opposition to Hitlerism and National Socialism. A second major group of politically organized nationalists were the old National Socialists. For the most part, these were men of the middle-Nazi ranks; the small fry who were caught up in the de-Nazification after the war; officers in the Hitler Youth; middle functionaries; military commanders who were not able because of de-Nazification or because of a personality structure which made success in the postwar

91

environment difficult to achieve economic respectability. This group of National Socialists was also made up of two distinct wings: (1) those National Socialists who were willing to reject aspects of the National Socialist experiment, who wished at least ostensibly to work within a democratic framework provided by the postwar period, who wanted to rehabilitate their past and its ideology if not fully restore the practices of the Third Reich, and (2) those National Socialists who desired a resuscitation of a genuine National Socialist regime, who were unrestrainedly blatant in their attacks on the democratic process, who were intent on subverting existent political parties and practices. The conservative nationalists were by and large active in the formation of parties in the period between 1945 and 1948. The National Socialist element begins to make itself heavily felt on the right wing of German postwar politics in the period after 1948. A third group of politically organized nationalists makes its appearance later on in the postwar period about the same time as the articulated swing of public opinion towards nationalism in the '60s became noticeable. These nationalists are the 'modern nationalists'. They are the advocates of a modern German integral nationalism as the ideological cement for a society: hierarchically structured and elitist, managed and conflictless, efficient and undemocratic, technocratic and irrevocably illiberal. They are pragmatic Fascists and are essentially a postwar growth rather than a true blend of the postwar nationalist groups that had organized before. (Although old-fashioned nationalists, especially traditionalists, seem susceptible to this new mode.) They have mobilized the postwar unpolitical ones (not previously organized nationalists) so that these form a majority in the membership and lower leadership ranks of their current, organized Nationalist Political Movement, the NPD. They consider and label themselves conservatives, and in this questionable self-appraisal they have been joined recently by the old Nazis with whom they coalesced.[1] They are especially interesting in that they provide a possible bridge to the major German political parties to the right of the SPD in the Federal political spectrum.

As a matter of fact the lines between organized nationalists in overtly national German political parties and in the major German political parties, including the SPD, were relatively porous during the period before 1960 as well. As a result, an added complication arises for the analysis of the plethora of nationalist political parties that arose during the postwar period. Organized nationalist political groups merge with each other and break apart and multiply like amoebas, and members of various overtly nationalist parties, indeed whole organizations, move without great difficulty to and from German establishment parties. In fact they are wooed and recruited.[2] This meant that nationalist and even neo-Nazi and/or authoritarian wings existed within the ostensibly non-nationalist German political parties. Here the attempt will simply be made to introduce some of the major postwar nationalist political parties in Germany that are typical of the various nationalist groups illustrated above. The least important group for future influence was to be the conservative revolutionaries. Interestingly enough, it was this element among the nationalists that was first active. Reinhold Wulle and Joachim von Ostau were typical of the intellectual anti-Nazi conservative revolutionaries of the Weimar period. These men maintained contact with people like the Secretary of State Erwin Planck, General Kurt von Schleicher, Georg Strasser, and even Colonel-General Ludwig Beck, all of whom were conservative opponents of the National Socialist regime.[3] Ideologically Wulle and von Ostau's politics were not altogether compatible. Wulle's concern for blood-and-land values and Christian idealism squared badly with von Ostau's corporate socialism. Both however were typical exponents of a cultural pessimism, irrationalism, and anti-liberalism which was part and parcel of the conservative revolution. In January 1945, during the last tortuous months of the 'Thousand Year Reich', Wulle established an illegal political organization, the German Reconstruction Party (DAP). With von Ostau's help, Wulle attempted to remould and reinject the precepts of the conservative revolution into the postwar period. On October 31st of 1945 the DAP was officially founded. The ideas of the conservative revolution however were not able to catch fire in a postwar Germany which had had enough idealistic storming. The DAP was obliged to fuse with the German Conservative Party. The German Conservative Party (DKP) was a traditionalist conservative grouping. It had no place for the corporate socialism of elements of the DAP but could accept the conservative idealism of that party. The DKP stressed Christian values, property rights, the organic community with the family as the main social 'germ cell', homelandism — a regional particularism which will be encountered in all conservative nationalist groupings — federalism and decentralization of political and economic power, agriculture as the fountainhead of Germany's strength, monarchy as an accepted form of political life and as the best form of protection against anarchy, and traditional pre-industrial moral values, true decency, etc., as the mark of Germanism.[4] The fusion between the DAP and the DKP joined conservative revolutionaries with assorted traditionalists, monarchists, and agrarianists, and the uniting factor, as so often in the past, was concern for German rights and German nationalism. The party that emerged from the fusion of the DAP and the DKP (the German Conservative Party) was the DRPKV (the German Rightist Party Conservative Union). Illustratively enough Hermann Klingspor, a typical traditionalist conservative nationalist was elected chairman of the party. However, despite the relative moderation of its leader, the party's campaigns throughout the periods of 1946 and 1947 included demands for the immediate granting of independence for the German people and an end to all occupation, the return of expellees to their homelands in the Sudetenland, Silesia, and Pommerania (the new Polish administrative provinces) plus the restitution of all expropriated German property in these areas.

As early as 1946, then, Weimar conservative revolutionaries and Wilhelmine traditional conservatives were counting on appeals to the expellees to strengthen the "national" position. These one-time East-erners, who had been critical for the deveopment of pre-Nazi German nationalism, and who had in the main indicated stronger support for Hitler than voters in other areas in Germany, were courted back into specific German nationalist folds; it began with the inception of or-ganized political parties and continues to the present. Even the Ger-man nationalists' relatively moderate DRP (KV) was banned by the British authorities from engaging in any electioneering in 1947. De-spite this and other harassments by the British authorities the party was able to gain an average of slightly over 5% of the votes in those districts of North-Rhine Westphalia in which it ran, and 3.3% in Schleswig-Holstein. In Lower Saxony the party appeared on the bal-lot in only four districts and gathered only 3.8% of the total vote cast in the land. However, the party was able to garner 10% of the vote in Gottingen in Lower Saxony. Significantly enough one of the main organizers responsible for the success, the chairman of the Gottingen district organization, was Adolf von Thadden, then 27 years old and typical of the rabble-rousing National Socialist rehabilitators that were finding their way into the postwar nationalist movement. The DRP

(KV) was a North German construction; similar movements were encountered in the American zone, for example the NDP of Hesse headed by the traditionalist conservative Heinrich Leuchtgens, and perhape Alfred Loritz's WAV in Bavaria.[5] Essentially these conservative fusions did not survive the creation of the Federal Republic after 1949. However, a party of traditional Wilhelmine German conservatism was successful in Germany from the period of 1946 to 1960. This was the so-called German party with its power base in Lower Saxony.

The German Party began its political life as the Lower Saxony State Party in 1945. It began as a federalist and particularist regional party with strong monarchist tendencies and a strong element of homelandism. Ostensibly it gave up its regionalism in June of 1947 when it constituted itself as the so-called German Party.[6] This change was made to suit postwar conditions and to open the party to expellees and refugees who were moving into Lower Saxony from East Germany and Eastern European areas. But the party remained very much the party of Lower Saxony's self-employed skilled artisans and farmers, a Wilhelmine party of the old middle-class with strong monarchical tendencies. It is interesting to note, however, how from a position of regionalism and traditional conservatism a nationalist party, the German Party, is born. In the eight theses of the German Party, the party emphasizes its regional homelandism but addresses itself to the entire German people and not only to those of Lower Saxony. Every one of the eight theses begins with the word Germany. And the party in its agitation in 1948 and 1949 maintained the ostensibly contradictory elements of regional federalism and nationalism as central to its political raison d'être. In addition, it remained a typical party of the Christian (Protestant) old middle-class North German "flat lands" (plains), but it was willing to engage in volatile support for the honour of soldiers who were returning by now in large measure and for a right of return of refugees and expellees to their Eastern homes. This traditionalist, essentially regional, conservative party, utilizing nationalism as an integrational ideology to gather voters who were neither indigenous to the region nor necessarily economically conservative, was able to do remarkably well in the elections for the first German Parliament in August 1949. It received 17.8% of the vote in Lower Saxony, 18% in Bremen, 13.1% in Hamburg and 12.1% in Schleswig-Holstein, by far the most successful percentages of votes cast that an essentially regional party and indeed that an overtly nationalist party achieved in federal elections in Germany in the postwar period. For ten years after this election, the German Party played the role of the establishment nationalist right within the Adenauer Governments. It remained true to its conservatism, in its support for agrarianism, the old middle class, and private industry, and in its support for Adenauer's anti-Communist policies. It remained true to its conservatism in its official constant rejection of any kind of alliance with the parties of extreme nationalism that were attempting to establish a foothold in the North German areas at this time. The long-time head of the party, Heinrich Hellwege, who was also for some time a minister in Adenauer's cabinets, and who eventually joined the CDU in 1961, rejected any kind of Harzburg Front. Its most prominent propagandist and theoretician, another Adenauer minister, Hans Joachim von Merkatz, produced the clearest idea of the conservative function in postwar Germany. The national idea was, according to von Merkatz, an essential part of conservatism, part of the idea of the homeland. Conservative policies were policies based on the family, on faith and morals, on history and personal freedom, on property and law.[7] But the party also contained as one of Adenauer's ministers Hans Christoph Seebohm who pandered to the expellees and established himself as the spokesman for the extreme right of the German Party. Seebohm acted out his political career as one of the political bridges between the forces of traditional conservatives and more extremist right-wing radicalism. More extremist nationalist groupings were also found in the German Party, but not in the regional stronghold Lower Saxony. North-Rhine Westphalia and Berlin, but especially Hesse, supplied much of the organized more extremist elements in the German Party.

The important fact remains that it was only as a traditionalist conservative group that the German Party was able to maintain its position in postwar Germany. Its strength in the surrounding northern plain areas Northern Hesse, Bremen, Hamburg, and Schleswig-Holstein deteriorated through the '50s, most of it flaking off on Adenauer's broadly based Christian Democratic Union. The party eventually was swallowed up by the CDU, the bulk of its representation in the parliament in 1960 was gobbled up by the CDU. It is a moot point whether Adenauer's restorative CDU had become as conservative as the German Party or whether the German Party had been educated to the more moderate positions of the CDU. It is also probable that the essential Protestantism of the German Party became less of an issue in

German politics in the late '50s. The attempt of elements of the German Party to carry on as the whole German Party in alliance with the Expellee Party (BHE) (more will be said about this party later) failed dismally. (In 1961 Hellwege, for example, joined the CDU.) The party recruited strength from Wilhelmine, security-minded traditionalist conservatives; adventurism was not part of their conservative bag in postwar Germany. In addition, strong anti-Marxism and anti-Communism shut many of the traditional conservatives off from developments within the more extreme nationalist German Parties in the '50s. The neutralism of these extremist nationalist groups, which may have developed as a reaction against Adenauer's success in uniting conservatives and middle-of-the-road Germans in his CDU, repelled many nationalists who might have found a home in one or another of the extremist nationalist parties. The extremist parties were for the most part the work of the second sub-division of nationalists, the old National Socialists. It is of course necessary to point out here that these old National Socialists were not for the most part old; they were young ex-soldiers, ex-SS, and ex-Hitler Youth, people whose ideological convictions had been shaped either by the conservative revolution or by the National Socialist experience in the '30s, or both.

Whereas traditional conservatives looked back ideologically to the Wilhelmine era and were security-orientated, the conservative revolutionaries and especially the young National Socialists identified with many of the strictures of the National Socialist period, even though many of them, perhaps the majority, were to a degree ready and willing to renounce Hitler and the tactics of the National Socialists. They brought with them much of the ideological wash of the National Socialist anti-plutocratic elements, and pseudo-socialistic verbiage, but they were essentially, economically and ideologically, displaced young authoritarian German nationalists seeking political and moral rehabilitation. Their first real success came within the framework of the DRP (KV). In 1947 the young radicals in the DRP von Thadden, Falk, and Schlüter, were able to pace the DRP to victory in the Wolfsburg city elections. The DRP captured almost 70% of the popular vote and this represented an enormous switch from the 75% who had voted for the SPD, the Social Democrats, in 1946. Wolfsburg was not a typical city, it was filled with refugees and expellees, and demobilized ex-soldiers who were about to begin work at the Volkswagen plant. It was the veterans who had voted for ex-military men. "Not one of the 17 suc-

cessful DRP candidates was over 40 years of age."[8] Indeed the previously mentioned success in Gottingen immediately followed this
Wolfsburg election. The same type of blatantly neo-Nazi panegyrics
were limitedly successful in the Bundestag elections of 1949. The DRP
sent five men to the Bundestag including Adolf von Thadden. The
election campaigning and especially the antics of such as Major General
Otto Ernst Remer however was much too radical for many of the older
conservative members of the DRP. It proved too much for those party
members who were not interested in a resuscitation of the National
Socialist regime in all its boisterousness and militancy. Remer's fame
rested upon his active suppression of the anti-Hitler conspiracy of
July 20, 1944. Remer along with others, including one von Thadden
crony Falk, were expelled from the DRP and went on to form the
SRP (Sozialistische Reichs Partei). The DRP was then left with those
Nazis who still wished to work within the legal framework of the
Federal Republic.[9] The party lost its extreme elements (and the word
extreme is quite relative in this context) to the SRP. In addition, its
conservatives wandered off to the DP or indeed to the established
bourgeois parties. The DRP was only able to reach a fusion with the
NDP in Hesse and so form the new DRP, "Deutsche Reichs Partei".
The new DRP was consistently unsuccessful at the polls and throughout the '50s lived as an organization, a rallying point for the so-called
nationalist opposition, without much hope and much more than 1%
of the national vote, and without even the regional successes common to the postwar nationalist right. The establishment of economic
and political security, the social and economic restoration in Germany,
and the integration of "contrite" National Socialists had robbed the
DRP of its potential. Its own schizophrenia between neutralist and
national Bolshevik tendencies and out and out anti-Communism and
anti-Sovietism caused its inability to ripple the tide of events in the
'50s. But the DRP maintained its organization and essentially the apparatus was the party. The apparatus eventually came under the control of the anti-Communists von Thadden, Schuetz, and Hess.[10] It
was very much out of this party that the NPD was formed. The DRP
was much like the 1964 NPD, a party led by Nazis willing to conform
with the new German parliamentary structure and the new European
realities.

Those who had not been willing to compromise massed in the early
'50s for one blatant attempt at a resuscitation of National Socialism

and an assault on the Federal constitutional State in Germany within the organizational framework of the SRP, the Sozialistische Reichs Partei.[11] The SRP was led by Fritz Dorls, an ex-Strasser lieutenant in Germany and one of the early major exponents of the conservative revolution who had then cast his lot with Hitler, Gerhard Krueger, a former SS lieutenant colonel and senior councillor (Oberregierungsat) in the Reich Security Office, and Major General Remer. It became obvious that it was this type of nationalism, heady and uncompromising in its adherence to the National Socialist experiment that would be most attractive to unreconstructed National Socialists and extremist nationalists at the dawning of the '50s. The circumspection of the DRP was far too "opportunistic" and "bourgeois" for the old comrades. Huge chunks of the DRP organization went over to the SRP. For example, 80% of the state organization in Lower Saxony defected. But the SRP was also able to attract strength from the German Party (DP), especially in Schleswig-Holstein, and indeed the hopping from one nationalist party to another was a favourite sport not only of elected representatives in this period but of voters and the local organizations of the parties as well. It is important to re-emphasize that one deals here with nationalists and with members of the German right who had more in common with one another than with the established structure that was developing within the Federal Republic, and that personal economic and/or communal connections and considerations sometimes played a more significant role in party musical chairs than ideological puritanism.

The divisions that have been emphasized above indicate the lack of unity on the right and help to blow away the myths that postwar nationalism and right-wing excess in Germany adhered only to the National Socialist pattern. The National Socialist pattern was simply one of many competing patterns in this period, and indeed the fate of the SRP made it obvious to nationalists that an overt attempt at repetition of National Socialism would be impossible. The SRP made very little attempt to hide its identification with the aims of National Socialism and its desire for resuscitation of the experiment. In Gottingen the head of the SRP spoke of the Nazi party as the "SRP's great predecessor." The following are statements by SRP functionaries: "Germany would be better off today if we had a man like Adolf Hitler again"; "I think the policies of the National Socialist Party would be for the most part correct for today's situation"; "We carried the responsibility in the Third Reich and we are ready again today to undertake responsibility." And in a letter to party comrades the leadership of the party had to apologize for a leaflet in which certain qualifications were made against dictatorship.[12] The party in its first try garnered 11% of the vote in Lower Saxony. Actually the success seems to have caused disintegration in the organization of the SRP as it became apparent that neither the occupation authorities nor the developing Federal German government would tolerate such a successful blatant successor organization to the National Socialists. The facts of German postwar political life were becoming established and although nationalist tendencies and National Socialist proclivities were still strong within the society, potential nationalist elites were not willing to risk legal and/or economic difficulties for the prosecution of these goals. The overwhelming majority of Nazis organizationally engaged before 1945 were not available for a blatant National Socialist assault on the society. The minority that were left preferred in the same ratio the anonymity of the ballot to the judicial and social spotlight of an organizational role. In addition, the unsure social conditions of 1949 and 1950 gave way by 1951 to the 'Wirtschaftswunder' in Germany and the number of unemployed of 1.5 million, mostly among masculine potential workers and ex-soldiers in the age group susceptible to nationalist and National Socialist tendencies, melted away as more secure economic conditions provided jobs. The willingness to support extremist political groupings sank apace. But the legal aspect retained its importance. As Tauber has pointed out, "the SRP lost much of its swagger and air of invincibility when the Bonn Government in November 1951 made good its threat after all and asked the Federal Constitutional Court to begin proceedings against the SRP."[13] The Court banned the SRP on 23rd October 1952 as a subversive political party. The only other party which was federally banned in Germany was the Communist Party. (The DRP was banned in the Rhineland Palatinate). The Party property was confiscated, substitute organizations were prohibited, and party members were deprived of all their seats on federal, state, and local levels. A reservoir of voters remained as communal elections throughout the 1952 period showed. But internal bickerings within rightist groupings, bickerings which are only explainable through the multifaceted conceptions of nationalism and political activity inherent in the German right of the postwar period, helped crush attempts at unity for the Federal elections of 1953. Extreme nationalists found their homes in various anti-Marxist, anti-Soviet, traditional conservative or ostensibly middle-of-the-road German political parties like the DP or the CDU and, most spectacularly, the FDP.

The FDP, the Free Democratic Party, is interesting for this analysis not so much because of its function as a nationalist party, as it was never a nationalist party in the sense that the German Party and certainly that the DRP and the SRP were. Rather, it harboured within it strong nationalist tendencies which were especially prevalent in the North-Rhine Westphalia and Hesse state-organizations. The party was constantly rent by conflict between more liberal state organizations such as Baden-Wurtemberg, Hamburg, and Berlin and the national "liberal" groups. In their election programme for 1952 the organizations of Hesse and North-Rhine Westphalia called for the same kind of national *rassemblement*, and a "German" national programme found in the German Party.[14] Especially in North and Middle Hesse the FDP was dominated by nationalist groups. The nationalist character of the Hessian FDP is indicated by its political coalition in 1949 with the Hesse NDP and the fact that the 'dintinguished' conservative Leuchtgens pulled down an FDP seat in the Bundestag in 1949. He eventually went over to the DRP. A certain movement from the FDP to more rightist parties is also apparent, and the best example for this activity was the leader of the NPD in Hesse, Heinrich Fassbender. But even more prominent FDP people in Hesse, for example August Martin Euler, left the party to join nationalist conservative groupings and eventually the German party.[15]

This short analytical excursion into the FDP is interesting because it indicates how difficult it is in postwar Germany to pinpoint levels of nationalism by party affiliation. In a party like the FDP, where extremely liberal tendencies coexisted with nationalist predelictions that bordered on both those of the extremist and traditionalist nationalist parties, it is hard to zero in on the organized political forces of nationalism. This is especially true after 1952 when the DRP exists as a self-supporting apparatus rent with ideological strife, the SRP disappears, the German Party coalesces with the ruling CDU, and a rash of splinter nationalist parties emerge and disappear. The FDP is also interesting because it was the party that was most susceptible to an extreme nationalist attempt to influence German politics through the political parties but without an overt political organization: the in-

filtration attempts of the Neumann group. Neumann had been Goeb-
bel's protégé in the Nazi Ministry of Propaganda and had hung on
to Hitler in Berlin through the calamitous 'Goetterdaemmerung' of
Spring 1945. He left Berlin on the 2nd May of 1945 and emerged in
West-Germany after the 1950 amnesty declaration in which many ex-
Nazis were released from prison. Through Ernst Achenbach, the
FDP's ranking member in its foreign affairs committee, Neumann was
able to get in touch with many wellplaced people within political
parties and to develop his neo-National Socialist circle. Achenbach
"the deportation expert in the Nazi Paris Embassy" during the war,
put Neumann into contact with parliamentary FDP secretary Heinz
Wilke and FDP state chairman Friedrich Middelhauve who were more
than willing to recruit into the FDP old Nazis in order to assume "the
FDP's responsibility towards the right."[16] Neumann's eventual aim
was to control nominating procedures in the organization of a major
German party. He was not as successful with the BHE, the Expellee
Party, although he did register some success in that grouping. It was
in the FDP that the infiltration of his Nazi cadres was most successful. Nevertheless, as soon as the light of publicity was shed upon the
Neumann circle it disintegrated. When the British arrested Neumann
the cadre organizations simply melted away into the parties in which
they had been injected. Political agitation had never been their strong
point. Men like Achenbach and Siegfried Zogelmann, also associated
with Neuman's circle, remained active in the FDP into the 70s, although
the Free Democrats are ostensibly now a left party. Achenbach's activities seem to have extended to protecting Nazi colleagues with records of war crimes in France well into the 70s.

Throughout this consideration of organized nationalist groups runs
the thread of the refugee and expellee problem in the Federal Republic. The concept of Easternism as an important component of
German nationalism was discussed in Chapter II. The problem of
refugee groupings further complicated considerations of German nationalism in the postwar period. The refugees brought with them the
traditional nationalism of the Eastern areas which tended to be more
extreme than that of the rest of Germany. They were as well, economically dispossessed and socially dislocated people who had to start
with less than those citizens already in West Germany before 1945.
The problem of the refugees is not made simpler by an analysis of
the political party that ostensibly represented their demands. The

BHE was at once the social interest party of the regionally and' economically dislocated refugees and expellees, and a nationalist group. It was not overtly a nationalist party. But as Niethammer reports, "it was a function of the structure of the BHE as an interest party that two thirds of its leading politicians were one-time Nazi functionaries."[17] The engaged politicians of the BHE were Eastern traditional nationalists, which meant they were susceptible to national extremism, but not willing to engage in the kind of extremism that the SRP had emblazoned on its banners. They were, interestingly enough, not as susceptible to the Neumann infiltration as the ostensibly less nationalist FDP. It is also significant that the BHE was capable of coalescing with the SPD in various state governments, for example Bavaria and Hesse.[18] The BHE was rocked by constant crisis, as might be expected in a party with strong normative rightist sympathies which was not above coalescing with the established left of the German spectrum for social-economic gain. It was the least national Hessian wing of the party which was most successful achieving in 1954, 7.7% and in 1958, 7.4% of the cast vote in the state elections. Indeed from 1955 into the '60s it ruled with the powerful SPD in Hesse in a coalition government and so was able to represent the social interests of the numerous refugees in North and Middle Hesse as well as providing them with mild ideological panaceas in the form of political 'Easternism'.[19] It is also interesting that the Hessian SPD in this period is the most left wing of all the SPD state groupings, and the SPD in South Hesse builds the absolute left wing of the SPD. But the BHE eventually followed its essentially traditional nationalist course and fused with the German Party in 1961.

It was the German Party and the BHE, parties with a certain socioeconomic following, which were the only nationalist groupings to function with any success at all throughout the period of economic development and success in the 1950s.[20] The fusion, however, was a dismal failure: 2.8% of the national vote and steady disintegration on the state levels ended the career of these postwar parties. It is apparent from this very short and cursory analysis of nationalist German organized political groupings in the postwar period that, although successes were possible here and there on a regional basis, and although certainly both an extremist nationalist and traditional nationalist reservoir was approachable by organized nationalists within Western Germany, no nationalist party was able to establish itself to the right of the CDU and the CSU. The following chart, however, indicates just how strong rightist parties were.

CHART I

State	State election before '49	Federal (Bundestag) election '49	State election	Bundestag election '53
Baden-Wurt.		9,7	12,0 (2,4)	8,2 (0,1)
Bavaria	7,4 (7,4)	35,3(14,4)	35,2 (2,8)	20,5 (1,5)
Bremen	3,9	18,0	30,0 (7,7)	25,0 (3,0)
Hamburg	0,3	14,3	9,1	15,6 (1,6)
Hesse			(0,1)	9,4 (0,2)
Lower Saxony	18,2 (0,3)	(8,1)	28,2(13,3)	31,5 (3,5)
North-Rhine Westphalia	0,8 (0,5)	2,1 (1,8)	3,6 (1,9)	3,8 (0,1)
Rheinland Palatinate			3,4 (0,5)	5,4 (2,5)
Schleswig-Holstein	3,1	14,0 (1,9)	37,4 (4,4)	17,4 (0,9)

State	'57		'61	
Baden-Wurt.	4,9	7,0 (0,6)	10,0	3,7 (0,7)
Bavaria	24,6	9,7 (0,5)	18,0 (0,6)	4,5 (0,5)
Bremen	22,0	17,5 (1,4)	23,0	5,2 (1,1)
Hamburg	1,0 (0,7)	7,4 (0,8)	5,3 (0,4)	2,0 (0,9)
Hesse	9,4	12,6 (1,3)	10,9	4,7 (0,6)
Lower Saxony	27,9 (3,8)	23,9 (2,3)	24,5 (3,6)	7,8 (1,6)
North-Rhine Westphalia	4,9	5,9 (0,7)	2,2 (0,6)	1,4 (0,5)
Rheinland Palatinate	2,8	6,2 (2,7)	7,0 (5,1)	2,9 (2,3)
Schleswig-Holstein	21,5 (1,5)	13,0 (0,7)	7,8 (1,1)	4,9 (0,9)

The figures in parenthesis include those of extremist nationalist parties. (DRP, DRP KV, SRP, etc,) WAV is also included. BP and DP are of course outside the parenthesis.

The figures in the chart include the combined election successes of the DP, both DRPs, the SRP, the BHE and the comparable German nationalist groupings which were not analysed in this chapter, especially the BP and the WAV in Bavaria. The WAV corresponded in a certain sense to the pre 1950 DRP and the BP corresponded closely to the DP. No FDP results are included and no analysis is presented for the many splinter nationalist groups.[21]

What is immediately apparent here is that, with the exception of Bavaria and especially the BP, nationalist groupings were strongly Protestant and for the most part centred in the North German plain. It is exceptionally interesting to note that North-Rhine Westphalia, by far the most populous German state, the most heavily industrialized, and furthest along on the road to a more modern social structure was one of the least susceptible to any kind of nationalist blandishment. As the Chart also indicates, nationalist parties disintegrated by and large by the middle '50s, and by the beginning of the '60s they had reached their absolute nadir point, both in organizational strength and in attractiveness to the voters. It was at this point that the NPD emerged out of the organizational ashes of the second DRP. It was a party of those who were holding on to the will-of-the-wisp (for that is certainly what it must have appeared to objective political observers) of a *rassemblement* of national opposition to the political system that had developed in the postwar era. It was an opposition that harkened back to the organizational camaraderie of the National Socialist period; it aimed still, especially in the apparatus circles of the DRP, at a rehabilitation of some of the ideas of National Socialism, certainly of its idealistic aims, and also of the men who followed the National-Socialist siren song in modern German life. It attracted to it those traditionalist conservatives who had as yet not made their peace with the postwar era and who continued to pursue the goal of particularist conservative ethos and Wilhelmine nationalism. These conservtatives for the most part are still to be found among the now homeless members of the old German Party.

The alliance of the German Party and the BHE proved a dismal failure, and so the DP was faced with an oncoming election in one of its last strongholds, Bremen, and needed the support of a few thousand extra voters to retain seats in the Bremen city-state Parliament. The DRP obliged with election help, and the so-called Bremen model became the model for the establishment of the new NPD which would "break the cartel of Bonn's monopoly parties as a fourth great party."[22] But this fourth great party for all its pretension was only, with great difficulty, able to elect four representatives into the Bremen city-state diet.

DRP election returns for the early '60s had been catastrophic. In

Lower Saxony in the state elections of 1963, the DRP lost 16% of its vote from the previous all-time low of 63,000 that it had achieved in the 1961 Federal elections. It received 1.5% of the popular vote, 53,000 voters in the ostensibly most nationalist of German areas. The DRP seemed to be threatened with oblivion. Von Thadden, who had remained true to the party and was its organizational mind, was forced to cast about for any solution.[23] It was not surprising that the DRP settled on Fritz Thielen's Bremen rump-DP. Here was the respectability and rehabilitation that the ex-Nazis had been seeking and that had alluded them throughout the '50s. Here was a milder and more congenial form of nationalism devoid of Weimar drummings of the conservative revolution and the smell of neutralism. The NPD would continue to try to rehabilitate National Socialism, but it was not certain that the party that was founded in the capital of Lower Saxony, Hannover, in December of 1964, would really attempt to preach, let alone to practise National Socialism within the radically changed political contexts of the '60s. It remained to be seen whether this new party would be any more successful in integrating the various forces of nationalism in postwar Germany than the past mixed organizational bags had been. The traditionalist conservatives were strongly represented especially in the party's central committee. The old National Socialists from the DRP, however, were aiming at a rehabilitation of the ethos of National Socialism and personal respectability. In addition, the third group of nationalists who had neither emotional ties towards Wilhelmine structures nor towards National Socialism was emerging in Germany, a group of modern nationalists and pragmatic Facists.[24] These modern nationalists within the NPD, centred regionally in Bavaria and in Baden-Wurtemberg, would try in the course of the '60s to shake loose the DRP wing (the critical organizational wing of the party) from its National Socialist sentimentalism and idealization and make it a modern dynamic rightist political groupng firmly based on the functional needs of the '60s and '70s. It was always von Thadden's strength that he could juggle political movements and sub-cultures within the extreme right of the German political spectrum with a great deal of alacrity. This organizational skill plus the "outcast" complex in the NPD which he played upon most skillfully allowed him to manipulate events, and his DRP maintained its control of the party. Von Thadden gave the party the image of a parliamentary nationalist group with strong attachments to middle-class notions of private property, cultural conformity, and parliamentary participation while maintaining the language of and the ideological attachment to the National Socialist period in the party press and often in election campaigns. In doing so, however, he ran into another paradox: The party attracted real right-wing adventurers into its ranks like the swastika smearers who had brought the DRP into disrepute in 1959 and early 1960 in the Rhineland.[25] This fourth element in the NPD, although probably small, has been able to make itself felt, has hindered von Thadden's attempts at respectability, and embarrassed and angered both the traditional conservatives and modern nationalists within the NPD. This fourth group is the volatile significant minority who would use nationalist ideals as an excuse for physically violent forays into political activity. In 1965, at the time of its inception, the NPD however was dominated by traditional conservatives and the rehabilitating National Socialists of the DRP. The old DRP triumvirate of von Thadden, Schuetz, and Hess did their organizational work very well. The state NPD party chairmen were rarely old DRP members although many of them came out of the National Socialist movement. Managers in the state party organization staff, were old DRP members and allies of von Thadden. Table II indicates this relationship.

This relationship within the party was even more apparent in the national directorate. The national conservative from Bremen, Fritz Thielen, was ostensibly the head of the party, but the directorate was packed with old DRP members and Lower Saxony allies of von Thadden. Of the members of the party directorate as of 1964/65 45% were ex-DRP members, 55% were old National Socialists whose party number antedated Hitler's seizure of power in 1933. An additional 17% were party comrades whose party number was issued subsequent to 1933. Only 28% of the members in the party national directorate in the period 1964–65 had neither been National Socialists nor members of the DRP. The members of the party directorate from Lower Saxony were 45% of the total and the offices of the party were the old DRP offices in Hanover.[27] In addition, the NPD took over the DRP's newspaper (put out by Schuetz's publishing house) the *Reichsruf*. It became *Deutsche Nachrichten* (DN). So the organizational structure of the new NPD and its propaganda organ were both dominated by the triumvirate of von Thadden, Schuetz, and Hess. Indeed it was these publications that had secured the economic existence of von Thadden, Schuetz and Hess during the period of

surprising then that *DN* and *DNZ* had a large readership. *DN* readership grew quickly in the period between 1965 and 1968. Forty-three
thousand papers published weekly by the NPD and the Schuetz Verlag
compare very favourably with the 72,000 *Vorwaerts* ("Forward") that
the SPD publishes weekly. But this is nothing compared to the volatile *DNZ*. Published independently in Bavaria, with excellent contacts to elements in the CSU and refugee organizations, the *DNZ*
was able to maintain its number of publications to 124,916 published issues weekly in the 70s. This made *DNZ* the fifth largest weekly in the
Federal Republic.[30] It is, however, important to stress that *DNZ* is independently nationalist even with regard to readership, German nationalists avoid "party label" products. The number of issues of *DN* and
DNZ read by the end of the year 1968 and membership in extreme nationalist organizations were both slightly receding (from 38,700 in 1967
to 37,000 in 1968, about 30,000 of whom were NPD members, and from
137,000 to 128,000 printed issues of DNZ — 88,200 to 80,000 sold copies —
and 43,000 to 40,000 printed issues of DN.[31] In this period this slight recession in extreme nationalist support in Germany was probably a
reflection of the inner-party struggle within the NPD. By 1969 it was
to become a landslide with about 8,000 cancelled memberships. Membership figures for 1969 seem to have peaked at 27,000 and fell
through 1970 from 24,000 to 22,000.[32] The difficulties of the NPD in
1969 and 1970 will be discussed later. The party resignations reflected
in the cancelled memberships meant a large scale negative balance
in the constant coming and going of members that was typical of the
NPD; especially resignations by important members plagued the
party. As early as 1966 the NPD had lost 1,800 members primarily,
as Kuehnl points out, from the traditionalist or consevative wing
of the party, and in November of 1966 Franz Florian Winter who
had been chairman of the Bavarian wing of the party resigned
stating that within the NPD "a group had pushed itself into
the forefront that had not forgotten anything and had not
learned anything."[33] Winter, an ex-CSU and GDP member, was a
typical conservative. Perhaps more interesting was the resignation
from the NPD of the deputy secretary of the Federation of Expellee
Youth (BHJ=Bund der Heimatvertriebenen Jugend) Frank Lauterjung. He stated as his reason for leaving the NPD that a dangerous emotional nationalism was being bred there, and that this nationalism was
not realistic. He, Lauterjung, could not belong to a party that was

supposed to lead Germany into a better future without divorcing it-self from the past and from old ideas.[34]

Here were the first stirrings of a nationalism among younger Germans that was neither fixed on traditionalist Wilhelmine conservatism nor on National Socialism but was imbued with a more realistic, more modern, but nevertheless virile extreme German nationalism. The "modernists" wanted their nationalism to conform with the possibilities available in postwar Europe; they wanted their Fascism pragmatic. The inner-party crisis of 1967, however, in which Thielen was removed from his position as head of the party and summarily thrown out of the NPD, showed the organizational strength that the old DRP maintained within the party. Fully 93% of the delegates to the party convention in the Spring of 1967 which removed Thielen, rubber stamped von Thadden's preeminence. The party in 1967 seemed to be very much in the hands of the rehabilitating National Socialists. It was important now to ask whether the NPD was truly a successor organization to the National Socialists and would eventually follow the same kind of goals the National Socialists had followed or whether it was simply a party of old Nazis hankering for respectability and hanging on against the thrusts of a new nationalist generation. In addition, it would be important to find out just who supported this party. Throughout 1966, 1967, and 1968 the NPD was remarkably successful in communal and state elections. It was voted into the State Parliament of Hesse, Bavaria, Rhineland Palatinate, Lower Saxony, and Bremen. Looking at NPD memberships there is no doubt that the membership of the NPD is primarily middle class and old middle class at that. By the end of 1968 fully 47% of the NPD's membership were either self-employed old middle class or skilled workers in the middle-class businesses.[35] On the basis of 142 members of the leadership elite of the NPD, Niethammer calculated that 41% were self-employed, 20% were in the civil service, and 33% were employees in other occupations. Niethammer points out, however, that more and more new middle-class members were finding their way into the leadership of the NPD i.e., people employed with middle-class incomes who are not self-employed or skilled artisans.[36] This tendency is not apparent for the membership as a whole.

There are three ways to discover just what sociological groups within German society were most attracted to the NPD. The first is through an analysis of the membership of the NPD and its leadership group to show that part of society which is most actively engaged in the propagation of extreme nationalist positions. Then, secondly, one can analyse the potential NPD voters and NPD supporters in the Federal Republic and attempt to extract percentages of support among particular occupations, educational levels, religious groupings, regional antecedents, age and sex groups, etc. This potential can be established by direct questioning of individuals as to their eventual inclination to support the NPD or by related questioning on the basis of attitudes that would 'presumably' lead to NPD support. A third way is to analyze election returns, to establish regions of NPD support and the types of area in which NPD voters can be found.

The most ambitious attempts at describing NPD potential are to be found in the studies of Scheuch and Liepelt.[37] Liepelt established percentages to his question which social groups would vote for the NPD. On this basis Liepelt postulated that the NPD differentiated from other parties in its broad appeal to various social groups, but clearly the old middle-class self-employed and farmers were over-represented in the percentages of those encompassed in the questionnaire. In addition, a relatively higher percentage of unskilled workers (especially those in the smaller enterprises) showed a pro-NPD potential (although the overall percentage of skilled workers was the highest noted for any professional group).[38] This late 1966 analysis is corroborated by a later analysis by Klingemann whose figures for farmers, small business men, and workers show similar trends and an above-average propensity to be NPD supporters.[39] Scheuch's 1966 figures are on the whole less clear, but here too the self-employed show a high propensity of NPD sympathy. Farmers with an average propensity towards NPD sympathy, show a much lower propensity to oppose the NPD in this Scheuch analysis. What makes this kind of structural analysis on the basis of professions so difficult is that a whole series of other factors play their role. Looking at percentages can be very dangerous – there are jumps in the figures over month to month intervals even in the most reliable testing data. (If such indicators can be called reliable without steady incessant testing.) The same problem encountered with public opinion polls is inherent in these potential support studies. In occupational groups, for example, real differences are found from one month to another, income factors play an important role in occupation groups although it is not clear on the basis of the statistics available what kind of a role. What does seem to be clear, and this is evident from practically all studies made is that when the respondents' economic prognosis are pessimistic the tendency within all job groups to support the NPD and/or extreme nationalist position is higher. When the individual involved maintains an optimistic prognosis the tendency to support the NPD is lower.

The reservoir of potential authoritarians and potential nationalists is still large in Germany. Therefore it should not be surprising that within all social groups one discovers certain tendencies to support nationalist parties especially if none of the established parties fill this political role. However, these tendencies vary not only in regard to economic hopes or fears but also in regard to age factors, sex, regional considerations, social ties to organizations such as unions, the church, clubs, professional societies, etc. What seems clear in analysing such tendencies is that higher educated, self-employed, Protestant or non-religious members of social and professional organizations that are not trade unions are the most inclined to support the NPD. In addition, certain refugee groups (the Sudenten Germans, for example) show high pro-NPD sentiments and extremist nationalist proclivities (for example one third of the Bavarian state Parliament NPD delegation are Sudeten Germans). The official refugee press is especially volatile.[40] Those least inclined to support the NPD are workers with a medium educational level, who are members of trade unions and who are practising Catholics (membership in unions and membership in the Catholic church are, for Liepelt at any rate, the most important considerations. The tie to an important sociopolitical organization relatively immune to the structures of nationalism is central for him). Here the comparison with Weimar indicates that it is just this type of person who maintained loyalty to the parties of the Weimar coalition, the SPD and the Centre. In addition, regional areas with Weimar pro-Nazi voting patterns maintain these now and show high NPD returns.[41]

In order to complete the picture one must compare membership and election results to get at an NPD potential within certain regions. Bavaria and Lower Saxony, Schleswig-Holstein, the Rhineland Palatinate and Baden-Wurtemberg show larger percentages of membership in the NPD than their percentage of the population of the Federal Republic.[42] For Hesse the figures are almost equal, but it is interesting to note that there is a decline in Hesse as in Bavaria for this period and, although this is not reflected in the charts below, the majority of the NPD members came from Middle and North Hesse, an area which was strong FDP territory. NPD election results on the state level (with the exception of Hesse 7.9%, Bavaria 7.4% and Hamburg 3.9%) are reflected in Table IV.

TABLE IV[43]

Comparison NPD Total State election returns and NPD voting patterns by age and sex groups in 5 States.

State	average	45/60 total	45/60 men	45/60 women
Rheinld.-P.	6,9	8,6	12,5	5,5
Schlesw.-Hst.	5,3	7,4	10,3	5,2
Lower Saxony	7,0	9,2	12,4	6,1
Bremen	8,8	11,1	14,8	8,2
Baden-Wurt.	9,8	12,0	17,1	8,1

State	average	21/30 total	21/30 men	21/30 women
Reinld.-P.	6,9	5,5	7,8	3,0
Schlesw.-Hst.	5,8	4,4	5,8	2,8
Lower Saxony	7,0	4,9	6,5	3,3
Bremen	8,8	7,1	9,6	4,4
Baden-Wurt.	9,8	8,1	10,9	5,3

The Table also indicates higher NPD percentage among the 45–60 year olds. In each state this age group proved to be the largest age group voting for the NPD and the relatively small number of 21–30 year olds was the smallest age group voting for the NPD. In addition, it is obvious that men in this age group tend in a relationship of almost two to one towards stronger support of the NPD. Interestingly enough, this 2 to 1 relationship is carried through the age bracket of 21–30 year olds as well.

TABLE V

Comparison of all age and sex groups on State and City levels.

State elections

age group	Rheinl.-P. 1967 (6,9%)		Schlesw.-H. 1967 (5,8%)		Bremen 1967 (8,8%)	
	men %	women %	men %	women %	men %	women %
21–30	7,8	3,3	5,8	2,8	9,6	4,4
31–45	10,6	5,1	7,6	4,2	12,6	6,8
46–60	12,5	5,5	10,3	5,2	14,8	8,2
over 60	7,1	2,9	7,6	3,2	7,2	3,9

City returns

age group 39	Wiesbaden (NPD 6,4%)		Darmstadt (NPD 5,5%)	
	men %	women %	men %	women %
21–30	7,9	3,0	4,1	3,5
30–45	7,2	5,1	7,4	5,0
45–60	12,2	5,9	12,7	6,3
over 60	8,6	3,2	9,8	3,7

TABLE VI

Total NPD Vote Percentages as of 28, 4, 1968, by age and sex groups

age group	% NPD voters	men	women
21–29	8,1%	10,9%	5,3%
30–44	10,9%	13,6%	8,0%
45–59	12,0%	17,1%	8,1%
60 and up	7,7%	11,2%	4,9%
total	9,8%	13,4%	6,8%

TABLE VII

Membership fluctuation in the NPD by age groups

age group	new membership	resignation	fluctuation tendency	age structure of the party end 1968
till 30	36%	35%	strong	25%
till 45	31%	30%		29%
till 60	22%	20%		31%
till and up	11%	15%	weak	15%

A group of figures for the two socially differently structured and more prosperous cities in Southern Hesse, Wiesbaden and Darmstadt (Table V) show relatively similar NPD voting patterns and seem to bear out this analysis. Indeed nationwide figures show the same pattern. Membership figures further strengthen this argument (Table VII). Indeed, it is fair to say that for all elements of German society the age group 45–60, the group that spent much of its formative and educational years under National Socialism, is the most susceptible to the appeals of the NPD and the most loyal to the party.[44] This seems especially true of highly educated people. An investigation of the Divo-Institut in the year 1966 of all educational groups in Germany i.e., those with grammar school education, those with high school education, those with university education indicated that university graduates of the Nazi era showed the most positive reception of the NPD. Of the university graduates having graduated during the years 1933–45, 12.5% were positively inclined to the policies of the NPD. Indeed, the next highest grouping, with 8.2%, were those with a high school degree (the so-called Abitur) that were also educated in the years 1933–45. Interestingly enough, the lowest percentages were the 2.6% of those who graduated from university before 1933 and 4.6% of those who graduated from university after 1945. The 12.5% figure for university graduates between 1933–45 is more than 50% higher than the next highest 8.2% figure and almost twice as high as the next highest figure (interestingly enough, 7.2% for those with an Abitur after 1945).[45] In Klingemann's analysis, university graduates whose financial hopes had not been fulfilled were found most likely to support the NPD. A significant number of high school graduates without a college degree probably nurse similar resentments.[46] The only variation from the high 1933-45 results in this test was for post-1945 grammar school absolvents who showed a slight increase 6.8% over 6.5% in support for the NPD. It is interesting that the group educated before 1933 seems the least susceptible to the NPD but would probably support conservative nationalists. Of course, this study does not weigh or really analyse the postwar generation of sceptics towards nationalism that is covered in Chapter III.

In addition to age group differentiation, which is particularly strong in regard to the NPD and which is generally significant in considering modern political trends, there are other factors apparent in election returns which solidify some of the arguments found in sociological support studies. For example Protestant areas return larger percentages for the NPD. This is particularly true in Bavaria where Middle Franconia, the only real Protestant majority area in the land, gave the NPD the over 10% (12.2%) of the vote it needed to get its representatives into the Bavarian State Parliament. The returns for Baden-Wurtemberg corroborate that religious affiliation is one of the key aspects of electorate behaviour in regard to the NPD (as indeed it is in regard to election behaviour for all parties in Germany). Protestant election districts like Oehringen and Crailsheim (60.8% and 75.4% Protestant) gave the NPD 14.8 and 14.5% of their vote in the 1968 state elections. Catholic districts like Saalgau and Beberach (87.3% and 79.8% Catholic) gave the NPD 6.5 and 6.0%. The economic and social structure of these districts is otherwise similar. The state average for the NPD was 9.8%.[47] The same pattern can be found in the Rhineland Palatinate where the NPD achieved an average of 6.9% but more than 11% in Protestant areas like city districts Pirmasens 13.6%, Zweibruecken 12.3%, and country districts Worms 14.4%, Alzey 13.5%, and Kusel 15.5% or in Hesse's NPD stronghold, in country district Alsfeld (81% Protestants 12% NPD), and of course in the overwhelmingly Protestant areas Lower Saxony with their strong nationalist tradition. Interestingly enough, Schleswig-Holstein is the only exception to this rule of inverse ratio between Catholic and NPD.[48] However, even a cursory glance at the chart will indicate that other factors play their role. A high percentage of farms in an area and a high percentage of self-employed will add to the tendency to support the NPD. In addition, Oehringen, Crailsheim, and Tauberbischofsheim, three state election districts with the highest NPD total for Baden-Wurtemberg were economically depressed areas.[49] The same situation held true in Hesse, in Bad Hersfeld where a difficult situation in the textile industry existed and in Dill Kreis where iron mines were closed, high percentages of 10.7% were garnered by the NPD.[50] Our Baden-Wurtemberg chart also indicates that it is small town areas that tend to support the NPD. This seems to be born out by a study of the percentage of NPD supporters carried out by Allensbach in 1966.[51] The NPD strongpoints seem to be in cities with populations of between 2000 and 20,000 which give the highest relative and absolute percentages of NPD supporters (34% of NPD supporters; 29% of the population as a whole, trailed by villages under 2,000 voters — 24% : 22% — and cities with between 20,000 and 100,000 voters — 18% : 16%). Urban centres (over 100,000) show a clear minus in relative NPD support. Almost one quarter of all NPD supporters come from urban centres, but 33% of the voting population live in cities over 100,000 in size.

The NPD seems to do well not only in the smaller cities but in cities with mixed economic forms in which traditional agriculture has been joined by new industry in Germany. These cities vary between 10,000 and 100,000 in size.[52] The Alsfeld area is a typical example. Here, 42% of the population are engaged in agriculture, 35% in industry and 32% move from one branch to the other.[53] And in addition suburban commuter towns seem, especially in Baden-Wurtemberg, to be susceptible to high NPD percentages. Of course there are exceptions to the urban rule, for example Mannheim, an industrial town which gave the NPD 12.1% of the vote and the high percentages in Wiesbaden and Darmstadt, both of them large and prosperous communities. Communal problems, the ability of local NPD politicians and their position within society, a plethora of 'neighbourly' contacts and attitudes also helped form the relationship between the community and the NPD.

The party's election successes in the middle 1960s were sudden and surprising since the NPD was constantly shaken by internal dissent and since its leadership had been remarkably successful at losing elections in Germany since 1950. Not only was the NPD at a disadvantage financially. Big firms have not contributed to the NPD, and the party was shut off from the major financial aid that the Federal German Government grants political parties represented in the Bundestag. Many reasons have been offered for the election success of the NPD: (1) The first real establishment of a super-regional nationalist party; (2) The economic insecurity of the 1966–67 period; (3) The renaissance in nationalist ideas found with the non-overtly nationalist leadership elite in Germany (4) The reaction against the non-nationalist trends and permissive cultural and moral standards of modern society; (5) The reaction against the international political situation and the detente between the US and SU; (6) The weakness of the Erhard Government and consequent feelings of political insecurity which heightened economic insecurity within some sections of society; (7) Local structural problems, such as those of agriculture, and the old middle-class generally; (8) The restoration of pre-1933 economic practices and social elites in Germany which spawned the same kind of rightist nationalist party; (9) Political Gaullism first in France and then in Germany which awoke national ambitions; (10) The CDU/CSU's opening towards the left during 1966 (admittedly after initial NPD successes) which shocked many traditional conservatives and made protest voters out of them; and last, (11) the important fact that the politically shell-shocked period of the postwar era had essentially come to an end, and this brought with it a new type of nationalist, who found in the NPD a ready home if not a congenial organizational leadership. It is interesting to note that most of the members of the NPD, and those who tend to support the NPD, reject much if not all of the National Socialist experiment.[54] This rejection is based on the ideological and operational excesses of the National Socialists and a continuing strong hankering for security in Germany.

The middle '60s spawned a new breed of nationalists in Germany capable and willing to fuse a new kind of modern nationalism with pragmatic Fascist ideas into a rightist parliamentary party which maintained the trappings of national opposition and still propagandized the ideologies of yesteryear. It is a relatively easy matter to prove that the NPD is a successor party to the National Socialists, especially if one's analysis is based primarily on works like the *Political Lexicon* of the NPD or perusal of *DN*. Indeed, Fred H. Richards in 1967 made a rather convincing point for point comparison between the 1965 manifesto of the NPD and the 25-point programme of the National Socialists of February 24th, 1920. The national rights of the German people and their right to self-determination, the need for centralistic control and government, anti-plutocratic strictures, strong pro-middle-class and farmer statements, anti-materialistic and communal service platitudes, tough education for youth and central sports education, fulminations against cultural permissiveness and pluralism are central to both. Often the same words are used, the style is very similar and the NPD programme is in fact much longer and much more all-inclusive.[55] This comparison was possible even though quite obviously NPD party programmes and manifestos are less concerned with National Socialist complexes then the clumsy, unusually heavy-handed *Political Lexicon*, and the nostalgically extremist party paper *DN*. Both of these publications and selected NPD party speech patterns are wellsprings of extremist nationalism and still fit the 1950s pattern of agitation.[56] Anti-Semitism, biological thinking, and racism still play a role in *DN* although it is a rapidly decreasing role and even at its high point in 1965 only made up 8.7% and 7.4% respectively of the percentage of ideologically extremist newsprint in *DN*.[57] Indeed, although some authors stress the anti-Jewish aspects of NPD thought and the necessity of anti-Semitism for the ethos of the party, an anti-Semitic proclivity, although certainly not on the wane especially among the old National Socialists and leaders of the NPD, is not something that is stressed.[58] Since 1965 the real emphasis (i.e., since *DN* has been *DN*) has been on patriotism, emotional and integral nationalism, and outspoken Germanism. Fifty-nine percent of the copy was found to be xenophobicly chauvinistic and more volatilely colored nationalistic and another 14.4% of the copy dealing with ideology was found to be of the same slant.[59]

Quantitative trend analyses of *DN* into the late '60s have not been made, but significant changes between 1965 and 1966 in regard to the main targets of *DN* criticism were worked out. Significantly the main increase in copy critical of the world in general and the Germany situation in particular was specifically anti-Bolshevist or anti-Soviet Union. In 1966, 22.5% of the criticism voiced in the *DN* was anti-Bolshevist in nature. In 1965 it had been high at 17% but it had trailed criticism of the Bonn system and anti-pluralism which in 1965 accounted for 25.3% of the critical copy in *DN*. In 1966 this complex had dropped to 17%. Another major complex was the anti-socialist, anti-union and anti-liberal syndrome which rose from 14.3% of critical copy in 1965 to 17.5% in 1966. Anti-Western positions, anti-Americanism and anglophobia remained fairly constant between 16.5% and 17%, whereas broadly based historically apologetic considerations of the war-guilt question remained the same at 13%.

In the pages of *DN* and on the election hustings, aspects of National Socialist tradition still find their way into the agitational style of the NPD. Kuehnl writes that in their basic thought patterns the National Socialist Party and the NPD are identical.[60] This is probably true to a degree, to the relatively high degree that the nostalgic National Socialists within the NPD, the old DRP people, and assorted other old-fashioned nationalists have their hand in the print pot or lend their voices to the election drummings. The saga-like biological sophistry of NPD directorate member Professor Ernst Anrich smacks of the racism of the Nazis.[61] Directorate member Professor von Gruenberg's haphazard flirtations with neutralism (his last and most notorious escapade into this was his condemnation, in *DN*, of those who had quickly condemned the Soviet Union after their invasion of Czechoslovakia in the summer of 1968) harkens back to the Hitler-Stalin Pact and the national neutralism of the '50s. The constant references to re-education after occupation and to "Morgenthau's boys", world "Leftism", and to the whole questionability of the de-Nazification and war-guilt complexes still fill pages. But these are perhaps more cries of self-righteousness, bitter as they are and unpalatable as they remain, than harbingers of a new National Socialism. National Socialism existed in its particular epoch, the terminal nostalgia and self-righteousness remain important with much of the NPD leadership that still control the party directorate and the party newspaper. But even here a slow change is coming towards a more pragmatic variety of Fascism and a more modern conception of nationalism. The anti-alien aspect of course remains. The Germanism remains and the concern with the middle-class moral imperative remains, as well as the continued pandering to Easternism, and national paranoia. But these are all revised into new formulas. Blatant anti-Semitism, as was mentioned above, is no longer an important aspect of either the NPD or its propaganda in *DN*. It still pops up, especially when nostalgic National Socialists take to pen.

Professor von Gruenberg's report on French Prime Minister Pompidou's visit to America and the Nazi professor's polite but unmistakably grim "advice" to "leftist Jewish" demonstrators is typical.[62]

Even the so-called guest workers' problem played less of a role than it did in 1967 and 1968, and in 1967 and 1968 the guest workers' problem played more of a role than anti-Semitism. Of course the guest worker is not ignored and unflattering references are relatively constant. The 'pragmatic' Fascists in Baden-Wurtemberg have made much of this issue in the State Parliament. "Communist subversion of guest workers" is a better issue than a resuscitation of anti-Semitism in a country where there are hardly any Jews left (30,000, half of them over 60).[63] In an intensive study of DN based on a three-month period in 1969, and especially the four weeks before and after the election, no anti-Semitism and little anti-guest worker strictures were encountered.[64] Anti-pluralism was more evident as well as strong attacks on political enemies within the Bonn system, e.g. the trade unions and the SPD. Here, however, the NPD has let latent anti-Semitism slip in. Former DGB (the ex-German federal trade union association) head Rosenberg, a Jew, has always been the target of sly innuendos, and the unions were thus somehow "semiticized".

Guilt by association is a favourite NPD tactic. A good example is the masthead of DN on March 13th 1970 after the Austrian elections: "All of German area ruled by Socialists" with pictures of Ulbricht, Brandt, and Austrian socialist leader Bruno Kreisky, whose SPO had just won the Austrian national elections. Kreisky's Jewish parentage is also well known to DN readers. The intention is clear here. Especially strong attacks were made against the students' leftist intellectuals and the mass media. Attacks on the Bonn system were not addressed towards its removal but to an eventual more hierarchically structured, less permissive and thus less corrupt leadership in the system, that could be offered by the NPD. The issue of "rising" crime rates is exploited fully.[65] Here both DN and the tenor of NPD election campaign speeches squared.[66] The party newspaper as in the years 1965 and 1966 addresses much of its interest to the old middle class, refugees, and those soldiers who served under the National Socialists and those who serve now. It also attempts to act as a spokesman for right-wing intellectuals.[67]

But even in the DN stronghold of nostalgic Nazis and old-fashioned extreme nationalists, one encounters an adaptation of the political struggles of the late '60s and early '70s. The anti-Bolshevism of Peter Kleist and Erich Kernmayer, profound contributors to DN and to neo-extremist nationalist propaganda throughout the '50s and

'60s, has triumphed over the neutralists. *DN* has continued to strengthen its anti-Bolshevism and anti-Soviet position. This brings it into the restorative pattern of German politics in the postwar era. It adapts the NPD to elements of foreign policy thinking, evident on the right of the CDU/CSU. Its attitudes on the military and its condemnations of internal leadership ("innere Fuehrung") bring it in line with much thinking within the Bundeswehr.[68] The antiplutocratic and socialist elements of the conservative revolution, that marked much of National Socialist propaganda, have disappeared completely. The NPD and especially its modern pragmatic Fascist wing support the capitalist system and support principles of private enterprise. Authority and efficiency and economic conservatism are becoming more important as principles to the NPD than the ideological imperatives of the '30s. A curious blend is being established between typically Fascist political ploys (for example stress of a preindustrial conception of the moral imperative, anti-intellectual proclivities, attacks on uprooted and decadent social groups like intellectuals, Communist infiltrated mass medias, cultural subversion of the people, appeals to ethnocentrism) and a spurious modernity.

Election speeches are patterned in much the same manner as *DN*. These speeches, prepared in Hanover, are standard for the whole party. The central idea is guaranteed through strict selection of speakers and prepared texts. NPD election speeches are perhaps a more important source of party ideology and practice than those of other parties. One pattern speech deals with internal leadership and the weaknesses in the army that have been caused by temporization and democratization. The expellees are addressed with a hard line on the Germany problem. The borders of 1937 plus Sudetenland are said to be the borders of any German state. Indeed the question of the guest workers and cultural intellectual decadence plays its major role on the hustings, as does the rehabilitation of Nazis and the oblique reference to foreign capital and sellout. The pragmatic Fascists, although they were probably the majority in the party before the 1969 elections, had not as yet been able to completely take over, von Thadden had been clever enough to keep his majority in the party directorate. This was true up to the disappointing federal elections of 1969 and after as well. In February 1969 attempts by the Bavarian 'pragmatists' to unseat von Thadden proved fruitless. Bavarian 'modernist' and sharp stylist, Bavarian state chairman, Senatsrat Beno Hermannsdorfer's at tacks on von Thadden simply strengthened the North German. Hermansdorfer's support remained limited to his regional followers, not even all the Bavarians supported him. Significantly, the attacks centred on Anrich and von Gruensberg, the National Socialist neo-ideologists, and not directly on von Thadden. But over 90% of the delegates rallied to the old standard and apparently neither the Bavarian organization nor the supposedly modern Baden-Wurtemberg organization maintained a certain majority of pragmatists.[70] In addition, constant bannings of NPD meetings and the constant anti-NPD demonstrations created a feeling of camaraderie for and aura of solidarity with the embattled von Thadden. But von Thadden is flexible and in the overall leadership of the party the so-called unpoliticals, those who have not come to the NPD from organized nationalist political parties, and the younger DRP people, who were pragmatic Fascists while still in the DRP, have between them 55% of the 142 leadership positions that Niethammer calculated in 1969 for the party.[71]

Since the pattern speeches quoted above are held all over the country — the NPD maintains a strict control of its speakers and being a speaker is one of the main insignia of higher party standing — the party is able to completely determine what is being said in the countryside. Its attempt at tight, indeed authoritarian, control is based on this information control of DN and of speeches and speakers. In its propaganda, nostalgic nationalism can play its role but the pragmatic aspects of this new Fascism make themselves felt through the technocratic abilities of the new breed. Typically, 'modernists' have been able in some hard infighting to modify neo-National Socialist principles, advising for example, that National Socialist autarchy give way to participation in the European Community. The pragmatic Fascists support German participation in the EEC with a number of economic reasons, but they plead that the EED is unavoidable since it is the only way to combat the Soviet menace, American imperialism and the threat to the white race that the coloured peoples portend.[72]

Again a strange mix of modern economic rationalism and bourgeois scary social horror stories mark the typical attitude of the pragmatic Fascists. Niethammer has best analysed this conflict within the NPD and has regionally pinpointed the pragmatic Fascists. They are, as has been indicated, for the most part to be found in

Southern Germany below the Main river line. Bavaria has always been a recalcitrant extreme nationalist province for the North German Protestants and, as the Hermannsdorfer affair shows, remains so. Baden-Wurtemberg, however, has become a major rallying point for pragmatic Fascists. Half of the parliamentary fraction of the Baden-Wurtemberg NPD was between the ages of 32 and 44 and was college trained. These are not the socially displaced members of the old nationalist parties. They are physicists, project engineers, economists, lawyers, etc. They are at home in big firms, having worked for organizations like Shell, IBM, Siemens.[73] And they are, interestingly enough, far more aggressive, far more flexible, and better informed in parliamentary situations than the old-fashioned nationalist wing, the nostalgic National Socialists of the NPD. Generally the NPD Landtag delegations have dismal records. Alacrity and intelligence are found only in Bavaria and Baden-Wurtemberg. It is only in Baden-Wurtemberg that the NPD was able to get a resolution passed, dealing, significantly enough, with penal reforms.[74]

The 'modernists' are out to embarrass especially the CDU and CSU into eventually agreeing with NPD positions. This was apparent in Bavaria, in parliamentary and panel discussions of student difficulties, and the 'modernists' are not above praising especially CSU politicians, for national positions. The following quote from *DN* of August 18th, 1967 is a good example. After a podium discussion between CSU, FDP, SPD, and NPD members *DN* wrote: "At the end of the discussion Stoppel of the CSU gave an assessment of the necessities of the German people that could not have been better formulated by a national democrat."[75]

The pragmatic Fascists are sincere and eloquent in their conviction that they can pull other German parties over to the right. One of the leading lights of the Baden-Wurtemberg parliamentary fraction, the economist Basler, whose eloquent support of managerial positions would do credit to any organization man, said in Baden-Wurtemberg State Parliament: "We are not your enemies, we understand and respect you, but we think that you are ignoring aspects of politics. You represent the Christian, the social and the liberal components of politics and that rightly so. But there is something else that we all have, that binds us all together, that is that we are members of one people that has grown together as a community over the centuries. We think that this community is in danger, yes, that it is threatened with dissolution, not only superficially in terms of East and West but also internally, and that is the greatest danger that all ties should be destroyed and dissolved. That is what we are fighting."[76] This appeal to the integral aspects of the national vertical is the key to the position of pragmatic Fascism that will undoubtedly be the determinant for the NPD and/or any similar group in the '70s. On a whole series of political positions there is a relative identity between the NPD and either supporting social groups or political parties established within the current German spectrum. This is especially true in the field of foreign policy, where the NPD rejects ratification of the non-proliferation treaty and sees the Soviet Union as being weakened with "mathematically calculable certainty through the rising strength of China." The NPD hints strongly that America is not a completely faithful ally, is allowing permissiveness to eat up its power, and that it is necessary to build strong political military economic and cultural European ties to take advantage of this situation and mitigate its dangers. The NPD calls this line towards Europe and America "a new position for the end of the century which does not have anything to do with 1933."[77] Of course 'Ost Politik' Brandt, the treaties with the German Democratic Republic and the four power treaty are considered great sellouts. The parliamentary system is accepted and in fact the NPD is a party of parliamentarians, but it is those aspects of the parliamentary system, elements of parliamentary government which can be manipulated for restrictive social purposes that are interesting for the NPD.

Both the nostalgic National Socialists and the pragmatic Fascists were disappointed in their attempt to enter the Bundestag in the elections of 1969. The NPD could manage only 4.4% of the vote, a disappointing result since the party had been far more successful in communal and state elections up until 1969. The NPD lost in percent of total vote as compared to the last state elections (figures in parenthesis indicate NPD % of total vote in federal election 1969): 1.5% in Schleswig-Holstein (4.3%); 2.8% in Hesse (5.1%); 4.4% in Bremen (4.4%); and in Baden-Wurtemberg 5.3% (4.5%), here as in Bremen a loss of over 50% in NPD voters; 1.7% in the Rheinland Palatinate (5.2%); 2.1% in Bavaria (5.3%); 2.5% in Lower Saxony (4.6%). The federal election figures for North-Rhine Westphalia were 3.1%, for Hamburg 3.5%, for the Saar 5.7%. Regional strongpoints, however, remained intact; for example the Rhineland Palatinate with

affect state elections more than federal elections (North-Rhine West-phalia for example the most populous German land had never been susceptible to nationalist political parties); (3) of a fact of postwar German political life that all "smaller" parties seem inevitably more successful in local and state elections where voters will risk casting their ballot for a smaller party that may not jump the 5% hurdle. The communal elections held in the Rhineland Palatinate three months be-fore the federal elections seemed to bear this out. The NPD had been enormously successful in its strongpoints and gained, in these areas, an average of 1.6% over the state elections of 1967. This had been considered by the NPD "a test of its development."[79] The party crowed that "in all six districts [here differently drawn and smaller than fed-eral election districts] and four district free towns in the state in which it campaigned, it would now be the third strongest party." (There are 28 election districts and 12 district free towns in the state.) Indeed in Alzey-Worms the NPD's success with 15.3% of the vote contributed most to the breaking of the SPD's absolute majority. Again such im-portant areas as Kaiserslautern city (10.95%) and Kaiserslautern countryside (11.9%) and Pirmasens city (9.7%) returned strong NPD percentages. For the state as a whole, however, the NPD only gar-nered 2.4% of the vote and the NPD's interpretation that it would do better in the state elections of 1970 than in the 1969 federal elections was self-deceptive. In North-Rhine Westphalia the NPD with 1.1% was far below its federal election result of 3.1%; in the Saar which with 5.7% had led all German states in the federal election the return of 2.7% was a shocker. But the most disastrous returns were from Lower Saxony, the heartland of nostalgic National Socialism. A 3.2% NPD return eased von Thadden and his friends out of the Landtag (the party had garnered 7% in 1967, and in the federal elections had still managed 4.6%). The NPD seems to be going the way of its pred-ecessors in postwar Germany. The 1972 federal elections in which the NPD could garner out 0.6% of the vote, and its strength in its strong-holds dissipated even further, bore out this assessment.

One of the major reasons for election failure must be that the party is still bedeviled and will probably always be bedeviled by violent persons who seek in the nationalist ethos an excuse to resolve their own aggressive drives. Although it is true, as was pointed out, that the amount of anti-Semitic excesses has declined, political violence is still very evident. The NPD was associated with two major scandals shortly before the 1969 federal election. An NPD member tried to bomb the headquarters of the German trade union federation in Mainz, and the head of one of the NPD's security squads (squads used to keep order in election-campaign meetinghalls) shot two students. This replay of yesteryear, punctuated the constant rioting, pummelling, and general noise at NPD election meetings (caused by clashes between helmeted NPD security guards, young leftist students, and trade unionists) must have hurt the NPD, especially in the eyes of the national conservative or 'unpolitical' burghers seeking law and order and psychic and physical security. Security conscious nationalists (and indeed authoritarians) are still able to find a home in the CDU and CSU which waged a hard essentially nationalist state and federal election campaign against the SPD's new opening to the East. Indeed it appears that that is just where the lost NPD voters turned in 1969 and especially in 1972. Shortly before the state elections in 1970 a conspiratorial group with stocks of weapons was uncovered in North-Rhine Westphalia. The group was made up of NPD members, and shortly before, men dealing in weapons smuggling to Tyrol were caught, again NPD members. All of this runs contrary to the goals of those directing the party from whichever wing they may come. But the party continues to attract violent, volatile types and this remains one of the party's main weaknesses. Its members really do not and probably will not always live up to its image, however much the NPD try to shake itself free of the violent types and to blend traditional conservatism in Germany with modern nationalism and pragmatic Fascism.

The National Socialist experience must be ignored more and more. Von Thadden realized this since even past-oriented political parties are subject to the inexorable influence of the reality in which they live. But even he failed to 'purge' the party of its 'hobbyhorse' (his phrase) nationalists. His resignation from the party's leadership on November of 1970 was a sign that the 'pragmatists' were moving on to less volatile fields. Much of the cream of the Baden Wurtenberg group was drummed out in June '71; party membership dropped to 18,000, (12,000 by 1974). Martin Mussgnug Thadden's replacement was obviously a caretaker for the impending election disaster in '72."[80] The NPD or similarly oriented groups must eventually seek the modern dynamic nationalist rebirth its 'modernists' propagate. It will try to give this nationalism a functional *raison d'état* based on a German managerial capitalist elite and hierarchical organizational forms in a disciplined society. It will be a party that will try to build a bridge to certain potentially 'friendly' elements in the German political and social process. It will not in the future be terribly interested in rehabilitating National Socialism. It will let the drum beat and the national flags just fade away. It will seek power now for a German national elite in Europe and a decisive German military position on the Continent. It will try then to make a new reality out of a lost discredited dream. And even if it fails, and indeed its inability to shake itself loose of old fashioned extremisms indicates that it certainly has failed, and the NPD goes the way of the DRP, the pragmatists in the party will have considered themselves successful if they can pull the other parties to the right.

Keeping the CDU/CSU honest is another and perhaps more important aspect of organized nationalism in Germany than the fluctuating strength of these parties. The CDU/CSU has steadily swallowed the right; the question of successful digestion remains unanswered. The NPD is hard hit now, and as long as it contains nostalgic Nazis and one or more of the big established parties satisfy the nationalist needs of a security hungry electorate the NPD will never be more than an imitating, ominous reminder that extremist, nationalist tendencies are still latent and strong enough to influence German politics. The danger and the political effectiveness of organized nationalism rests with the effect and indirect influence that the articulated positions of modern nationalism and pragmatic Fascism have on susceptible social groups and on other political parties competing with organized nationalists for much the same kind of voter. The Bundeswehr and the CSU have been isolated and selected for analysis in this book because they seem to best satisfy the prerequisite for susceptibility.

Notes

1. The NPD is stressing conservatism more and more in its official pronouncements. Cf. *Wertheimer Manifest 70*, the newest manifesto of the NPD, especially the portion on the preservation of timeless values. In addition, cf. *Deutsche Nachrichten*, April 17th, 1970, in which von Thadden calls the party a conservative party, and especially *DN*, December 26th, 1969 with its consideration of the conservative writings of Armin Mohler, and the stress of conservatism as the strongest anti-anarchistic element in the society. This strong revival of conservatism in the NPD by forces within the party, which were responsible earlier for the isolation and

defeat of the conservatives in the leadership group, is an element that has become more and more apparent since the Bundestags elections of 1969. Cf. as well *DN* February 20th, 1970.

2. There has been a constant flow of individuals and organizations in and out of various nationalist parties and into various establishment parties as well. NPD members have been assiduously wooed by both the CSU and the CDU. Cf. *Die Welt*, November 24th, 1966 for CSU recruitment. The situation in Lower Saxony before the state elections of June 1970 was a typical example of the CDU's recruitment of NPD members.

3. Tauber, op.cit., pp. 47 ff. For consideration of conservative resistance to Hitler especially in regard to Schleicher and Beck cf. J. Wheeler Bennett, *The Nemesis of Power*, London 1953, *passim*.

4. Tauber, op.cit., pp. 57 and 58 for the conservative manifesto. Almost all the information regarding this period of German nationalist party development has been culled from Tauber's excellent study.

5. The WAV was a protest party which attracted the same social elements as other nationalist parties.

It showed its true colours with the emergence of Neo-Nazi Karl Meissmer as its dominant figure. By 1950 it had lost any significance. Cf. Tauber, op.cit., pp. 101–107.

6. H. Meyn, op.cit., *passim*. For the most part the consideration of the Deutsche Partei, the German Party, is based on Meyn's excellent empirical study. For the establishment of the party as an extra-regional body see pp. 12 and 13. Meyn would qualify the appellation 'nationalist' for the DP.

7. Ibid., pp. 130 and 131.

8. Tauber, op.cit., p. 70 and especially footnote 66. This portion of Tauber's study is based on a British survey taken by the occupation authorities during this period.

9. Tauber, op.cit., p. 87, and for an excellent analysis of the NRP's position at this time. Niethammer, op.cit., p. 56 ff.

10. Von Thadden seems to have been the party's tactical and organizational genius. Schuetz handed the publications and helped with organization, Hess was responsible for propaganda and the best *bon mots*. The most typical and applicable and one that is quoted everywhere is a remark made in 1966 by Otto Hess: "As of 1950 I have always said, we are going to play woodwinds, oboes, clarinets, and strings but no more tubas and basedrums with cymbals."

11. For the SRP see Tauber, op.cit., p. 690 ff. Tauber's study is based for the most part on an analysis by Otto Buesch and Peter Furth of the Berlin Institute of Political Science, *Rechtsradikalismus in Nachkriegsdeutschland*, Berlin, 1957.

12. Reinhard Kuehnl, Rainer Rilling, Christine Sager, *Die NPD — Struktur, Ideologie und Funktion einer neo-faschistischen Partei*, Frankfurt, 1969, pp. 20 and 21.

13. Tauber, op.cit., p. 713.

14. M. Jenke, *Verschwoerung von rechts*, Berlin, 1961, p. 155 ff.

15. Cf. Joerg Michael Gutscher, *Die Entwicklung der FDP von ihren Anfaengen bis 1961*, Meisenheim am Glan, 1967, pp. 172–182.

16. For the Neumann Kreis see Tauber, op.cit., pp. 132–146
For Achenbach's and Middelhauve's and Wilke's role, pp. 140–143.
For Achenbach's unclear relations with Nazi war criminals in France and his current questionable activities in the Bundestag in this regard cf. Tagespiegel. 14, July 1974 and Suddeutsche Zeitung. 13 July 1974.

17. Niethammer, op.cit., p. 44 ff.

18. For the BHE see Franz Neumann, *Der Block der Heimatvertriebenen und Entrechteten 1950–1960*, Meisenheim am Glan, 1968.

19. Cf. Carl Juergen Meyer, "Die NPD in Hessen", unpubl. Diplom. paper, Otto-Suhr-Institute Berlin, pp. 15 and 16.

20. Cf. Meyn, op.cit., pp. 73 and 74, and Ernst Kastning, *Die Gesamdeutsche Partei in Niedersachsen* 1961, 1962, Diplom. paper, Otto-Suhr-Institute, Berlin, 1962. The work is cited by Meyn.

21. Table I, compiled by Horst Juergen Retzlaff in *Wie erklaert sich der Erfolg der NPD verglichen mit der Situation des Rechtsradikalismus vor 1966*, Diplom paper, Otto-Suhr-Institut, 1969. The chart is compiled on the basis of various statistical reports of the various German states. The WAV and the BP in Bavaria are of course not automatically synonymous with other German nationalist parties, but the WAV and certainly the Meissner wing of that party was a neo-Nazi group. Cf. Tauber pp. 101–108.

The BP was centred in Lower Bavaria with the exception of one election district, Passau, and four districts in Upper Bavaria, Altoetting, Ingolstadt, Rosenheim, and Traunstein. The Bavarian party was strong in these regions which are Catholic regions. This makes the Bavarian Party interesting since it is the only party with strong national tendencies and a regionalist base which is Catholic, unless one wants to consider the CSU as belonging to this category. For the CSU see Chapter VI. For a short analysis of the BP's election area see H. Kaack, *Wahlkreisgeographie und Kandidatenauslese*, Cologne, Opladen 1969, p. 45.

22. Niethammer, op.cit., pp. 61–66.

23. Tauber, op.cit., pp. 870–873.

24. Niethammer, op.cit., p. 97.

Niethammer's discussion of neo-Fascists, what have been called modern nationalists and pragmatic Fascists in this book, and post-Fascists, what have been called old Nationalist Socialists and nostalgic National Socialists in this book, gave much of the impetus to this writer's analysis which, however, varies from that of Niethammer in certain respects. For example, modern nationalists seem to be able to coalesce quite well with conservative traditionalist sorts and historical influences are not absolutely banned from the pragmatic Fascist's analysis of events and propaganda. Pragmatic Fascism remains Fascism, it is a curious blend of modernism and past-oriented normatives.

25. In late December 1959 in the Cologne area swastikas were painted on various Jewish cultural sites. This swastika painting led to an epidemic of minor Anti-Semitic incidents in Germany at this period. The initiators were young DRP members of the nationalistic parties in Germany, especially the National Socialist rehabilitators who have continuously attracted this type of individual, and it has probably cost these parties much of any election success that they might have

hoped for. For an interesting graphic analysis of anti-Semitic and right-radical illegal activities between 1965 and 1969. Cf. *Juedischer Pressedienst*, No. 9, 1969, pp. 12 and 13.

26. Niethammer, op.cit., p. 68.

27. Niethammer, op.cit., see his chart p. 236.

28. Tauber, op.cit., pp. 466–685.

This is a book within a book and deals minutely with ideas and publications of the neo-German nationalist movements. For a more specific treatment see Kuehnl, op.cit., pp. 53–61.

29. For Table III see Niethammer, op.cit., p. 51, and for consideration of nationalist leadership see Kuehnl, op.cit., pp. 56–61.

30. Kuehnl, op.cit., p. 60.

31. *Juedischer Pressedienst*, No. 9, 1969, pp. 17 and 18.

32. See the *Sueddeutsche Zeitung*, February 12th, 1970. For an analysis of resignations in the NPD and one extreme set of statistics for 1969/70 see *BZ*, February 16th, 1970.

Cf. *Frankfurter Allgemeine Zeitung*, September 16th, 1969 for the figures of 36,000 in 1969 and 24,000 in 1970 and for analysis of resignations from the NPD. For a specific analysis of Baden-Wurtemberg see *Die Welt*, January 11th, 1969.

33. Cf. Kuehnl, op.cit., p. 47.

34. Fred H. Richards, *Die NPD — Alternative oder Wiederkehr?*, Munich, 1967, p. 56.

35. Cf. the Chart in *Juedischer Pressedienst*, No. 9, 1969, p. 15.

It is based on information of the Ministry of the Interior and its reports on right-wing radicalism through 1968.

36. Niethammer, op.cit., pp. 249 and 250.

37. Klaus Liepelt, "Anhaenger der neuen Rechtspartei," in *PVS*, 8. Jg., H. 2, June 1967, pp. 237–271, and Scheuch, Klingemann, op.cit., *passim*.

38. Liepelt, op.cit., p. 243.

39. Kuehnl, op.cit., p. 237 and

Elisabeth Noeller Neumann, "Wer waehlt die NPD?", *Politische Meinung*, 12. Jg., 1. Heft, 1967, p. 25.

40. Cf. Liepelt, op.cit., *passim*.

Scheuch, Klingemann, op.cit., Table No. 8, p. 19. Kuehnl, op.cit., p. 242, especially his report of an analysis by Klingemann in 1968 which attempts to differentiate between conservative Protestants and the so-called certainly misnamed Protestant left, that is non-practising Protestants, conservative Proestants being 29.2 percent of the group supporting the NPD whereas the Protestant left makes up 34 percent of the pro-NPD percent group.

Of the traditional Catholics 7.0 percent support the NPD and this out of a percentage of the group questioned of 21.4 percent whereas the Catholic left i.e., the Catholics no longer tied to the church, make up 21.6 percent of the supporters of the NPD. For an analysis of the refugee press see Edgar Weick, "Gibt es einen Rechtsradikalismus in der Vertriebenenpresse?", in J. Fetscher, op.cit., pp. 95–124 and for the strength of the Sudeten Germans in the Bavarian NPD see Niethammer, op.cit., pp. 114 and 115.

41. Kuehnl, op.cit., pp. 266 and 267.

For example, in Bavaria, Middle Franconia, and in Hesse election districts like Bad Herzfeld and Dillkeis, Rhineland Palatinate, districts like Worms, Alzey, Pirmasens, and Kaiserslautern land and city, etc., gave the Nazis relative majorities in 1930.

42. *Juedischer Pressedienst*, No. 9, 1969, p. 16 based on the report of the Ministry of the Interior on right-wing radicalism in the Federal Republic.

43. Table IV was compiled by Retzlaff, op.cit., on the basis of the *Statistisches Jahrbuch* of Bremen, *Statistische Monatshefte* of Baden-Wurtemberg and "Rechtsradikalismus in der Bundesrepublik 1967," *Beilage zum Parlament* B 15, 1968.

Many of the same figures and tables can be found in Kuehnl, op.cit., p. 238.

44. Kuehnl, op.cit., p. 239; for Table V, Table VI, and Table VII, *Juedischer Pressedienst*, op.cit., p. 9.

45. Kuehnl, op.cit., p. 254.

46. Cf. Hans D. Klingemann, "Keine Saulen der Demokratie," in Scheuch, Klingemann, op.cit., pp. 63–70, especially Table IX which indicates as well the importance of foreign policy considerations for the educated groups.

Cf. (Table I on p. 71 which shows an enormous percentage of highly educated (university or *Abitur*) (22 percent tending to support the NPD, as opposed to 9 percent with middle *Matura* (high school degree, but two years less study than for the *Abitur* and not entitling one to university- study) and 8 percent with grammar school education; and Table II, p. 73 which indicates the ration of rising percentage for a tendency to support the NPD and high education plus low income.

47. Cf. Chart compiled by Retzlaff, op.cit., p. 10 on the basis of the *Statistischer Bericht Baden-Wuerrtemberg*, B III 2, March 1st, 1968 and July 16th, 1968.

48. Kuehnl, op.cit., p. 240.

49. Kuehnl, op.cit., p. 236.

50. Meyer, op.cit., p. 32 and cf. *Der Spiegel*, No. 47, November 14th, 1966 used by Meyer as his source.

51. Noelle-Neumann, op.cit., p. 27.

The figures here do not correspond exactly to those that Scheuch compiled, see Table VI, p. 17. However in both analyses cities with over 200,000 population are less inclined to be sympathetic to the NPD.

52. So in any event in Hesse according to Meyer, op.cit., p. 27 basing his analysis on a report by Divo for the FDP Federal Office.

53. "Report on the NPD in election district Giessen." By Hessian CDU Bundestag delegation July 3rd, 1970, unpubl. There are 55,000 people in the state district Alsfeld of whom 28,000 are employed.

54. This point was best brought out by Scheuch but is apparent in any analysis of NPD resignations and the growth of the so-called unpolitical group in the NPD that Niethammer follows so carefully. Niethammer, op.cit., p. 204.

55. Richards, op.cit., pp. 151–159.

56. An interesting example of the confusion that faces the NPD in dealing with the problem of the Jew in the postwar world is the *Political Lexicon's* treat-

ment of Ben Gurion which is relatively neutral but closes with the interesting allegation that in Ben Gurion's home it was not quiet enough for Adenauer and Ben Gurion to talk to one another. This relatively amusing portion of the *Political Lexicon* does not outweigh the more bitter passages such as the continuation of the myth that the Zionists were major enemies of Germany.

Kuehnl analyses NPD ideological positions very much on the basis of *DN* and the *Political Lexicon*, and that is probably one major weakness of the book which is otherwise excellent. Indeed neither *DN* nor *Political Lexicon* in the period 1965–68 give an accurate account of what is happening ideologically within the NPD.

57. Herbert Kohl, "Die Deutschen Nachrichten — Eine politologisch-soziologische Analyse des publizistischen Organs der NPD", *PVS*, 2. Heft, 8. Jg., June 1967, pp. 272–289.

The charts in question are on p. 283.

58. A contrary opinion is expressed by H. Bott in *Die Volksfeind Ideologie, Zur Kritik rechtsradikaler Propaganda*, Stuttgart, 1969. Bott stresses the necessity for continued anti-Semitism within the NPD and makes much of anti-Semitic references in NPD propaganda, especially *DN*. See p. 100 for references to the Six-Day War, p. 104 for references to Jews and unions, and pp. 132, 120 and 81 for references to powerful Jewish positions, etc. The guest workers according to Bott supply the same necessity for an 'enemy-of-the-people' ideology (see p. 93–97). For an analysis of anti-Semitism see P. W. Massing, *Vorgeschichte des politischen Anti-Semitismus*, Frankfurt/M., 1959 and

E. G. Reichmann, *Flucht in den Hass — Die Ursachen der deutschen Judenkatastrophe*, Frankfurt/M., 1968.

59. Kohl, op.cit., p. 283 and for all following figures.

60. Kuehnl, op.cit., p. 216.

61. For an analysis of Anuch see Niethammer, p. 80. Anuch's biological structures are matched by his neo-Splenglerism, see *DN*, August 11th, 1967.

62. Cf. *DN*, March 13th, 1970.

63. Cf. *Die Welt*, July 12th, 1969.

64. Cf. Chapter VI -B.

Although speech G. of "Speeches for an NPD meeting" a master speech for all of Germany, it rides the guest worker issue hard. Photocopied manuscript Federal Ministry of the Interior, Bonn.

65. Cf. *Sueddeutsche Zeitung*, July 18th, 1967.

Actually Germany's crime rate is much lower than that of most industrial nations.

66. Cf. Chapter VI -B

Compare *DN* with "speeches for an NPD meeting" (speeches A — H) photocopies of 1969 speeches made available by the Federal Ministry of the Interior.

67. Cf. Kohl, op.cit., p. 289.

68. Compare with Chapter V.

Cf. as well Rudolf Brandt, *Die Militaerpolitik der NPD*, Stuttgart 1969 and speech H from "Speeches for an NPD meeting".

69. "Speeches for an NPD Meeting," op.cit., speeches A, G, H.

70. Cf. for Hermannsdorfer revolt, *Sueddeutsche Zeitung*, February 16th, 1970.

Niethammer stresses the strength of the pragmatic wing within the Baden-Wurtemberg NPD, but even here it took a hard fight to defeat the von Thadden man Kuhnt as a replacement for old National Socialist Gutmann. A modern pragmatic Fascist Mussgnug (still an ex-DRP man) was elected in 1968 as head of the Baden-Wurtemberg directorate. Here again the weakness of the so-called modern nationalists or pragmatic Fascists within the NPD is illustrated. Not even in the anti-Thadden states like Bavaria and Baden-Wurtemberg can majorities be found to curb the nostalgic Nazis. Indeed modernists like Mussgnug and Stoeckicht in Baden-Wurtemberg are ex-DRP people and so indicate a certain proclivity towards old National Socialist tradition. This may help explain the waning of the Party in the 70s as well as von Thadden's continued control in the face of it.

71. Niethammer, op.cit., p. 250.

72. Ibid., p. 255.

73. Ibid., pp. 204–230 for Baden-Wurtemberg and for Bavaria, pp. 114–153.

74. Cf. DN, March 6th, 1970.

For the work of the NPD in the State Parliaments: Niethammer, op.cit., and Helma Grape, "Die Taetigkeit von NPD-Fraktionen in den Landtagen", unpubl. Diplompaper, Otto-Suhr-Institut, Berlin 1968.

75. Kuehnl, op.cit., p. 304, footnote 23.

76. Niethammer, op.cit., p. 229.

77. Cf. speech for "Day of the NPD – a new Europe, a new Germany, a new party." Uniform speech sent by the party directorate on May 9th, 1968 to all state units of the NPD for delivery on May 18th, 1968, p. 8.

Cf. p. 1–8.

Cf. DN, April 3rd, 1968 and NN, February 20th, 1970 for von Thadden's speech stressing European power potential.

78. Figures for this analysis were taken from the FAZ, October 14th, 1969. In Alsfeld land Protestant villages like Haarhausen (35.4 percent), Unter Sorg (32.6 percent), Hainbach (32.6 percent) gave the NPD one third of the vote, Catholic villages, Hoerkersdorf, Vockenroed, Ruhlkirchen from 1.7–0.5 percent.

79. Cf. Nationaldemokratischer Pressedienst from June 11th, 1969, No. 23, 1969 confirmed "a rising tendency for NPD."

80. Cf. Sueddeutsche Zeitung, Nov. 10, 1971.

Herald Tribune, Nov. 22, 1971

Sueddeutsche Zeitung, June 11, 1971

Berlin Tagespiegel, April 27, 1972

Frankfürter Allgemelne, Nov. 19, 1971

It is significant that Anrich became vice chairman of the Party and this helps explain its demise. Cf. Report of the Federal Ministry of the Interior. 1973/74 on Extremists in the Civil Service. The figure for rightist extremist youth groups rose from 1800 in '73 to 2000, still a very small amount.

position seems for the most part to have been personal but not political. Officers dissociated themselves socially as if the government and military of a country were a kind of German duelling fraternity. Hitler was never let into the fraternity but he ran the machine. In addition, a large number of the new generals made under the Hitler period and officers who had swelled the ranks of the army in the '30s remained true to Hitler till the end.[3] If for no other reason than this, it would be necessary to single out the Bundeswehr as an element in German society with a remarkable predisposition towards nationalism, indeed towards extreme nationalism. For it is for the most part just these Hitler officers who are now moving into positions of authority, of supreme authority within the German army.

Historically, then, the German army has been (1) an elitist-minded group that has invariably interfered in favour of conservatism and authoritarianism within German society; (2) a social group with highly delineated hierarchical and authoritarian social patterns and philosophical prejudices; (3) a group permeated with a nationalist ideology which varies on a scale from traditionalist to conservative revolutionary and extreme nationalism. These ideological elements are probably true to some extent for the officer's corps of most nations of industrial society. However, the intensity of these elements in the German historical tradition cannot be matched. Historically speaking, both in susceptibility and in initiation the German military has been if not a determinant factor in German national experience certainly a very major variable. This did not of course automatically mean that the Bundeswehr would resuscitate the old conceptions, or that the Bundeswehr would replay the role that German military structure has historically played. However, one can expect the same problems that face the military elsewhere in the world to face the Bundeswehr, and these problems usually lead to a restoration of some of the aforementioned historical patterns. Psychologists, French and Ernest, established in 1955 that the military was attractive for people with authoritarian tendencies.[4] Impressionistically it was always obvious that such hierarchically built social structures as police, military, etc., would attract this type of person. French and Ernest established this relationship with scientific rigour. Two years later America's major military sociologist Janowitz wrote that the modernization of the military career and the ensuing technological penetration of military hierarchies would not necessarily lead to democratization of

V

The Bundeswehr and Nationalism

Military forces are predestined by their very nature to be carriers of nationalist ideas. This was not always so. In the period before the modern national cycle armies were bound to political leaders and not necessarily to nation-states. Men fought for money, for adventure, or because they were unable to do anything else. Often they did not fight at all, they simply ran. The success of the armies of the French Revolution and indeed of the American revolutionary armies as well heralded the new integrating military factor of the nineteenth and twentieth centuries. The national vertical was utilized as a means of organizing masses of individuals, just as the mystique of nationalism was necessary as a galvanizing factor for this mobilization of resources. Both were necessary for the organization and development of national armies. Nationalism moved great forces of men to die for their country. The principle of dying for one's country would have seemed absurd to most soldiers in the period before the nineteenth century. A readiness to die or better yet to kill for one's country presupposes the acceptance, a wholehearted acceptance, of the integrating and mobilizing aspects of the nationalist myth. In Continental Europe, after the French Revolution, huge standing armies were the rule and army elites were very often recruited out of traditionalist, elitist, conservative elements of society. Traditionalist elites made their peace with the natonalist principle, indeed carried it into their bosom, and conceived of themselves now as a national elite; the combination of hierarchical conservatism and militarism was complete.

Nowhere was this more true than in Germany. Of all the modern industrialized states Germany had the most profound interlocking of traditionalist and militarist society. It was in Germany that the power of the atavistic social groups was greatest. France had its Dreyfus affair and the fall of Boulanger, in the United States and Great Britain the influence of the army was minimal, Italy was simply too poorly organized for such an influence, and neither Italy nor Austria-Hungary nor Russia were modern industrial states after 1870. In Germany, however, thanks to the historical patterns that were cited here previously, the Prussian officers' corps was able to develop a position of primacy. Chapter II illustrated how atavistic social groups inherent in the Prussian system of government were able to utilize the nationalist principle to mobilize the German citizenry and in a sense feudalize the middle class. Inherent in this process was the acceptance of power and militarism as features of national life. This in turn gave the army a free hand to continue its Prussian type of development. This meant a closer relationship between military and executive than existed anywhere else in the modern world with the possible exception of Czarist Russia, or Austria-Hungary. Certainly this relationship was more formally structured and disciplined and the results more significant in Germany.

The military traditions of Prussia go back to Friedrich Wilhelm I, called the Soldier King. This robust paternalist was willing to sacrifice most of the economic elements of his sandbox state to strengthen his military. His more worldly son, Frederick the Great, was constantly engaged in wars to maintain the independence of the Prussian state. Ironclad discipline became a watchword for the Prussian army, but it became obvious after its defeat by the French revolutionary forces that more was necessary. It was in the period after 1814 that ironclad discipline merged with messianic nationalism to construct the powerful German military machine. This, however, could not be done in Prussia alone. It remained for the establishment of the German Empire in 1870 to truly fuse this combination. Discipline and efficiency remained unweakened by the excesses of ideology. This too separates the German military machine from many before or after it. In the Empire the army was a power factor in its own right within the state. Neither the executive nor the parliament had more than limited influence over the military.[1]

Typical for this attitude in the Empire was the common use of the expression "glowing defence force", *schillernde Wehr*, which fondly expressed the nationalist's love for his military and indeed for his military leadership. Defeat in World War I did nothing to shake either the evaluative perception of the German army by the German citizenry or the cognitive overconfidence of the soldierly qualities of German nationalism. The fact that the German army was limited to 100,000 men by the Versaille Treaty did not limit its role as a power factor of the state since the army was deemed necessary to maintain social peace in an era of social conflict. Nor did defeat in any way change the basic attitudes of the officers' corps which remained traditionalist, national, and conservative. Indeed the small size of the army allowed the conservative and authoritarian elite leadership group to recruit exclusively from among their own, and so the leadership group of the army and its conception of its position within the society was shielded socially from any foreign influence. This made it easier for the German army to maintain its own psychological and organizational life. Its organizational independence made it immune to influences from the government; its psychological independence made it immune from any influence of a post-World War I nature. Not even the wildly heroic attitudes of the conservative revolutionaries were able to penetrate the conservative minds of the leadership group. A man like von Seeckt was certainly not a romanticist in the sense that Juenger's idealistic followers were.

The army elite considered itself trustee of the old monarchic system of government and its allegiance was to that system of government. Its nationalism was the disciplined nationalism of the nineteenth century, but its leadership, although organizationally free from civil fetters and psychologically insulated from ideological penetration, was forced to deal with other groups in the society. The fact that soldiers in the new German army could neither vote nor run for office freed the army even more from concern with the democratic political process. However, that did not stop General Seeckt and other officers from hatching dictatorial plans with members of the heavy industry. One of the plans included the development of the so-called national directorate.[2]

Despite the traditionalist, national, and conservative character of the army, it was not able to resist the post-Nazi penetration and takeover by Hitler's mutated conservative revolutionism. It saw the danger to its independence but was not able to react. Increased efficiency, better weapons and promotion possibilities, plus the essential nationalistic integrative factor appeased moral conservative antipathy. Op-

position seems for the most part to have been personal but not political. Officers dissociated themselves socially as if the government
and military of a country were a kind of German duelling fraternity.
Hitler was never let into the fraternity but he ran the machine. In
addition, a large number of the new generals made under the Hitler
period and officers who had swelled the ranks of the army in the '30s
remained true to Hitler till the end.[3] If for no other reason than this,
it would be necessary to single out the Bundeswehr as an element in
German society with a remarkable predisposition towards nationalism,
indeed towards extreme nationalism. For it is for the most part just
these Hitler officers who are now moving into positions of authority,
of supreme authority within the German army.

Historically, then, the German army has been (1) an elitist-minded
group that has invariably interfered in favour of conservatism and
authoritarianism within German society; (2) a social group with highly
delineated hierarchical and authoritarian social patterns and philosophical prejudices; (3) a group permeated with a nationalist ideology which varies on a scale from traditionalist to conservative revolutionary and extreme nationalism. These ideological elements are
probably true to some extent for the officer's corps of most nations
of industrial society. However, the intensity of these elements in the
German historical tradition cannot be matched. Historically speaking,
both in susceptibility and in initiation the German military has been
if not a determinant factor in German national experience certainly a
very major variable. This did not of course automatically mean that
the Bundeswehr would resuscitate the old conceptions, or that the
Bundeswehr would replay the role that German military structure
has historically played. However, one can expect the same problems
that face the military elsewhere in the world to face the Bundeswehr,
and these problems usually lead to a restoration of some of the aforementioned historical patterns. Psychologists, French and Ernest,
established in 1955 that the military was attractive for people with
authoritarian tendencies.[4] Impressionistically it was always obvious
that such hierarchically built social structures as police, military,
etc., would attract this type of person. French and Ernest established this relationship with scientific rigour. Two years later America's major military sociologist Janowitz wrote that the modernization
of the military career and the ensuing technological penetration of
military hierarchies would not necessarily lead to democratization of

the military ethos.[5] He pointed out the dangers existing for society in general from these modern patterns and the threat of the militarization of society. In a study made in 1969 for the Institute of Sociology in Berlin a young German sociologist, A. Canstetter, came to much the same conclusion. Command structures within the army were not being dissolved but were simply becoming more indirect and impersonal.[6] Much the same fears of a renaissance of authoritarian militarism in a modern garb are voiced by Oskar Negt. Negt, a Marxist theoretician, cites the dangers of a philosophical alliance of military and heavy industrial elites that will form what he calls the authoritarian efficiency or achievement society, the *Leistungsgesellschaft*.[7] Hierarchical structures, he maintains, will put a premium on efficiency and will develop political methods to force elitist conceptions of this efficiency down the throats of the rest of society. The corollary problem of economic merger, of military need, capital financing, and the technologies of production, the so-called military-industrial complex, has been covered at great length by American political scientists. A German analysis by H. D. Klingemann has pointed out that brand new industries with old German firm names and politico-economic ethos are at the beginning of a new development and that this development relates to the development of the production of weapon systems.[8]

The development of the German industrial capacity for military paraphernalia is one of the goals of German conservative politicians. (This will be especially apparent in the coming chapter on the CSU and Franz Joseph Strauss.) Klingemann points out that the development of this military-industrial complex is proceeding rapidly in Germany and is also increasing the pace of concentration of German industry.[9] "The production of modern weapon systems can only be guaranteed by big companies. As the development of the armament sector of the German economy after 1955 shows, mergers have been made consistently with an eye out for armanents contracts. It is possible to observe that firms that co-operate in the armaments market compete in the civilian sector. Nevertheless we will establish the hypothesis here that a partial amalgamation in this armaments market will have the tendency to diminish concurrent competition in other civilian markets."[10] It is obvious that development of this military-industrial complex will have an influence on the political structure of Germany. In both historical predisposition and psychological determinants and in terms of developing social function the Bundeswehr seems destined to play a conservative and potentially nationalistic role in German society. One may be doing the Bundeswehr an injustice. Nevertheless it seems justifiable to single out the military as the major element of society to which to give special attention in order to find out if "army and democracy are antithetical factors in Germany" still.[11]

In our considerations of public opinion in the '50s we noticed that nationalistic ideas were expressed mostly by men in general, and specifically those with 2–6 years of military service. In addition, as was pointed out in Chapter IV, the neo-Nazi parties of the '40s and early '50s appealed heavily to the demobilized *Wehrmacht* veterans. Most inclined to be rabidly nationalistic were those men with more than six years of military service.[12] Deutsch and Eddinger also reported that the majority of individuals who would be interested in military service would come out of those 25 percent who were nationalist or Nazi-oriented. "The number of Nazi sympathizers while small in proportion to the total population — you will remember about 10–16 percent — seems large in relation to those likely to volunteer for military service, and it could well be as high as 40 or 50 percent of this latter group."[13] In addition only one-eighth of the 'all-weather-democrats' seemed willing to enter the armed forces. The increasing reliance of all nations on professional soldiers with long-term contracts strengthen this particular trend in Germany and elsewhere. These groups then become, as they did in Weimar, self-selecting so that an initial predisposition towards authoritarian social structures and nationalism brings a larger group of such men into the armed forces and keeps them there. They then perpetuate their own ideas in this sensitive area. "Both of these factors operated in the days of the Weimar Republic and helped to produce a conspicuously non-democratic and potentially anti-democratic army."[14]

The same factors seemed to be at work in the '50s. Indeed in the middle '60s service in the armed forces seemed to have a pro-national effect on young men. Of those students polled who had served in the armed forces, 48 percent answered that they preferred living in Germany; of those who had not served in the armed forces only 39 percent answered that they would most like to live in Germany.

A trend towards acceptance of authority was also determined. Reservists were less likely to demonstrate than students who had not

served in the Bundeswehr. Of those male students who were reservists, 19 percent indicated that they had strong inclinations to demonstrate; 27 percent of the other students said that they had strong inclinations to demonstrate.[15] The Allensbach analyst speculated that a
certain self-supporting tendency could be established here. Perhaps
high school graduates with a positive attitude towards the military are
the ones who volunteer for service. On the other hand perhaps service
in the armed forces influences the young men. Nevertheless, the majority of students in Germany have not served in the armed forces.
Certainly these are not conclusive figures, but they do give a valid
indication of the persistence of nationalist and associated attitudes in
the military and they do seem to verify the fact that the military at-
tracts a certain type of individual – one more likely to be influenced
by nationalist blandishments. A tendency towards militant nationalism holds most true for all men in Germany between the ages of 35
and 50, and so it is not surprising that a service organization would
also indicate stronger tendencies in this direction than would the rest
of society. In addition, as Wildenmann has pointed out, volunteers
for an army in a society like the German society will probably show
status insecurities.[16] The status insecurities will be compensated for
by a disciplined acceptance of the ingroup ethos. It is necessary to
look at the development of the Bundeswehr in the postwar period and
try and get at its level of possible extremism, nationalism, and conservative traditionalism, and its inclination to take an active role in
fostering these attitudes in society.

Although the rest of the world was satisfying itself that Germany
was being rebuilt along strictly democratic lines, the attempts to rebuild a military organization were being carried out for the most part
by people without the least political reference to democratic systems.
Tauber has excellently documented the infighting that went on in the
early '50s between conservative nationalists and out and out radical
nationalists among ex-German officers over the question of support or
non-support for the Adenauer government. Churchill's famous postwar statement "My God, we've slaughtered the wrong pig" gave
wings to the feelings of self-pity that permeated the German officer
corps after war. The Americans and the British, with the French drag-
ging their heels reluctantly, found a ready and receptive response in
Konrad Adenauer for their plans to rebuild a German army which
would be firmly embedded in the Western defence system.[17] Veterans'

organizations which mushroomed in the early '50s were primarily radically nationalist in their composition, and belonged firmly in the rehabilitating camp of the postwar nationalist spectrum. The most important of them, the *Verband deutscher Soldaten*, seemed at the worst out and out pro-Nazi and at the best it seemed to reflect the political ideas of one of its most important political figures Gert P. Spindler. This Hitler Youth graduate was interested in establishing the 'efficiency achievement state' and what was called *Mitunternehmertum*, a kind of syndicalist economic system, patterned on the Spanish example.

But such domestic political ideologies remained diffuse and took a back seat to the demand for personal rehabilitation and the justification of past roles. The early '50s were marked by the struggle between attentist and/or radical nationalist elements in the German officer corps and those who were ready to support the Adenauer position. Some supporting Adenauer like Lieutenant Colonel Ulrich de Maizière and Count Kielmannseck were certainly genuinely democratic. Others like Baron Leo Geyer von Schwarzenbach were "arch conservatives but eminently CDU-orientated."[18] Part of the sordid infighting that went on to influence ex-officers to come back to the German standard was the financing by the Adenauer government with tax money, through secret funds, of the *Deutsche Soldatenzeitung*, the *German Soldiers' Journal* (once DSZ, now DNZ), the violently anti-Communist, anti-Semitic, and radically nationalist newspaper. The DNZ enjoyed a wider circulation among ultra-nationalists than any other right extremist publication. The Federal subsidy was DM 13,000 a month, quite a bit in the early '50s. Ironically enough, while 'America's loyal ally' Adenauer was secretly supplying tax funds to the DSZ, America's High Commissioner in Austria together with three other members of the allied council banned the DSZ from Austrian territories on the grounds that it was openly pan-German and neo-Nazi.[19]

The old DSZ, now the *German National Journal*, is the most blatant spokesman for extremist nationalism in Germany, surpassing the NPD's *Deutsche Nachrichten* in intemperance if not lineage, in eloquence, and probably in influence.[20] The govenment did not fully dissociate itself from the *German Soldiers Journal* until October 1958. The Federal Government however did attempt to keep the top brass of the military clean of excessive nationalists. A personal screening committee, the GA, was set up to screen potential higher officers. The GA was composed of 38 citizens whose anti-Nazi positions and history were "not open to doubt."[21] The screening committee, which by the way came into being against the wishes of Chancellor Adenauer, reviewed all applicants for military leadership positions from the rank of colonel upwards. Tested was the applicant's personal capability and democratic sentiment. Since 1,350 generals had survived World War II and only 50 generals were necessary for the building phase of the Bundeswehr, a selection possibility for the leadership positions in the new Bundeswehr was very high.[22] The personal screening committee was able to function then as a kind of filter for democratic officers, and it was hoped that in this way an excessively nationalist group of generals could be kept out of the service; it was one of the few governmental groups in Germany to oppose Adenauer successfully in the postwar period. The committee forced the dismissal of five high officers in the Defence Ministry itself, including Colonel Vett and Bergengruen who were two of the Defence Minister's closest collaborators. The committee reviewed 600 cases, rejected 100 potential officers, accepted 486, and found 14 conditionally suitable. Interestingly enough, among the "conditionally suitable" was Lieutenant General Adolf Heusinger. The screening council's doubts about Heusinger did not prevent him from becoming inspector of the Bundeswehr, the foremost position in the German armed forces. What is more important is that nothing under the rank of colonel was screened by this group so that in the '50s junior and field grade officers were able to enter the service no matter what their political allegiances may have been. Generally this group tended to be more radically nationalist than the old members of the German general staff. In addition, once veterans seemed to support the government's policies, their democratic passports were issued. Many ex-officers simply accepted the anti-Communist position of the Adenauer government and ranged themselves alongside the right-wing of the ruling coalitions which included the ultra-conservative Deutsche Partei from Lower Saxony and the extremely conservative elements of the CSU. Tauber writes: "Consequently, while acceptance of re-armament and of the Western treaty structure and rejection of neutralism did increase sharply among organized veterans, it would be very hard to show that there was anything like a proportionate increase in the acceptance of liberal democratic parliamentarianism and a rejection of various authoritarian alternatives . . . Identifying more or less narrow policy preferences with 'democracy' clearly suggested that those who preferred different policies were somehow less democratic. This suggestion threatened to undermine the assumption of good faith of the opposition party upon which rests the political dialogue which is Western democracy."[23] The Adenauer government, to the extent "to which it wished to avoid anything that could jeopardize a re-armament happy climate, had to be considerate of traditionalist, nationalist, and even militarist sensibilities."[24]

The army, then, from its inception, was an incubator of historical traditional nationalism of both the conservative and extremist variety in postwar German society. Two great differences remain however in relation to the Weimar period: 1. The public in Germany was clearly anti-military and the position of the soldier in German society never re-attained the absolute command of public respect and deference that it had in the past. 2. The re-armament of Germany was embeded in the Western defence system. Germany did not rearm until its military potential was absorbed in the NATO alliance and was clearly bound by the Western European Union. The capacity and operative scope of the German army was limited from the beginning. Since the Bundeswehr was an alliance army it was open from the start to a Western communication of ideas. The nationalism of the Weimar period would necessarily be restructured by this kind of new social experience.[25] In addition institutionally, the German Bundeswehr is embedded in the German Constitution in a different fashion from any previous German army. After a hard domestic political battle about the establishment of the Bundeswehr in the early '50s the primacy of the political decision-making organs was secured.[26] The channels of command which were so heatedly guarded by the military in the Weimar Republic have been firmly established within the Ministry of Defence. The control of the armed forces reverts to the Federal Chancellor in the event of war. In this way the framers of the Constitution tried to make sure that the goals, structure, and organization of the Bundeswehr would be subject to the parliamentary government and to parliamentary will.[27]

In order to guarantee that the institutionalization of democratic control over the armed forces would function an attempt was made to educate or re-educate the officers and especially the non-commissioned officers. A new leadership style was instituted with the remilitarization of Germany. The old Prussian military tradition which stressed extreme discipline was replaced by the so-called idea of the civilian in uniform. Graf Baudissin and Graf von Kielmannseck are associated with these reformist ideas for the new Bundeswehr. It was hoped that soldiers would be secured against the excesses of their officers and that the participation of civilians in the armed forces would bring civilian ideas from the domestic society into the life of the military.[28] The establishment of the *Schule fuer innere Fuehrung*, the school for internal democratic leadership, and an 'ombudsman' for the troops, it was assumed, would also help to institutionalize democracy in the Bundeswehr. There seems to be no doubt that both these institutions have had little success in achieving their aims. The school of internal democratic leadership has not been particularly successful in training or in restructuring the thought patterns of German officers. General Count Baudissin, the most prominent reformer in the German army, was not able to take real control over events. In the fall of 1961, Baudissin was promoted to the head of the NATO college in Paris and was thus no longer able to influence the German army's development. He is now Professor of Strategic Studies at Hamburg University. Almost all the ombudsmen, no matter what their political proclivities, have been in political hot water. The Bundeswehr has developed a tremendous sensitivity towards political investigations into its affairs which neither the disaster at Nagold, in which recruits died apparently at the hands of sadistic trainers, nor anything else has been able to shake. The Bundeswehr, for example, resented the parliamentary outrage at the remarks of Captain Karl Adolf Zanker in 1956. Zanker, speaking before a naval training company at Wilhelmshaven, supported the roles of Nazi Admirals Raeder and Doenitz in World War II. Zander said, "both admirals were condemned for political reasons . . . by an international court of the victor powers according to a law which had been created purely for that purpose . . . everyone of us old navy men . . . knows . . . that no blame [is] attached to the person of our two former supreme commanders. I want to say to you today quite frankly . . . after many talks with high officers of the Western powers I am certain . . . that they recognize that the grand admirals had done nothing but their duty to their people."[29] Zanker however was only seconding what the CDU government in Kiel had already undertaken, i.e., to unanimously confer an honorary citizenship of the city on Admiral Raeder, a convicted war criminal. Only the intervention of the Danes and the Norwegians who threatened to boycott Kiel caused an end to the affair. It did leave the officers, however, convinced that they were the stepchildren of society. When ombudsman Admiral (ret.) Heye criticized the service's authoritarian practices in 1965/66, it was he who had to go. This type of military self-pity and identification with the World War II period has not remained isolated. In addition, officers in the armed forces have indicated that they would be more than willing to move against student demonstrators. In Hamburg in 1968 the commander of the army officers' school there sent his cadets into a church to defend the conservative Hamburg theologian Professor Thielecke against demonstrators and/or to prevent the demonstration.[31]

This kind of activism was not evident in the Bundeswehr in the '50s. Then the officers were for the most part trying to rehabilitate themselves. In the '60s, however, a counterattack was initiated against the reforms of Baudissin and others, and in a sense against the course of German social development. The ideas of the officers' corps and their assessment of socio-political events in the society are exceptionally important for the development of ideas among the troops. Especially the inspector, . . . and the commanders of the defence areas, the commanding generals, the division commanders, the school commanders, and the members of the staff are crucial for opinion-making within the officers' corps and through the officers' corps to the rest of the troops. These groups are not united in their views and so one cannot expect a common attitude in all affairs. Nevertheless a certain conservative attitude seems to have developed. This is all the more important since the Bundeswehr, as do all armies, maintains its own information and communications networks which can also be hidden under a plethora of secret and confidential stamps and an inner communications network. It is through this network that not only functional ideas of a military nature can be passed along but also social and political values. The public at large does not view these military communications and publications, and so one does not get a clear picture of the intensity of nationalist or authoritarian values until some big mistake is made by the military command. This makes the investigation of nationalism in the military very difficult since neither the military nor the Ministry of Defence seem at all interested in publishing either the nationalist panegyrics of some of its officers or statistics on the amount of nationalist or anti-democratic sentiment in the services.

Nevertheless certain strong restorative, national, conservative tendencies are apparent. Perhaps the most obvious of these are the symptomatic attempts by officers to change the uniform of the Bundeswehr. When the Bundeswehr was established the uniforms were kept very simple, almost civilian in style. At the beginning of the '60s many changes were made in uniforms, changes that reminded one of the colourful martial uniforms of previous German armies. Indeed here the romantic traditions of other armies in NATO may have played a role in influencing the Germans who felt that their uniforms were drab in relation to those of their NATO allies.[32] The last such development was the suggestion by the German army that berets similar to those worn by the French be instituted for German paratroopists. The influence of organizations like the American Special Forces or Green Berets or the French Paras on the German army and especially on elitist groups within the German army has unfortunately not been analyzed; nevertheless it is interesting to note that contact with other military units does not have an exclusively salutary effect. If we posit nationalist or anti-democratic developments in the allied military organizations we can also expect that these developments will have their effect in weakening any resistance to these political movements within the German armed forces.

For the time being, however, this is a minor consideration in comparison to what has happened within the German armed forces themselves. The political heads of the Bundeswehr from 1956 to 1969 were national and/or conservative. Of the ministers Strauss, von Hassel, and Schroeder, the first two especially are exponents of nationalist tendencies within Germany. It was primarily Franz Josef Strauss as Defence Minister who attempted through the purchase of the Starfighter to establish a nuclear weapons carrier for the German.[33] In addition it was Strauss who used the Ministry of Defence and its ties to other nations (in this case Spain) to attempt to limit the freedom of the press in Germany.[34] After Strauss' departure in 1962 Kai Uwe von Hassel, a North German national conservative, continued the attempt to gain for the Germans a certain say in the deployment of atomic weapons and their utilization. The projects MLF and ANF were lanced by his ministry in the period between 1962 and 1966.[35] Through the Bundeswehr the German Government wished to gain a certain amount of influence on the utilization of atomic weapons in central Europe, and the military command supported and encouraged the Defence Minister in all these initiatives. The coupling of these attempts at a larger measure of military independence with the rise of an *Ersatz* German Gaullism associated with the CSU's Strauss, ex-State Secretary for foreign affairs and party foreign affairs spokesman v. Guttenberg, and the national conservative wing of the CDU, typified by ex-Parliament President Gerstenmaier, cast doubt upon the purely tactical interests advanced by the German Government. Nevertheless one could still explain away this concern with nuclear planning in Central Europe by simply postulating the same kind of strategic thinking for any state in Germany's position. The combination of this concern with atomic weapons, the rise of neo-nationalism and other restorative tendencies, and nationalist propaganda within the military was more significant. The *Traditionserlass* (statement on tradition) by von Hassel's Ministry on the character of the Bundeswehr in 1965 coincided with the previously mentioned governmental neo-nationalism and with the ambiguous German position on nuclear weapons. In the booklet *Bundeswehr und Tradition*, published by the Ministry for Defence in July 1965, national awareness, love of the fatherland, and an oldfashioned nationalism were stressed. Much attention was devoted to symbols for the perpetuation and cultivation of oldfashioned tradition: (1) The German eagle as an emblem of the Federal Republic; (2) the red, black, and gold flag; (3) The Iron Cross as an example of morally fixed soldierly heroism. At the same time this *Traditionserlass* was issued, flags of old German units were issued to the various units. Von Hassel said, "the new flags for the Bundeswehr will indicate to every soldier what we are for and what we are against."[36]

This concern with national martial traditions coincided with a certain attempt at understanding between the US and the Soviet Union and the weakening of the position of the reformers within the Bundeswehr. "The Traditionserlass and the issuance of flags for the troops in a period of beginning detente indicates the weakness of democratic understanding in the social conceptions of the military leadership of the Federal Republic. The military leadership indicates very little tendency, very little desire to identify with the democratic institutions."[37]

Indeed these traditional replants are indicators of a nationalist counterattack against the reforms of Baudissin and others that began with intensity with Baudissin's removal to Paris in 1961. In 1963 in a series of statements to the troops General Hess stressed nationalism and elitist militant character in the army: "Patriotism to our Western cultural homeland is essential. [The word used here for "Western" is *abendlaendisch*, a very interesting formulation, which is semantically associated with Spengler and used by ultra-right circles in Germany today.] These characteristics of leadership should be utilized to straighten out the softness and high standard of living weakness in the society of the Federal Republic."[38] Hess demanded an extension of military values into the society. This dual trend towards nationalism and social militance is also carried through in the political education of the troops. The separate instructors can always choose their own examples from German military history. This of course is fair as an educational method. However, generals who served Hitler to the end with an absolute sense of discipline have served as examples for the troops. This is not surprising, as the Defence Ministry itself was willing to name troop units, ships, and barracks after military people whose record was not absolutely clean in regard to National Socialism. (The best example was the naming of a new rocket destroyer after the controversial Admiral Luetjens of WW II.)

In the late '60s the educational directives of the head of the educational system of the army stressed a military romanticism within the patriarchical leadership ethos. References to the unbroken tradition of an army that conceives of itself as an elite factor for order, that will defend the country against the nihilism of a modern pluralistic society permeated the directives.[39] General Kaarst the officer responsible for the Bundeswehr's educational directives reflected on some of his views in a letter to the Professor of Politics at Hamburg University, Hausmann. Kaarst directed his polemics against "the opportunism without belief systems and the lack of absolute moral standards so that authority disappeared and anarchy seems around the corner." His romantic attitude towards the state in politics appeared in his desire to resuscitate the old corps spirit, the fraternity spirit in Germany. The conservative revolution of his youth peeks through the lines. "To shoot with cannon and mortars, to throw hand grenades and fire grenades, to fire from tanks, to move away mines, to drop bombs, etc., are just simply not bourgeois professions."[40] Kaarst writes in addition: "If we ignore the political background of the Nazi regime the soldierly education of that period was efficient and successful."[41] With such direction to the educational system it is not surprising that strong nationalist, and extreme radical national publications at that, have made their way into the libraries of the troops. National conservative and even neo-National Socialist literature dots the barracks' libraries. Examples of these books are von Manstein's *Verlorene Sieger* (Lost Victors) and Grimm's *Volk ohne Raum* (People without Space). In addition one encounters the writings of Kurt Ziesel, an author who preaches authoritarian, nationalist forms of government and extolls a kind of soldierly death in terms that would do Ernst Juenger credit. Books of the volatile nationalist Hans Joerg Studnitz and pamphlets by his ideological bedfellow Winfried Martini are also standard works in these libraries. These books play upon the unsure status of the professional soldier and attack reformist elements within the army. In his polemic book *Rettet die Bundeswehr* (Save the Bundeswehr) Studnitz attacks the concept of *innere Führung* (inner leadership), to him it is a useless hindrance for the national army. Studnitz not surprisingly also attacks the ombudsman for military questions. "With him," Studnitz writes, "the parliament was able to weaken military authority in a way that not even Hitler was able to do." Studnitz tries to compare the concept of an army controlled by parliament to that of an army controlled by Hitler. And the tenor of his argument is that armies should be independent of governmental control. The difference between parliamentary and single party control is ignored by him. The concept of the civilian in uniform is for Studnitz comparable to Hitler's attempt to put his party emblem in army uniforms. "Those who are surprised about this [the attempt to make the army an army of civilians in uniform] should remember that the concept of the Bundeswehr is more closely tied to that of Hitler's conception of the Wehrmacht than Seeckt's ideas for the Reichswehr. In the same way as in the Third Reich the government is attempting to politicize and to unionize the soldiers who wish nothing but to be apolitical."[42] Winfred Martini makes many of the same arguments and his conclusions are that "politically the Bundeswehr is now really much less free than the old Wehrmacht."[43]

A serious attempt was made to discover just how much this traditionalist, conservatively oriented, and nationalist propaganda was affecting the political habits of the bulk of the Bundeswehr. Wildenmann led a serious sociological study in an attempt to determine how soldiers would vote in coming elections. The analysis was made in 1968. One should emphasize that this was a period in which there were still elements of economic recession in the Federal Republic, that the student demonstrations had reached their peak, and that the flight of the NPD had apparently reached its zenith for the decade. The year of the analysis seems to have been the peak year for political nationalism in the Federal Republic, and trends in 1969 tended downwards. The main result of this investigation was a prognosis about potential possible NPD voters in the armed forces. Wildenmann postulated (according to the magazine *Der Spiegel*) that within the civilian sector of society the NPD in 1968 could reckon with from 10–15 percent possible supporters.[44]

Wildenmann discovered between 20–25 percent support in the army. At the beginning of 1968, the head of the Bundeswehr de Maiziere pointed out that only 0.5 percent of the members of the Bundeswehr were also members of the NPD. Von Thadden, the head of the NPD, claimed that 1,500 Bundeswehr members were organized in the NPD, 250 of these were officers and 750 non-commissioned officers. For 1969 an inofficial figure of 700–800 has been quoted indicating that the drop in NPD membership hit the armed services as well.[45] Especially noticeable was the sympathy that the NPD enjoyed at this time among young officers.[46] The reasons given for support of the NPD were the feeling that the army was too weak to defend Europe and Germany and opposition to the Baudissin concept of internal leadership.[47] In addition, a lack of respect by the population at large and difficulties in getting along with civilian society seemed to influence many soldiers to try their luck with extreme nationalism.[48] The NPD has seized upon these factors, and the military programme of the NPD stressed restorative and national tendencies.[49] The NPD demanded the resuscitation of the German general staff, the administration of the troops by military people and commanders (at the present time the military is administered by a civilian administrative section with between 175,000 and 180,000 employees), the re-establishment of military courts of justice and the end to internal leadership. The NPD maintains that internal leadership "seems to be democratic but must mean a disturbance of order and discipline in the military areas."[50]

The NPD has also sought to win members of the armed forces as candidates for the German Parliament. In 1965, three of 17 military candidates for the Bundestag were members of the NPD, a large percentage for such a small party. One year later, in state elections, 31 soldiers up to the rank of major campaigned for the NPD for positions in State Parliaments. One (Captain Wolfgang Ross of the army) made it into the Bavarian Parliament. In 1969 nine soldiers, six of them officers, campaigned for the Bundestag. The highest ranked NPD candidate was Ernst Thomson, a captain in the Navy.[51] These figures leave no doubt that there are stronger propensities towards the NPD in the military than perhaps in any other social group in Germany. It is only fair, however, to point out that the military is made up primarily of Protestant men, and it is this group within German society that leans in any event most strongly towards both extremist nationalism and the NPD. More interesting, perhaps, are the other results of the above study that indicate that soldiers and civilians vote differently. Not only was the tendency towards the support for NPD apparent in Wildenmann's study but a tendency towards more conservative parties generally. For example in the election districts where large numbers of soldiers are stationed the vote for the CDU was about 60 percent over the national average, the vote for the SPD about 35 percent under the national average. Professional soldiers especially seem to have sympathized with the CDU and the CSU. These sympathies seem to grow with the time that one has put in in service.[52]

It remains difficult, however, to really perceive what the men in the ranks, and that includes junior officers, are thinking. The army is a heterogeneous group and no really firm attitudes have been established. But one can generalize that strong tendencies exist within this hetereogeneous group towards authoritarian thought patterns and nationalist leanings. This is all the more true of the general officer ranks. The tendencies observed in the early '60s have continued and are every bit as strong today as they were then. A study made by the leadership of the army in 1970 indicated clearly for the first time what the ideas of the army elite were. This study as well as the one by Wildenmann have not been released for publication by the Defence Ministry. But both studies did leak to the press. The study called "Thoughts for the Betterment of Internal Order in the Army" was developed at the initiative of Defence Minister Schroeder and signed by the Inspector General Schnez.[53]

The study reflects quite typically the thinking of the entire army leadership. It was prepared by the inspector of the army, his deputy, the commanding generals of the three corps, and the head of the educational system. It represents accurately the ideas that come down to the troops from the general officer ranks. The study seems to plead for a reform not only of the Bundeswehr but for society as well; for example paragraph 7: "The military leadership must not desist from pressing necessary demands even if these demands cannot be carried out because of political reasons at the time that they are made."[54] This paragraph seems to mean that the military leadership reserves for itself the right to attempt to reform society in order to increase military efficiency. The society at the present time is seen as in opposition to the needs of the military. Military needs are garbed in traditionalist robes. Authority must come from the individual's position in the hierarchical structure and not necessarily from his personal capabilities. "The illusory demand for an authority arising out of personal qualifications of the superior officer automatically brings the army and its officers into a difficult situation." The hierarchical structure then is the key to military authority. This control must be maintained through strong associations with the traditions and the nationalistic past of Germany. "The troops are still being condemned to an ahistorical conception and do not have a committing awareness of tradition . . . political and military leadership must identify themselves clearly with German soldierly traditions, . . . the money that has been allocated for the artistic decoration of buildings in which troops are maintained should be used more directly in the future to illustrate soldierly activities and to strengthen an awareness of tradition."[55]

All these examples indicate that the leadership group of the army is reacting sharply to the changes that are current in Germany society. Obviously the attitude of young people is one of those changes that affect the leadership of the army the most. The military establishment is confronted with sceptical German youth and the rising numbers of conscientious objectors in Germany; an enormous increase in the last year has caused the army some concern. We have seen that commanders were not above sending troops out to hinder demonstrators. The entire problem of the youth affects commanders and strengthens them in their authoritarian and nationalistic leanings more than it does leaders of other sectors of society.

Nothing seems to have changed since 1962, when the conception of society that the army leadership wished to present to its soldiers was developed and published. Four basic principles of society were stressed. The overall conception is one of a kind of social harmony which was a part of the thinking of the conservative revolution of the Weimar period and an integral part of anti-democratic German nationalism throughout the nineteenth century. Important is the stress on the need for efficiency in the society: (1) Society is organized for maximum achievement and efficiency. Productive capability not special privilege decide how positions in society will be distributed. (2) Society is middle-class without social differences between upper and lower classes. (3) Society is not a mass society. Society is divided into many separate social groups which give society its structure. (4) The centre of authority in our society can be localized. Society does not have any amorphous structure and there is no authority of the whole group. A system of order, discipline, and authority guarantees that the elite can carry out its authority function. "Especially in a free society discipline and authority are absolutely necessary if the society is to function."[56]

Although this study recognizes the various pluralistic groupings in society, it does not recognize any conflict between them nor does it recognize any radical democratic solution to social problems. It supports an elitist, structured, hierarchical social conception. It is not surprising then that the generals in the armed forces were shocked when the Ministry of Defence allowed soldiers to join a union. The Inspector of the Bundeswehr, Tretner, resigned when this directive from the Defence Minister was issued.[57] We could probably expect this kind of reaction in many armed forces, certainly the combination of traditionalist thinking, latent nationalism, authoritarian structures, and a German society which contains within it strong reformistic elements make for a serious problem for the German military leadership. The entire question of the status of the soldier in today's international system must be particularly difficult for the Germans. Educated on the nationalism and glory of another era as many older officers were, and the German officers' corps is one of the oldest in the world (average age 46),[58] they have not been able to adapt to the needs of German democratic society as it is developed especially in the late '60s. In the '60s the restorative tendencies of the '50s were recognized, and the attack on them began in many areas of society. The virulence of traditionalist and nationalist sentiment in the army is a reaction to these attempts at reform.

In addition to these conflicts the army is faced with a problem of internal control that reflects the problem faced by society at large. Authority in the army depends very much on hierarchical position and the personal leadership of troops, but efficiency within the army depends most often on technological knowledge. Cantstetter in his analysis indicated the conflict between those who wish an army with command structures based on specialization and technological ability and those who wish to maintain an army based on traditional control functions.[59]

The conflict between functional structure and traditional forms of authority structure is quite prevalent in discussions within the German army. The aforementioned General Kaarst has come out strongly and not surprisingly for traditional forms of control. Kaarst feels that the army leadership should accept only a temporary functional necessity for technological control and should maintain its traditional hierarchical patterns.[60] Viewed functionally the authoritarian structure of the army is as oldfashioned as are the traditionalistic and nationalistic thought patterns of its generals. The percentage of soldiers carrying out purely military functions i.e., doing the fighting, has sunk in modern armies to below 15 percent. The need for technically qualified soldiers has caused an enormous increase in the number of technologically programmed servicemen in the middle ranks.[61] Men in these middle grades never command in the sense that officers in the nineteenth-century armies commanded and have little patience with spit-and-polish discipline. But the army is full of officers who in the postwar period were not able to succeed in the new German economy and who were status-threatened persons when they embarked or re-embarked upon a military career. This new threat within their own social group, within the area where they thought that they were safe from the dangers of a technological society must increase their tendency to identify with previous patterns and to seek a new reason for these patterns in the modern age. Negt points to the romanticization of the efficiency principle within the army, the so-called *Leistungsfreude*, joy through accomplishment efficiently disciplined as one martial solution to this problem.[62] The need for hierarchical structures stressed by military men combines the psychological need with a kind of sophistic pseudo-technological romanticism to produce a military aspect of modern society. In other words "our military elan and our national obedience and our traditional leadership qualities are necessary for a society that really wants to establish efficiency and accomplishment." The dangers inherent in this kind of thinking for democratic society are only too evident. The officers' corps in the Bundeswehr, especially in the general ranks but including many non-commissioned officers and younger idealistic officers, could easily again be a major galvanizing element for German nationalism. This nationalism would not be necessarily pro-NPD or even extremist. It would certainly be traditionalist, socially conservative, antireformist, and romantically militant. In this it seems closer now to the right wing of the CDU and the bulk of the CSU than to either wings of the NPD. It is relatively quiessent now under the SPD/FDP coalition and especially under SPD defense ministers. But a recent study by prominent SPD members presented a none too sanguine picture.[63] The political and ideological mixed marriage of the romantically authoritarian and the technocratic pragmatic Fascist cannot be excluded from Germany's future. But its eventual definition will depend on the level of social conflict in Germany and the resiliency of history's legends.

Notes

1. Cf. Chapter II and among others Juergen Schmaedeke, *Militaerische und parlamentarische Kontrolle*, Luebeck, Hamburg, 1966, p. 13 ff.

Gerhard Ritter, *Staatskunst und Kriegshandwerk, Das Problem des Militarismus in Deutschland*, Bd. 1, 2. Aufl. Munich, 1959, p. 28 ff.

Gordon Craig, op.cit., *passim*.

Rudolf Wildenmann, "Politische Stellung und Kontrolle des Militaers," in: Koenig, ed., *Beitraege zur Militaersoziologie*, Cologne, Opladen, 1968, p. 74 ff.

2. Schmaedeke, op.cit., p. 91 ff.

3. J. W. Wheeler–Bennet, *The Nemesis of Power*, op.cit., *passim*.

4. E. G. French and R. Ernest, "The relations between authoritarianism and acceptance of military ideology," in: *Journal of Personality*, 24, 1955, pp. 181–191.

5. M. Janowitz, "Military elites and the study of war," *The Journal of Conflict Resolution*, Vol. 1, 1, 1957, especially p. 18.

6. A. Cantstatter, "Technisierung und Autoritaet," Diplom paper in sociology, October 15th, 1969, unpubl., Free University Berlin, *passim*.

7. Oskar Negt, *"In Erwartung der autoritaeren Leistungsgesellschaft,"* in: Schaefer/Nedelmann (eds.), *Der CDU–Staat*, Munich, 1967, pp. 200–237.

8. H. Klingemann, "Wirtschaftliche und sozale Probleme der Auf- und Abruestung," in: *Beitraegessur Militaersoziologie*, op.cit., pp. 239–270.

9. For concentration in German industry see Grosser, *Konzentration ohne Kontrolle*, Cologne, Opladen, 1969.

10. Klingemann, op.cit., p. 265.

11. K. Buchheim, *Militarismus und ziviler Geist*, Munich, 1951, p. 21.

12. Deutsch, Edinger, op.cit., pp. 40–45.

13. Ibid., p. 44.

14. Ibid., p. 44.

15. Institut fuer Demoskopie Allensbach, *Student und Politik*, Summer 1967, op.cit., p. 60 ff.

16. Wildenmann, op.cit., pp. 82–86.

17. Tauber, op.cit., pp. 266–316. For the French position in relation to the problem of rearmament of Germany cf. especially J. Mosh, *Histoire du réarmement allemand depuis 1950*, Paris 1965. Cf. as well Gerhard Wettig, *Entmilitarisierung und Wiederbewaffnung in Deutschland, 1943–1955*, Munich, 1967.

18. Tauber, op.cit., p. 296.

19. Tauber, op.cit., pp. 300–302.

20. Cf. Chapters IV and VII.

21. Tauber, op.cit., p. 302. Cf. as well W. Baur, "Deutsche Gernerale," in: *Beitraege zur Analyse der deutschen Oberschicht*, hrsg. Wolfgang Zapf, Munich 1965, 2nd ed., p. 114.

22. Cf. Erler, "Politik und nicht Prestige," in: Erler und Jaeger, *Sicherheit und Ruestung*, Cologne 1962, p. 87.

23. Tauber, p. 299.

24. Ibid., p. 299.

25. Wettig, op.cit., p. 613 ff.

26. Cf. Ludwig W. Friedeberg, "Zum Verhaeltnis Militaer und Gesellschaft in der Bundesrepublik," in: Picht, ed., *Studien zur politischen und gesellschaft-Situation der Bundesrepublik. Die Bundeswehr*, Bd. 2, Berlin, 1966, p. 24.

27. Cf. Grundgesetz der Bundesrepublik, Art. 65a.

28. Cf. Erich Hermann, "Innere Fuehrung. Erlaeuterungen zu einer kurzen Begriffsbeschreibung," in: *Wissenschaftliche Rundschau*, No. 9, 1969, pp. 492–507, and Tauber, op.cit., pp. 306–308.

29. Tauber, op.cit., p. 309.

30. Ibid., pp. 309–311. In this development officers' opinions are confirmed by the closed communications system of the army, cf. Wildenmann, op.cit., p. 61 and the officers' own conceptions of what was and is historically necessary. The lack of social flexibility simply increases incomprehension of what happened to the German officers' corps during the Nazi period.

31. Cf. *Der Spiegel*, No. 4, 1968, pp. 27 and 28.

32. Cf. Helmut Grosse, "Die Bundeswehr in der Gesellschaft der Bundesrepublik Deutschland," Beilage zur Wochenzeitung *Das Parlament*, B 470 V 241, 1970, p. 18.

33. Cf. Gerhard Brandt, "Ruestung und Wirtschaft in der Bundesrepublik," in: Georg Picht, op.cit., Bd. 3, especially p. 310 ff.

34. The *Spiegel* affair in 1962 is the most prominent example of this attempt. For an excellent analysis see J. Seifert, "Die Spiegel-Affaere," in: *Franz Joseph Strauss − Ein Typus unserer Zeit*, ed. by E. Kuby, Munich 1963, pp. 233–314.

35. James L. Richardson, *Deutschland und die NATO*, Cologne, Opladen 1967, pp. 66–85.

36. *Information fuer die Truppe*, 3, 1965, p. 158 and cited by Negt, *Bundeswehr und Tradition*, ed. by Bundesminister fuer die Verteidigung, July 1st, 1965, FUBI 4 AZ 35–807.

37. Negt, op.cit., p. 226.

38. General Major Hess, in: *Information fuer die Truppe*, 12, 1963, p. 786 quoted by Negt.

39. *Der Spiegel*, No. 25, 1969, p. 75.

Or consider this order of the day by General Vechtritz, Commanding General of the 1st Corps: "What we soldiers think of ourselves is a possession that no one can take from us." *Spiegel*. No. 3, 1970, p. 16.

40. *Der Spiegel*, No. 25, 1969, p. 75.

41. Ibid., p. 76.

42. See H. G. von Studnitz, *Rettet die Bundeswehr*, Stuttgart, Degerloch, 1967, especially p. 100 and von Studnitz, "Abschied vom Herrn," in: *Student*, No. 9/10, January/February 1970, p. 2.

43. W. Martini, "Der Baudissinismus und seine Fehlspekulationen," in: *Student*, op.cit., p. 4.

44. See *Der Spiegel*, No. 8, 1968, p. 28 ff.

45. *Frankfurter Rundschau*, August 23rd, 1969.

46. Ibid., p. 29.

47. Ibid., cf. as well Kuehnl, op.cit., pp. 244–249.

48. See von Friedeberg, op.cit., p. 25 ff.

49. Cf. Chapter IV.

50. *Der Spiegel*, No. 2, 1968, p. 29 and R. Brandt, *Die Militaerpolitik der NPD*, Stuttgart, Degerloch 1969.

51. Kuehnl, op.cit., pp. 244–249 and *Frankfurter Rundschau*, August 15th, 1969.

52. *Der Spiegel*, No. 8, 1968, p. 28 ff.

53. *Der Spiegel*, No. 1-2, 1970, pp. 22–27.

54. *Der Spiegel*, ibid.

55. *Frankfurter Allgemeine Zeitung*, January 1st, 1970, p. 6. *Der Spiegel*, op.cit., pp. 22–27.

56. *Information fuer die Truppe*, No. 6, 1962, quoted by Baur, op.cit., p. 127.

57. See Dietmar Schoessler, "Militaer und Gewerkschaften", in: *Beittraege zur Militaersoziologie*, op.cit., p. 137 ff.

58. *Der Spiegel*, No. 6, 1970.

59. Canstatter, op.cit., *passim*, and Janowitz and Little, *Militaer und Gesellschaft*, Boppard, 1965, p. 61 ff.

60. Canstatter, op.cit., pp. 56–58.

61. Cf. J.H. von Heiskel's "Militaer und Technik", in Picht, op.cit., pp. 66–158.

62. Negt, op.cit., *passim*, and Kuehnl, op.cit., p. 351 footnote 9 as well as the book cited.

W. Scholl, *Fuehrungstechnik und Fuehrungskunst in Armee und Wirtschaft*, Bad Harzburg, 1965.

63. G. J. Moneta, K. H. Hansen, E. Horn. Bundeswehr in der Demokratie Macht ohne Kontrolle? Frankfurt a.M./Köln, 1974. This study makes aptly clear that the much heralded, anti-authoritarian theses of the so called "Democratic Leutenants" of 1970, was a fly by night affair.

are doctored before release and closed meeting protocols are never laid open. The computer cards stay locked up, financing is not discussed.[4] In addition, a deep sense of particularistic, provincial mistrust faces the foreign (non-Bavarian) investigator.

One should not only be from Bavaria to be assured a measure of political trust, one should preferably be from a middle-sized town, old-family and middle class. (The only exceptions to this are the Sudeten Germans.) Bavaria was not hit badly by ground fighting during the War. The countryside and small towns were spared the holocaust, and the Bavarian social structure survived the war relatively intact. Post-war political activity quickly took on a pre-World War II nature. Old political ties and familiar voting percentages were noted: "The Bavarian Peoples Party [the Bavarian wing of the Weimar Catholic Centre Party] maintained a constant 26–30 percent of those eligible to vote. The CSU should be considered the direct successor party to the Bavarian Peoples Party. As of 1949 it was unable to gain new supporters. In fact its percentage sank slightly to 24 percent of the eligible voters."[5] This relative weakness was one of the reasons for the CSU's lack of individuality in the '50s. But the party's percentage for national election were far better than its state percentages. After its first enormous success in the first state election of 1946 (40.5 percent eligible voters, 52.3 percent votes cast) it began to feel the competition of the conservative, farmer oriented, federalist Bavarian Party (BP), the neo-nationalist WAV (which after initial successes quickly collapsed) and later the refugee-oriented BHE. The CSU's steady increase in strength throughout the '50s culminated in its striking position of absolute dominance in Bavaria in the '60s, and was made at the expense of the BP, the WAV, and the BHE, all of which had strong rightist and/or neo-nationalist tendencies.[6] The CSU was able to co-opt a significant percentage of the large body of conservative voters in Bavaria who had traditionally refused to support a Catholic political party. A perusal of the election results in Bavaria during Weimar indicates that this "extra-clericalist" conservatism existed in Catholic ranks as well. About 15 percent of the Bavarians eligible to vote (about 20 percent of those voting) from 1920 till 1933 voted DNVP or Nazi. Liberal or leftist parties fared worse than the national average. Bavaria as a political culture is no more conservative than other regional areas in Germany but it retains this conservatism throughout an organized federal land. In this it is perhaps still analogous to Rhineland Palatinate or Baden Wurtemberg, although in the latter case certainly a more significant Protestant liberal tradition prevailed. It is different from these states in the essential conservatism of its established Catholicism. The Rhineland has always been more open to the liberalizing influences of Holland and, more important, it was institutionally and to a degree ideologically independent of its major conservative party. Whereas the CDU leadership must consider the heterogeneous mix of German society, the demands of the more liberal urban centers, of the unions and workers, Protestants and Reform Catholics, the CSU has had no need to align with such groups. It is a party which has throughout the late '60s maintained its absolute majority of those voting. It added to its clericalist-oriented Catholic middle-class and farmer voters, nationalist refugees and national conservatives of various stripes. The CSU became a party of paradox. It purportedly represented a region and it adopted the role of the nationalist conservative spokesman. "For Bavaria, Germany, and Europe", the masthead of the CSU's mouthpiece *The Bavaria Courrier* trumpeted since the early '60s. Interestingly enough, Strauss' formal leadership of the party dates from 1961. Although Bavarian German nationalism is not simply a function of Franz Joseph Strauss' leadership of the CSU, its steady volatile expression coincides with his accession to the number one spot in the party.[7] Indeed a national conservative role seems to be one of the main integrative factors of the CSU. Its regionalist antecedents seem only to strengthen this support for an avidly nationalist conservative leadership. The party as a whole and its general secretary in particular mistrust elements in the allied CDU and are not above challenging them.

The CSU sees itself and Bavaria to be the vanguard of Union policies (CDU/CSU) in German domestic and foreign affairs. Strauss gave the best example of this thinking before the CSU state party meeting in October 1966. Strauss' remarks may have been inspired by the state election in the offing in November or by the CSU's autumn 1966 attack on the Union/FDP Erhard government. Probably the latter played its role. But the essence of the speech was independent of the tactics of the day-to-day political struggle. Strauss' talk was entitled: "Bavaria's *German* task". In it he stressed the role that the CSU had played and, more important, *was* playing in keeping the Union and Germany steady along the paths laid out in the fifties: "You [the CSU] can take credit for playing an outstanding role in the development of the fundamentals of our [German] political structure and in the Federal Republic's successes . . . You can take credit for having been, and especially now, being the most united representatives and representation of the Union in the Federal Republic."[8]

For Strauss, not only was the CSU the crucial variable in the Union, Bavaria was the critical variable in Germany: "It was of immense importance that among the parts of the federation that partook in the construction of Germany's new institutional state order a land like Bavaria was found, in which the conceptions of state independence, state awareness, state personalities, state responsibility, and state mindedness could be refurbished."[9] Strauss didn't say 'national', but of course that is what he meant. He complimented the Bavarians on the fact that their nationalism could not be misconstrued as reactionary, and that is why Bavarian regional national impulse was so important for the development of the Federal Republic. In any event the existence of an intact Bavaria had been perhaps as important for the creation of a new Germany as Prussia had been for the old. "Perhaps people will realize later the influence that a state with such deep historical roots as Bavaria could have for the rebuilding of the free part of our fatherland after the destruction of Prussia."[10] Strauss considered the two main salutory influences (apart from healthy nationalism) the restoration of the capitalist system and of the military. Strauss is right. Eddinger and Deutsch among others have poined to the influence of Bavaria and the Rhineland in the construction of the Federal Republic and in the staffing of its elites. The conservative Bavarians felt right at home in a Federal Republic where Wilhelmine political and social verities enjoyed a renaissance. In the coalition talks with the SPD in 1966 they were the tail that wagged the CDU dog, in the election campaign of 1969 they seem to have set the nationalist anti-reformist tenor for the Union. Their influence on the CDU's domestic and especially foreign policy in the 70s and especially after the CSU's success and the CDU's failure in the '72 elections has been even more manifest. In Strauss they have the most dynamic Union politician. CSU support organizations the so-called 'friends of the CSU's, have begun to appear outside of Bavaria, and there is steady talk of the party's expanding into the rest of West Germany.[11] In analyzing the CSU one must look at two things — the party's make-up as a reflection of its Bavarian stamping grounds and Franz Josef Strauss the party's intellectual and political leader, national spokesman, and creator of foreign policy and nationalist verity.

CSU and Bavaria

Although Strauss maintained that the CSU was able to rescue Germany's national honor during the late '40s and make German state independence etc. respectable again after WW II, the party was almost banned by the American occupation authorities.[12] In some areas of Bavaria (for example around Wuerzburg) the CSU was considered too reactionary to be licensed. Essentially it was Joseph Mueller, the most important personality in the founding years of the CSU, who reingratiated the CSU with the Americans. Mueller had been a member of the Canaris group during the war and a member of the resistance against Hitler.[13] But Mueller's conception of Christian social policies suffered the same fate as that of Berlin's social crusader Jakob Kaiser in the CDU. The CSU allied itself quickly with the landowning big farmers (very often aristocrats) and later as soon as the economy was resuscitated, with big business. Typical of the CSU's fondness for aristocrats — especially those with large estates — is the party's record in Lower Bavaria. Here, where large forested areas make huge private property control profitable and where pre-industrial respect for the gentry and the priest is notorious, aristocratic land-holding families formed the backbone of the state organization leadership of the CSU. The families Heyte-Montgelass, Haniel-Niethammer, Spreti and Poschinger were (and still are) either all at once or at least separately represented in the secretariat of the Lower Bavarian CSU since its inception. Indeed one representative of a noble family chaired the secretariat more often than not.[15]

Bavaria is a land with long historical memories and an exaggerated reverance for the past. If you lay a map of the Brandenburg family dukedoms at around 1750 (Kulmbach, Erlangen, Bayreuth, Ansbach, Neustadt-Aisch) over a voting pattern chart you get astonishingly different voting patterns than if you lay a map of the old bishoprics Wuerzburg and Bamberg down. A difference of 10 or 20 km means in most communities the difference between a typically Bavarian pattern CSU) or a non-Bavarian pattern (FDP and/or lately strong NPD minorities). Obviously religious dichotomies play their role here. The Catholic areas are CSU and the Protestants deviate. The crassness of this deviation reflects long memories. Traditions may be something to respect, and the Bavarian aristocracy may be worth preserving, but the concentration of land in their hands may be one of the reasons that Lower Bavaria with 28 welfare recipients for every 1000 persons has the highest poverty quotient in Bavaria, and is the only Bavarian area with an over average quotient for Germany.[16] In addition cross relationships exist between CSU aristocracy, economic elitism, and extreme political conservatism. The case of Prince Georg von Waldberg zu Zeil und Trauchburg is an excellent example. Prince Georg, whose holdings, mostly land in Swabia, amount to about 800 million DM, belongs to the CSU and the CDU, but his close political ties are with the right-wing Catholic CSU studded *Abendlaendische Akademie*. His newspapers support conservative and national positions and he himself was a CSU candidate for parliament.[17]

The traditionalist tie to the landed aristocracy is not simply a case of reverse 'noblesse oblige'. It is one instance of the CSU's connection to moneyed interests. The CSU is pro-capital and anti-labour. No doubt the CSU would deny this. But the symptoms of anti-laborism are all there. The CSU is associated with three labor organizations. The CGB, (the federal Christian Labor Union), the South German *Werksvolk* (Working People), and Kolping. These groups feed the CSA, the CSU's labour-oriented sub-organization with 7,800 active CSU party members almost all of whom are skilled workers or from small business operations. Its leader Hans Stutzle was once Labor Minister for the Federal Republic. But even pet labor influence within the CSU was never great and is now minimal. It would be impossible to compare it with the relatively strong Catholic worker element in the CDU under former Labor Minister Katzer. The CSU and especially the Working People and Kolping approach labor relations in an evolutionary communal manner. Modern industrial conflict is anathema to them. Indeed as their membership stems for the most part from small firms and skilled craftsmen, there is a traditional pre-industrial mentality which has nothing to do with the mass unions of Germany's modern economy.[18]

The real anti-labor philosophy of the CSU comes out in the minutes of a secret meeting of the economic advisory council of the CSU during the Bavarian metal workers' strike in 1954. In its commentary on the strike the CSU had issued a "serious warning to the unions" and CSU deputy Elsen read an official party statement complaining that: "It is not responsible in the interests of the land and its people to continue to accept the heavy social economic and political damage that is now being done."[19]

State secretary Nerreter went further. He demanded that "the laws be enforced properly." New legislation was not necessary; quick police action was. The police should be "sent in if a dangerous situation exists before criminal acts can be committed." "The city police were not good enough . . . the emergency squads (a kind of para-military force of new recruits) should be increased." It was imperative to have a "clear limitation of the right to strike", with "compulsory arbitration."[20]

Director Lang, the meeting's chairman, argued that "the right to strike was not only a matter for the union." Lang insisted on limiting the right to strike and legislating compulsory arbitration.[21] Compulsory arbitration and limited strike rights were proposed with absolute unanimity. The "responsible" employees, those interested in "order" (Elsen) had to be protected. There was "no absolute right to strike" (Hatzunger) "just as there was no absolute freedom" (sic).[22] The CSU's position here is obviously far to the right of that of the Union and there is no indication that these 1954 positions have been mitigated today. It would be difficult to prove this assumption because no secret documents of the deliberations of the CSU about the 1969 wave of strikes in Germany have fallen into the hands of eager researchers. On the other hand, the circumstantial evidence is convincing. Of the six major lobbyists for big business and anti-labor policies who have managed to get a seat in the Bundestag (as elected representatives) two have made it over the CSU lists: The late Dr. Wolfgang Pohle from the Flick concern and Dr. Gisbert Kley from Siemens. Of the four others three are from the CDU, one from the FDP.

Perhaps more important here than the high percentage is the fact that the CSU went after non-Bavarian industrialists and offered them a high place on Bavarian state lists. Pohle was not assured a safe place on the CDU lists and got one from the CSU and the treasurer's position in the party as well. He was elected to parliament in 1965 and in 1969 held down the number nine place on the CSU list. Kley is a new acquisition for the CSU parliamentary delegation.[23] The CSU of course is the absolute enemy of union or worker participation in the decision making process of industrial firms. This participatory practice, adopted with some success in the European Coal and Steel

Community, is favoured by the labor unions in Germany to insure that investment policy is structured to avoid job loss and provide means for workers to move into executive positions and to learn how to handle them. The CSU is absolutely opposed. Strauss' ideas on this subject are indicative. He is pro-entrepreneur and their right to control investment. In Germany, however, firms are short of capital and operate largely with bank financing. In the case of Krupp (among others) the government had to step in (in 1967/68) to prevent bankruptcy. The tight credit structure made the labour unions and others outside the executive economic hierarchy nervous, and an independent commission of experts supported the principle of 3:2, i.e., 3 representatives of the management, and 2 labor in firm directorates. It is 1:1 in the Coal and Steel Community.

Strauss' solution for the coming problems of the technological restructuring of German industry is "cooperation between management and labor representatives"; he avoids the words labor union. He states: "For questions that effect the employees [which these are he does not specify] better information and consultation should be organized. The basic idea of trusting cooperation implies an obligation for both partners." This is simply another expression of paternalism. The economic power remains where it has been in Germany, in the hands of management There is no reason why the CSU should not be a big business party. Capitalist interests in Germany have usually been nationalist but not always extreme, and at times elements of the big business community have been far less rabid than the rest of the country (as, for example, in 1913). On the other hand, Strauss' economic positions imply support for the development of military industrial technological complexes in Germany since his support for business is tied to a predilection for state investment in national weapon's technology.[24] In addition and perhaps more significantly, Bavaria is not heavily industrialized. The CSU is a party of the Bavarian Catholic conservative middle class, Catholic farmers, and women who vote the party into power. The membership is old and new middle-class dominated with 13.1 percent skilled workers, 20 percent farm owners, 5.6 percent self-employed, 6 percent employees, 6.5 percent civil servants and 3.5 percent academic professions, a total of 54.7 percent. (The figures are from 1964). CSU records interestingly enough do not define the other 45.3 percent or merely as housewives, pensioners, etc., and so are a bit suspect.[25] These groups have few economic interests if any in common with the industrial giants that the CSU has embraced. Therefore as in the past an anti-modernist pre-industrial moral ethos of community society and nationality has to substitute for functional unity. German industry is, after all, important; German workers and white collar employees apparently not so important. Germany dare not become an "American license province."[26] German efficiency and excellence can only be achieved by strengthening the German entrepreneur. Strauss coats his middle-class CSU listeners with a big business brush: "The middle class is . . . an essential, integrative part of the overall economy and of social policies." But here Strauss means the self-employed middle class with their huge percent of Germany's total economic product. Of 84,500 industrial firms in Germany 83,500 (total turnover till 50 million marks) handle, according to Strauss, 43 percent of the total industrial turnover. Interestingly enough 500 firms with a total turnover 100 million handle 39 percent. Concentration is actually farther advanced than that.[27] But Strauss paints a positive picture for the small businessman as he does for the suspicious, anti-modernization farmer. He gives the farmers' economic problems a fairly short shift; their sociological importance and the critical nature of their ties to "home, state, and property" are stressed.[28] Pre-industrial homilies and the integrative force of the moral imperative — the old nationalist brew — are the broadening mainstays of the CSU's tightrope.

The essential character of the CSU is Catholic small town. Precise figures of membership are hard to come by, but some are available, and on the basis of one *Beisitzer* (member without vote) in the CSU state council for every thousand party members cautious extrapolation is possible. The Catholic Lower Bavaria with 14,000 members and Upper Palatinate with 13,000 lead Upper Bavaria with 12,142, Swabia with 11,000, and Lower Franconia with 10,000. Middle Franconia with its concentration of Protestants has 7,000, probably mostly in the Bamberg area. A couple of comparisons are possible here. Munich, the Bavarian capital with a population of over a million and a concentration of political and economic activity which makes party membership in the ruling party eminently desirable, has 4,000 members. Lower Bavaria's population equals approximately that of Munich, but lower Bavaria has twice as many CSU members. Nuremberg-Furth, a Protestant area of approximately 600,000, has only 2,000 CSU members, mostly Catholic. Augsburg, a Catholic city of

200,000, has only 635 CSU members, of whom 3 percent are Protestant. A 9 percent figure for Protestants is probably an accurate one for the whole CSU. Twenty-six-and-a-half percent of all Bavarians are Protestant. In Middle Franconia with 60.8 percent Protestants only 30 percent of the CSU members are Protestant.[29] The small-town character of the party is recognized by the leadership. At a party directorate meeting called to deal with this problem K. Schaefer complained that "90 percent of the CSU members moving from the country into the city are lost — despite contacts and persuasion to join the big city wards."[30] Indeed the CSU does not control a single important city council in Bavaria. Munich, Augsburg, Nuremberg, Regensburg, etc., are all administered by SPD mayors and majorities.[31] Large elements of the CSU are in fact anti-city. Statements by Bundestag representatives on appropriations cited at the CSU directorate meeting were peppered with this mistrust: "Do you think we want to give the red cities money?" And: "We don't want people to move to the cities from the small towns where they will vote SPD. We want them to stay out and not vote SPD".[32] But Dr. Lades, the CSU mayor of Erlangen, knew how to rewin the cities for the CSU. Not through social reform or communal economic projects but through national conservatism were urban voters to be gained. "The conception of Fatherland, that which is conservative and that which preserves the state, hasn't been stressed enough by us."[33] And Oskar Schneider, the Catholic secretary of Nuremberg city CSU organization, blamed the church for not being "willing to fight the Sozis [SPD] the way the CSU has been fighting and in the national way."[34]

It is surprising Schneider talked this way since the church in Bavaria is an open ally of the CSU. There are three major leadership wings in the CSU, one is the extreme nationalist conservative group which included the late editor of the Bayernkurier and one time Strauss' personal representative Marcel Hepp, one time Justice Minister Richard Jaeger, Professor von der Heyte, law professor and arch conservative from Wuerzburg, and Walter Becher, the head of the Sudeten German refugee group. (The new editor Michael Horlacher is also quite conservative and dependent on Strauss.) This group has ties through the Abendlaendische Akademie ideologically and personally to the Catholic conservative wing led by the bearded Bavarian ex-Agriculture Minister Alois Hundhammer and ex-Culture Minister and head of the CSU

Bavarian state parliamentary representatives Ludwig Huber. The Catholic group organized till about 1965 in the Petra Kreis is as anti-Communist as the first group, but the primary authority in social matters is seen in the church not the state. There is no doubt that it is a strongly authoritarian group, and it is supported by much of the Bavarian church press especially the bishopric publications of Regensburg, Passau, and Wuerzburg.[35] The third group is what one might call modern conservative. Bavarian Minister President Goppel, Leo Wagner, the executive secretary of the CSU Bundestag delegation and Strauss' right-hand man in Bavaria, Max Streibl make up this group. Let us say they are the Nixons of the CSU and leave it at that. Strauss has forged a tight alliance of groups one and three and indeed has on a few occasions both sided with and combated the second group.[36] He probably feels, and correctly so, that the Bavarian church has nowhere else to go. The church's own internal conflicts between authoritarian and reformist courses will force it to support the party of social conservatism and force it to seek the integrative support of political conservative national ideology to hold its flock together against the neo-Erasmite Dutch "heresies".[37]

A whole series of remarkable affairs scared the Catholic hierarchy in Bavaria in the fateful late 60's. The most important were the Regensburg bishop's rejection of birth control, because it would weaken the white race against the coming colored storm, and the Defregger complex. Bishop Defregger was a captain in the Wehrmacht who ordered the shooting of two score Italian hostages in Filetto. The Munich Cardinal Doepfner refused to condemn him, and although the Italian town wishes to try him as war criminal he will almost certainly never be brought to trial. He has simply been "suspended" from his duties as a bishop. These two instances revealed a higher level of nationalist feeling in the Church than one might have expected from socio-religious election analysis. Indeed, according to Kuehnl, "no major Catholic organizations have clearly damned the NPD" and the Wuerzburg bishopric publication urged Catholic voters to vote NPD rather than FDP in the Bavarian state elections of 1966.[38]

Strauss, then, has been able to maneuver between the first and third group. He started his career with group three and the relatively enlightened *Ochsensepp* Josef Mueller. Strauss was Mueller's protégé but he ditched him in the late '40s and allied himself with the anti-

Mueller nationals and Catholics. He did this primarily in order to be sure of Jaeger who was important for him in Bonn. Strauss was after the Defence Ministry, and Jaeger was chairman of the Bundestag's parliamentary committee on defence. That Strauss politically and psychologically destroyed CDU-man Blanke, the Bavarian's predecessor in the Defence Ministry, is common knowledge. Jaeger's role was significant. The price was Mueller and strong social Catholicism. Since then Strauss has never attacked the extreme right of the CSU, and the extreme right of the CSU is no different from the modern nationalists in the NPD except that it is ambivalent towards open and past anti-Semitism.[39]

A constant series of affairs has dogged the CSU. Nazi pasts and neo-Nazi and/or extreme nationalist proclivities are part of the party's make-up. The Frauendorfer case is typical. Max Frauendorfer was deputy treasurer of the CSU. Frauendorfer was twice unsuccessful in getting on the CSU's election lists (once for the Bavarian Parliament and once for the Bundestag). Both times the Mueller group was able to stop him, but he continued to be influential in the CSU and to enjoy Strauss' protection. Ex-SS-*Sturmbandfuehrer* Frauendorfer had lived under an alias, Dr. Schreiter, till 1951. He had been Himmler's personal adjutant while the SS-chief was still police president in Munich (1933). He had had a long career in the Nazi Workers' Front and as chief editor of the *Reichsschulungsbrief* (Reich's educational letter) and as head of the *Reichschulung*. These were key posts for the dissemination of Nazi ideology within the SS. A special three-man group in the CSU — none of whom had been Nazis — claimed that Frauendorfer had never agreed to Nazi ideology and had really been in the resistance. Frauendorfer's whitewash was accompanied by an impassioned plea to the Chancellor, the Federal President and parliament by two important Munich right-wing CSU members, district chairman Erwin Stein and ward chairman Emerich Giel, that it was time "to issue a general amnesty for all crimes committed by Germans insofar as they were connected with the war or the situation created by the Nazi regime."[40] Giel's case is interesting. In 1967 he became a member of the publishing team of the *Deutsche National und Soldatenzeitung*.[41] Through him, Stein, Hepp, and Emil Meier, an ex-Nazi journalist and chief editor of the *Deutsche Konservative Korrespondenz*, a Catholic national conservative information sheet close to the CSU, maintained close contact to the volatile nationalist *DNZ* and its rabid editor Gerhardt Frei. Giel, by the way, replaced CSU member Frank Huber, Ludwig Huber's brother, in the *DNZ* publishing house.[42] Another contact point between the CSU and old and new Nazis is the neo-nationalist Sudeten German organization, the "Witkobund". Tauber describes the Witko Bund thus: "SS, SA, and Hitler youth leaders abound in the Witko League and completely overshadow and outweigh the comparative handful who have never been members of the Nazi Party . . . Needless to say the Witko League's leadership remains firmly in the hands of former Nazi functionaries and folkish authoritarians."[43] A prominent member of the directorate of the Witko League is Dr. Walter Brand, a one-time close associate of the chief Nazi in occupied Czechoslovakia, Konrad Henlein, editor of the Nazi paper there called *Die Zeit*. Brand is a member of the CSU and deputy president of the *Sudetendeutschlandsmannuschaft*. Deputy secretary of the directorate of the Witko Bund and leader of the Sudeten German refugee organization is Dr. Walter Becher, number ten man on the CSU election lists in 1969 and a CSU member of the Federal Parliament. Becher's literary efforts in occupied Czechoslovakia included references to "Jewish culture warts", "fat Jewesses", "Jewish culture destruction", etc.[44] Of the seven other members of the directorate of the Witko Bund four belong to the NPD. A third prominent CSU member and member of the Witko Bund is Herbert Prochazka. Prochazka was 22 years old at the end of the war. He was Director of the private bank Dierks and Co. in Munich. He was a CSU representative in the Bundestag in June 1969, at a time when he was arrested in Bonn for drunkenly bellowing this ditty:

Ein Volk, ein Reich, ein Fuehrer,
Wir werden immer duerrer,
Die Juden immer fetter,
Adolf Hitler ist der Retter.

One people, one empire, one leader,
We are getting ever thinner,
The Jews ever fatter,
Adolf Hitler is the saviour.[45]

Members with prominent Nazi pasts are found in all German political parties.[46] But the CSU members have far more personal ties to unreconstructed National Socialists, and the party seems to have more practising neo-nationalists and especially Sudenten Germans of the old stripe in high positions in its ranks. In addition, the CSU has had its share of questionable political affairs as a party and has not simply been embarrassed by individuals. In order to win communal elections the CSU has entered into election alliances with the NPD. To be sure these alliances either in the form of common lists or tacit support for CSU candidates by the NPD have always been criticized by the Bavarian state party leadership. Usually a letter of admonishment to the offending city leadership has informed them of the state CSU's formal opposition to any common action with the NPD. Certainly the FDP and elements in the CDU leadership have reacted with more vigor than the CSU in combating this kind of thing. In addition the CSU is the only repeater in a given area.[47] In 1966 the CSU and the FDP in the Franconian town of Kulmbach established a common election list with the NPD in order to capture the city hall. Kulmbach, a working man's town (55 percent blue collar) has a narrow SPD majority and a strong NPD following. Whereas the FDP state directorate passed a binding regulation forbidding the common lists (which unfortunately came too late according to Bavarian election by-laws), the CSU's displeasure was indicated in a legally meaningless letter by Strauss to the district leader Weiskopf. Weiskopf was furious and defended his district's decision: "This is simply a tactical election ploy. We want to save the extra votes from the SPD. In addition we have nothing against Dr. Wagner [of the NPD] he is a very decent fellow."[48]

In 1969 the CSU in Franconia was again involved as the NPD indicated that it would formally support the CSU candidate in that area. After a few weeks of hemming and hawing the alliance was dissolved. The fact of repetition however indicated that the state leadership takes no action against district and ward bosses who maintain excellent contacts to the NPD, that the voters in these areas accept these ties, and that the district CSU membership is immune to public extra-regional criticism. It is important to remember here that the socio-economic structure of CSU and NPD voters in Bavaria is similar. Women and practising Catholics vote CSU by an overwhelming majority, but the NPD can make inroads into males, farmers, and self-employed middle-class CSU voters and has, of course, especially in Franconia strong support among conservative Protestants. Both parties compete for farmers, craftsmen, and middle class, and for all their previous success in holding these groups election meetings in 1969 indicated that the CSU was in trouble in these socio-economic areas.[49] If one remembers how the force of nationalism has served as an *ersatz* for social solutions and a binding political factor just for these socio-economic groups then it is easy to understand why the hard-pressed Franconian CSU is most vulnerable to alliances with extreme nationalism.

Perhaps more significant than the district alliances with the NPD was the entire tenor of the CSU's election campaign. The CSU emphasized its national and anti-Communist, anti-radical determination. The idea of passing the NPD from the right seems to have been most widely accepted in Bavaria. There is no doubt that Strauss with his heavy-handed anti-student strictures (they, the student demonstrators, are nothing but "animals" and "neo-vandals") fear-filled Cassandra cries in foreign policy and volatile anti-leftism was the central Union figure in the campaign. Indeed an extensive statistical comparison between the CSU's weekly newspaper *Bayernkurier* (over 100,000 issues a week) and the *Deutsche Nachrichten* and the *Deutsche National Zeitung* did not turn up significant differences for the four issues before and the four issues after the federal elections. Both qualitatively in propaganda tendency and quantitatively in newsprint spent and emphasis the CSU's weekly editorializing and reporting differed but slightly from extremist nationalist papers.[50] The bitterness and indeed danger of such a course was best illustrated by the establishment of a paramilitary CSU 'security' force during the campaign. Again Franconia provided the center of activity. Members of Nuremberg's police force signed up to join a CSU 'security' force. The recruitment of these policemen was handled "confidentially". (Many German papers claimed conspiratorially.) Nuremberg's SPD mayor Urschlechter did not get wind of the affair until one policeman complained. Other policemen have brought court action against the "informant". Urschlechter's complaint to CSU state Interior Minister Merk was allowed to gather bureaucratic dust. Most significant in the affair was the fact that an ex-member of military counterintelligence, a certain Max Laehrmann, was retained by the state CSU to run the security group and protect Strauss, this at a time when Strauss as a German Federal Minister could have summoned all the protection he wanted. When questioned about the off-duty police security corps, press secretary Kiel of the State CSU stated: "Any policeman is free to work for a political party in his free time . . . CSU members or friends in Nurem-

berg are working with us in an area in which they are proficient."[51]
From the above it seems apparent that the CSU is a party with
national conservative predelictions and a significant minority willing
to ally with nationalist extremism. Obviously the party feels it can
control these extremists and eventually swallow their voters much
as the Union did in the '50s. Indeed the 72 elections indicated as much.
The NDP fell apart in Bavaria. In 1969 in had 5.3% of the Bavarian vote,
its second largest total in Germany. In '72 it fell to 0.7% and this undoubtedly helps to explain the CSU's '72 success (from 54.4 to 55.1%).[52]
It is also obvious that the party maintains an ambiguous attitude towards
certain aspects of democratic practice and is anti-liberal and receptive
to all forms of hierarchically structured authority. It is a middle-class
party but big business has a major say in its policies. This basic economic
disfunction forces the need for emotionally integrative political positions.
The competing groups within the party, Nationalist, Catholic, and
techno-conservative also cry for a unifying hand. Both the policies and
the hand have been supplied by Franz Josef Strauss.

Franz Josef Strauss

"They let Franz Josef Strauss mount the barricades and they sit
behind them and play cards," — F. J. Strauss about his fellow party
leaders.[53]

Franz Josef Strauss is more than just a rallying point for the CSU.
He is more than just the cement that holds the various competing conceptions and sociological groups in this party together. He is a pace-
maker of modern German nationalism. He is typical of a definite
political style, he represents a German leadership variant of political
movements apparent in Western industrial society. He is the epitome
of a nationalist leader. He is this despite the fact, or perhaps because
of the fact, that his power base rests on a very strong regional grouping. His political weakness in Germany has been his political inability to cross the Main-line i.e., the river line that divides North from
South Germany. But this weakness has not hindered him from establishing decisive criteria for modern German nationalism. From his
position as undisputed leader of the CSU he has been able to develop
political attitudes which are more typical for the course of modern
German nationalism than are the divided flounderings of the NPD
and so-called extreme right-wing radicals. Strauss swims on the ex-

treme right of the German mainstream, and in so doing he has been able to help chart the course of that stream. A better metaphor would perhaps be to dam the course of that stream, since Strauss' function and the function of modern German nationalism as he represents it is to brake the normal functional flow of events from the nation into the larger reformed supranational groupings, and to maintain national social structures with unchanged national elite selection processes. This is not to say that Strauss and the CSU do not regard themselves as Europeans; indeed they purport to espouse European solutions. These solutions, however, are firmly tied to the national structure and especially to an increase in power for the German national state. In addition domestically, as the preceding chapter illustrated, the national position is used to pander to sociological groups which are threatened by modernism i.e., by the change inherent in technological and sociological developments. Furthermore it is at least possible to hypothesize that the attempt to rescue certain capitalist structures in Germany and to retain them in their pre-World War II form is a hisorical corollary to the successful attempt under the Wilhelmine monarchy to rescue an elite that had outlived its functional usefulness. Analogous to the feudalization of the German middle class we may be witnessing an attempt at its managerization. A comparison between Junkers and capitalist entrepreneurs may not seem valid, and indeed such a comparison is hypothetical at best. The point remains that in its so-called Europeanism the CSU is attempting to preserve strong elements of the nation-state and essentially the sociological structure of society which carried this nation-state throughout our modern cycle. Franz Josef Strauss is one of Europe's most eloquent spokesmen for these policies.

Strauss is more than just the political opportunist that some of his enemies see him as.[54] He may have been that at the beginning of his career, but he is now an inexorable part, indeed a leader, of a very distinct and very typical political movement. His personality and his political career are not to be the subject of this short study.[55] Nor will the attempt be made to repeat his moralistic strictures and bitter attacks on student protesters and leftist intellectuals in general. These are, of course, part and parcel of the categorical moral and cultural offensive inherent in modern and in oldfashioned nationalism. More important for this study will be the political positions that are the outgrowth of modern German nationalism.

Here, most important is Strauss' concept of the role of the nation. Strauss recognizes the historical functional character of the nation-state. He realizes too that the romantic framework that surrounded the nation-state was a psychological process to achieve goals like the unity and the efficiency of the state. He is aware that the function of the nation-state is not the same in the postwar period as it was in the early part of the twentieth century and utilizes the concept of organized space in proving his point. The organized space available to a European nation-state in the modern period is simply inadequate for the economic and security needs of European states. So far his argumentation would not differ from most analysts. He scores as well the aggressiveness of oldfashioned nationalism, and indeed he attacks those who would attempt to resuscitate this type of nationalism in Germany.[56]

The nation, however, remains for Strauss the moving force in Europe. Europe has no greater capital than the diversity of its national talents and the continuity of its national abilities. The cultural and spiritual civilizing strength of the nation-states is to be preserved and is necessary for the establishment of any kind of regional structure.[57] Strauss is of course no theoretician of nationalism and his ideas have meaning only in relation to his conceptions of Germany's future. Europe is for him a Europe of the nations, although there seems no difference in his conception of a 'Europe of the nations' and de Gaulle's 'Europe of Fatherlands'. Indeed Strauss is influenced by Gaullism. The difference between Gaullism and Strauss' late 1960s conception seems to be in the appreciation of who was to lead this regional structure of Europe. The structure itself is not granted any sovereign rights over states by either Strauss or de Gaulle. Strauss hopes for a feeling of 'Europeanness', but he insists on the life force or the life will of the individual people which he considers an elementary prerequisite for an intact spiritual unity.[58] What lies behind these ideas is the special situation in Germany. Germany holds for Strauss the key position in the entire regional development of "the European family". That is because there can be no Europe in which the Germans are divided, no Europe that ends on the Elbe or the Oder river. Strauss does not directly demand reunification before the establishment of Europe, but he demands freedom of movement throughout the European area including East Germany. Although he also seems to envision a re-extension of German influence which he euphemistically calls 'Europeans into Eastern Europe', at no time is he willing to give up German legal positions in the Eastern European area.[59]

The concept of the German nation may be modernized but an elementary political aspect of German nationalism remains the same: a large Germany or German area extending its influence into Eastern Europe. This is Strauss' Europeanization of German nationalism and indeed it allows him to appear as a Europeanist (which is necessary for it is a popular concept in Germany and especially popular in certain Catholic areas), but it also allows him to maintain a strictly inflexible policy vis-a-vis Eastern Europe and the German Democratic Republic. Europeanism then becomes simply another way of restructuring German nationalist policies and does not really afford any radical change with either Wilhelmine or indeed with more recent past positions. Indeed the necessity for Europeanism is tied very closely in Strauss' mind to the *Realpolitik* of German economic and political desiderata.

The so-called structural revolution in economic affairs and in the production process concerns Strauss mightily. Atomic energy, electronics, aircraft, plastics, and space technology are for Strauss essential keys to national power. Strauss, as other Europeans, sees the necessity for Europeanization of production processes in order to establish a competitive basis in relation to the United States and the Soviet Union. In addition it is just these industries — electronics, aircraft, petro-chemicals — whose boards of directors supply Strauss' major domestic financial sponsors. Strauss suggests a European investment system in which those industries with the most impact on the future should be supported. This process of public support and investment for key industries, he maintains, is what has helped create the technological gap between the United States and Europe and is making Germany into a "licence province of American industry."[60] In addition, it is these industries (with the exception of aircraft) which form the backbone of Germany's powerful economic position in Western Europe. Some commentators go so far as to claim that France's economy is falling into a structural dependence on Germany's, similar to Germany's and Europe's dependence on the United States.[61] Strauss stresses the tie between military investment i.e., investment in weapons production and spillover into key industries. Essentially what has developed here is the utilization of the Europeanization argument to foster certain German industries since they are the leading European industries in electronics and petro-chemicals. At least, Germany would probably, in Strauss' opinion, also quickly gain an important position in aircraft and space. In addition, Europeanization would allow Germany a research foothold, and this of course would give Germany a strong military say in European atomic industries and atomic strategy. The entire complex of economics cannot be divorced from the security considerations which Strauss always brings into play. His idea for a European investment fund is matched by his conception of a European weapons cartell.[62]

The European weapons cartell would not only serve as a means of lessening American influence but would also serve to complement the investment policies that would be co-ordinated on a European level. In other words, the creation of the vast European military and industrial complex is part and parcel of Strauss' modern German nationalism. It is also obvious that no change in the existing economic structures is anticipated; indeed one of the arguments that Strauss brings against participation by German unions in the decision-making process of major firms is that this participation would hinder European integration.[63]

Europeanization, then for Strauss means a strengthening of the private economic structure in Europe and especially in German industries that are hard pressed by foreign extra-European competition: electronics, petro-chemicals, and airframe industries. This reasoning complements the aforegoing German national necessity complex. Neither legal potential political positions are to be sacrificed in Eastern Europe nor is any change envisioned in current economic structures. The conservative preservative nature of this modern nationalism is obvious.

For Strauss the Soviet Union remains the aggressive power it was at the beginning of the cold war. Reinforced by its possession of atomic weapons and its successes in outer space the Soviet military presents a problem for German security which can only be successfully faced through the military organization of Europe's power. Here again Europeanization is made to hold still for Strauss' conception of the necessities of German strategic doctrine.[64] The American shield is simply not sufficient. There is the danger of "condominion coexistence". The doctrines of flexible response and limited war are simply inapplicable to the European situation. According to Strauss "the prosecution of a policy of no-victory will probably result in less

though they all vote CSU are "underrepresented" in the party according to Bavarian Labour Minister Pirkl; *Sueddeutsche Zeitung,* June 18th, 1970.

The 45 percent housewives, pensioners, and others remains deceiving. The figures for 1964 were the only ones available and were photocopied surreptitiously by Alf Mintzel.

26. Strauss, December 13th, 14th, 1968, op.cit., p. 30.

27. Ibid., pp. 32–40.

Cf. Grosse, *Konzentration ohne Kontrolle,* Cologne, Opladen 1969 and, H. Arndt, *Die Konzentration in der Wirtschaft,* Berlin 1960.

28. Ibid., pp. 16–18.

29. Information available at the Institute for Political Science.

30. Landesvorstand meeting of the CSU, May 13th, 1966.

31. The latest communal elections in Bavaria in the spring of 1970 have not brought any change to the situation, but the CSA has gained strength in the cities since 1972 and in state elections in 1974 took all of Munich's wards.

32. Ibid.

33. Ibid.

34. Ibid.

35. This regional Catholic press has been especially critical of the SPD government. See *Die Zeit,* November 21st, 1969.

36. Strauss has never been fully accepted by this Catholic wing of the party which has mistrusted his national ambitions and has not forgotten his beginnings with Joseph Mueller. Indeed Strauss has used the *Bayern Kurier* to attack the conservative Catholic group in the CSU; see

Die Zeit, December 10th, 1965 for Strauss' control on utilization of the *Bayern Kurier.* For conflicts within the CSU,

Die Zeit, September 6th, 1964; "Die Muenchener Prinzengarde" by Otto von Loewenstern. For conflicts with the Catholic wing of the party;

Die Zeit, August 23rd, 1963; "Ein Klotz am Schwert der CSU," Otto von Loewenstern; and

Die Zeit, July 12th, 1963; "Strauss und Bayerns Kirche," C. Amery.

This latter is a discussion of the anti-clerical Filser letters written in the *Bayern Kurier.*

37. For the situation facing the Catholic church cf. especially Gert Hirschauer, *Der Katholizismus vor dem Risiko der Freiheit,* Munich, 1966.

38. For the Wuerzburg publication as well as a critical assessment of the German Catholic hierarchy and neo-nationalism see

Reinhard Kuehnl, op.cit., p. 311 and pp. 319–313

The Defregger and the Regensburg complex are handled in various *Spiegel* over the year 1969.

39. Indeed the CSU, although it seems to contain some anti-Semites in prominent positions, is not an anti-Semitic party. Strauss for example has consistently maintained a very pro-Israel position. As Minister of Defence he helped engineer the deal in which Israel was able to buy a number of tanks from Germany. In his book *Herausforderung und Antwort,* Stuttgart 1968, Strauss openly praises the Israelis and indeed attempts to use them as a kind of model for Germany. Conservative non-Nazi right-wingers in Germany seem actually to consider Israel as

a kind of model for German behaviour. Their attachment to the state undoubtedly springs from nationalism, its militancy, and Soviet threats against it rather than from its socialism or Semitism, pp. 199–202.

40. *Die Zeit*, June 21st, 1963.

41. Kuehnl, op.cit., pp. 60 and 61.

For further biographical information of Stein and Meier see the Institute for Political Science in Berlin.

42. Ibid. Other prominent CSU members with ties to DNZ are directorate member Hans Neuwirth and F. A. von der Heyte.

43. Tauber, op.cit., p. 98.

44. Kuehnl, op.cit., pp. 37–39 as well as Tauber, op.cit., for an excellent study of the Witkobund, pp. 928–935.

45. See *Tagesspiegel*, June 17th, 1969.

46. Globke, Kiesinger and Schiller are examples, although the former two were far more prominent Nazis than the latter. Schiller for example left the party in the early '40s and accepted duty on the front, whereas Globke who helped write the Nuremberg race laws and Kiesinger who was the foreign office's liaison man to Goebbels' *Propagandaministeriou*, were far more prominent and important Nazis. Generally the SPD has a far better record on this account than either the FDP or the CDU/CSU. Schiller indeed has since left the SPD.

47. Most recent example of these connections with the NPD has been the CDU's acceptance of renegade NPD members in Lower Saxony. The CDU parliamentary land delegation in Lower Saxony accepted members of the NPD delegation; this has given the CDU delegation a majority over the SPD delegation and has destroyed the CDU and SPD coalition in Lower Saxony and resulted in new elections (the SPD narrowly won these). Indeed Lower Saxony with its regional nationalist groupings provided the most blatant case of this kind of 'national' communal coalition the "Buergerblock" of the North German port town Wilhelmshaven, in which neo-Nazi and national conservatives joined with the CDU and FDP to combat the SPD.

Cf. K. Hirsch, *Kommen die Nazis wieder?*, Munich, 1967, p. 121 and for right-wing radicalism in postwar Wilhelmshaven see

Tauber, op.cit., pp. 91–93 and Chapter IV.

48. *Die Zeit*, March 11th, 1966.

49. Cf. *Sueddeutsche Zeitung*, June 30th, 1969 in which the president of the central organization for German craftsmen, Wild, attempts to protect the CSU at a congress of middle-class organizations. Congress members had attacked the CSU for neglecting its middle-class voters. For difficulties pertaining to the farmers see *Sueddeutsche Zeitung*, June 21st/22nd, 1969 Strauss had a hard time defending himself at the conference of the German Farmers' Organization. Here again he had to be defended by aristocrat and estate owner Freiherr Otto von Feurig of the CSU.

50. Cf. among countless other sources *Frankfurter Rundschau*, May 13th, 1969; Kuehnl, op.cit., pp. 247–300;

CSU Party Congress, December 13th/14th, 1968, pp. 1–6

For an analysis of the *Bayern Kurier, DN*, and *DNZ* see Chapter VII.

51. Cf. *Frankfurter Rundschau*, June 11th, 1969 and June 13th, 1969, as well as *Der Tagesspiegel*, June 19th, 1969.

52. Cf. W. Falter "Die Bundestags wahl vom 19 November 1972," in *Zeitschrift für Parlaments fragen*. 4. Jg. 1973 Heft 1 March 1973 p. 122 ff. Süddeutsche Zeitung Nov. 25, 1972. The CSU's state election success in '74 (62%) is even more of the same.

53. Cf. E. Kuby, *Franz Josef Strauss — Ein Typus unserer Zeit*, Munich, 1963, p. 39 for an analysis the *New Statesman* and *Nation*, September 10th, 1960 and following pages for an unflattering consideration of Strauss' personality.

54. Ibid.

55. Ibid. Especially the chapter by Otto von Lowenstern, "Von Schoengau nach Bonn," which is a recapitulation of a series of articles in *Die Zeit* from 1962 and 1963.

56. F. J. Strauss, *Herausforderung und Antwort. Ein programm fuer Europa.* Stuttgart, 1968, pp. 114–118.

57. Ibid., pp. 118–124.

58. Ibid., p. 125.

59. Ibid., pp. 149–160.

60. CSU Party Congress, December 13th/14th, 1968, pp. 21–30, and CSU Party Congress, June 30th, 1967, Munich, pp. 33–42.

61. Francois Peru, *L'indépendence de la Nation*, Paris, 1969.

62. Ibid., pp. 37–38. (CSU Congress)

63. CSU Party Congress, December 13th/14th, 1968, op.cit., p. 13.

64. Strauss, op.cit., pp. 54–62. This is as good an example as any of Strauss' continuous harping on this subject. Cf. as well ibid., pp. 100–111.

65. Ibid., p. 66.

66. Ibid., p. 102.

67. Kuehnl, op.cit., pp. 297–299.

68. Strauss, op.cit., pp. 97–99.

69. Cf. Stuecklen's speech at the CSU Party Congress, June 13th/14th, 1969 in Munich. It is essentially a replay of Strauss' position.

70. Cf. Sueddeutsche Zeitung July 12–14, 1974 Berliner Abend 13 July 1974

VII

A Content Analysis of Three German Right Wing Newspapers in An Election Situation

The NPD's *Deutsche Nachrichten*, the CSU organ *Bayern Kurier*, and the independent *Deutsche National-Zeitung* are three right wing newspapers. To distinguish the attitudes propagated by the radical right papers (*DN* and *DNZ*) from the presumably national conservative ideas of *Bayern Kurier*, partly to establish their level of agreement, a systematic comparison will be followed.

In order to compare objectively the amount and kind of attention each paper devoted to each of ten key subjects Likert scales were constructed.[1] This makes it possible to weight statements about a subject or attitude object for their comparative extremity and then to show statistically either "the difference in concern the three papers show for attitude object x is statistically significant at the .05 level,"[2] or that "though their styles are different, *DNZ*, *DN*, and *BK* are almost equally preoccupied with x complex." Qualitative analysis of the relationships among attitudes and attention patterns in each paper accompanies and follows the quantitative analysis. The attitude areas examined are related to the previous analyses of right wing parties.

A. Authority-hierarchical order
B. Army and police
C. Technical and economic progress, achievement orientation, "relationship to modernity"
D. Pre-industrial and non-industrial economic sectors
E. National emphasis
F. Ingroup-outgroup, perception of threats and enemies, and fear mongering

189

G. Exaggeration of left radicalism
H. Conventional morality
I. Reunification and lost Eastern territories
J. European unity

These topics were chosen on the basis of traditional German nationalist ideology, and all of the statistical calculations and the complex counts as well as the statistical structure of the comparisons are the work of Professor Ellen Flerlage.

Ideological tendencies are related to socio-economic categories in accordance with the patterns of previous chapters. The quantitative analysis was based on a sample of eight issues of each paper, the four immediately before and the four immediately after the 1969 national election, which took place on Sunday, September 28, 1969. We hoped thus to maximize comparability, for it seemed logical that the papers would be more likely to concentrate on what they perceived to be the immediate political concerns of voters than would be the case at other times, and one could thus credit more of the variance between the papers to their editors' views and correspondingly less to accidental or random fluctuations in subject matter included in the sample of issues. However, not all the quotations we use here for illustrative purposes are from the set of issues analyzed quantitatively. The source of each quotation is noted in the text.

The comparison is based on the following analysis scheme, to be used with a Likert-type scale for each attitude object:

1. Assuming that every paragraph of text in these newspapers expresses the views of the editors, everything except want-ads, advertisements, and statements marked as quotations from other papers or letters to the editor will be counted.
2. The counting unit will be the paragraph, for a smaller unit, like the sentence or some specified interval around a key word, might not express the attitude fully.
3. A given paragraph is to be classified under a theme if that theme is so much as touched upon in that paragraph.
4. To account systematically for the impact of titled articles, as distinguished from scattered statements, if the attitude object appears in the title of an article, all paragraphs in that article will be counted as dealing with the theme in question, and such paragaphs as merely provide supporting information will be classified in the +0 category.
5. If the title of the article is sensational in its effect ("Brandt verraet Deutschland," "Brandt Betrays Germany" for example) each +0 paragraph

will be counted as +1, to take more accurate account of the probable overall effect on the reader.
6. Some paragraphs may thus be counted under more than one attitude
complex.

We shall present the data for one attitude area at a time in the
order in which they were listed.

A. Authority-hierarchical order

It would be hard and perhaps not even valid to use statistical procedures on the scattered and rather heterogeneous references to authority, need for hierarchical order, and so forth, which appeared in
this sample of issues. None of the issues analyzed was replete with
references to the need, for example, for strict parental discipline (although *DNZ* did have a three-paragraph article quoting Plato to this
effect on page 2 of its August 8, 1969 issue) greater efficiency in business through establishment of clear lines of authority, or even critical
discussion of the Bundeswehr's *Innere Fuerung.* Nevertheless the
latter constitutes nearly all of what the quantitatively analyzed issues
of *DN,* the paper most concerned with this complex, did have to say
about authority and hierarchical order. One might suppose it would be
worthwhile to count up and compare totals of references to the need
for order in the sense of "law and order", *Recht und Ordnung,* but
this would overlap the support for army and police complex. A set
of Likert categories ranking attitudes from traditional right to its
logical opposite is assumed to look like this:

+3—(most authoritarian pole) strong statement in favor of hierarchical
control or demand that it be established in some area;
+2—praise of the ideals of obedience and *Treue* (loyalty) to one's superiors,
for stern and 'decisive' authority;
+1—complaints about lack of hierarchical order, not enough parental discipline these days, too much democracy in the army; also more or less
normative statements about subordination of the individual to the common interest;
+0—neutral mention of authority, chain of command, etc. (but not counting
scattered words denoting more or less formal positions, e.g. captain,
fire chief . . .);
—1—complaints about authoritarian relationship, lack of democracy; mild
positive reference to broad democratic control;

—2—praise of something because it is democratic; clear statement of the "all men are equal" variety;

—3—recommendation of some measure to increase equality and broad popular control, decrease hierarchical control.

What actually appeared in the 24 newspaper issues analyzed ranges from *DN*'s blasts against Baudissin and other alleged champions of indiscipline and demands that 'Innere Fuehrung' be replaced by the iron discipline that made the Prussian army great to an article in *DNZ* (September 19, 1969, p. 11) entitled "Voters' Democracy or Party Dictatorship?" praising a somewhat idealized picture of the American electoral system largely on the grounds that it is more democratic than the West German system. By democratic the author means, however, not so much that the average voter has more control in any sense over what goes on in Congress, but that the (almost necessarily corrupt) political parties have less, and this colors each of the seven paragraphs. The distribution of references to the attitude object authority-hierarchical order is shown in Sample A. The reader can see the relevant statements were relatively sparse and it is hard to say anything definite about the differences between the papers except that *DN* has many more statements refering to authority and hierarchical order than do *DNZ* or *BK*, and unlike both of these *DN* has no entries in the negative or pro-democratic categories: The *DN* statements were concentrated on the single subject of the army, however. All three papers have made nasty comments at one time or the other about workers' participation in industrial management. This is only one aspect of their general opposition to the German Trade Union Association (DGB; see section G: exaggeration of left radicalism).[3]

B. Support for Army and Police

Most of what the quantitatively analyzed issues of *BK* had to say about the Bundeswehr was more or less technical consideration of the effectiveness of West German defence institutions, like what kind of armed forces will serve the BRD best as a means of deterring Soviet aggression. An additional aspect appears in *BK*'s January 24, 1970 issue, in the justification for General Schnez's controversial report on the condition of the Bundeswehr: ". . . Burdened with an undigested tradition the Bundeswehr came into the era of protesting youth. It had to maintain its demand for drill and obedience in the barracks against a beat generation. It is precisely these problems which General Schnez spoke of in the study bearing his name." In the article "Manoever: Roesselsprung und Bundeswehrreform" (September 20, 1969, p. 5) a *BK* correspondent discusses "three questions about the shape of the army" which this maneuver, Roesselsprung, had pointed up: (1) problems of provisioning large units; (2) the whole concept of territorial defence; and (3) the apparent uselessness of large militia units under realistic fighting conditions. *BK* has very little to say about the police. *DNZ's* attitudes toward armed enforcers of order appear chiefly in book reviews, and *DNZ's* choice of books includes a goodly proportion of military histories. *DN* devoted much more attention to the police and the army in the issues analyzed than did the corresponding issues of *BK* and *DNZ*. This is certainly related to the NPD's choice of the campaign slogan *Sicherheit durch Recht und Ordnung* (security through law and order). However, what is actually said about the police and army does not reflect a homogeneous need for order factor; seven out of the eight references to police in the August 29 issue, for example, explicitly or implicitly denounce SPD or otherwise left-influenced police officials who failed to provide adequate police protection for NPD rallies or did not allow them to take place at all because of portending scuffles between protesters and NPD people.

In *Deutsche Nachrichten* of October 3, though, there is an article entitled "Crime as a National Sport" in which three paragraphs of information on rising crime rates are followed by a demand for "thorough reform" of the criminal police, including better training and higher pay. Similarly, it is not easy to bring all *DN* statements about the army under a common denominator. *DN* mentions variously the need for "justice" in the draft system: it is unfair that only some of the eligible young men have to serve, the idea that *Ersatzdienst* (substitute service for conscientious objectors) should be made rougher so that fewer people would choose to serve their 18 months that way instead of in the regular army, the need to replace NATO with a European military alliance or community, institution of a three-tiered armed service with heavy reliance on "home defence units" or militia (see *DN* "Sonderausgabe" (special issue) August 1, 1969 p. 2) and the glory of the traditional army. The soldier à la Scharnhorst is the model for German manhood (*DN*, August 1, 1969), p. 1).

Of course all these views are ultimately related to the theme of social order through the notion of the army as a major socializing and/or educational agency: *die Schule der Nation* (a historical phrase which Chancelor Kiesinger also mentioned in the 1969 election campaign) or as one in the series of socializing agencies that form the German citizen. The article "Questionable Innere Fuehrung" (*DN* October 3, 1969 p. 14) ends with the following declaration: "The need for change is urgent. A Scharnhorst is needed not only for the army, but for the whole nation! May he rise out of that young generation of officers which in this (atmosphere of) pluralistic cowardice still has the courage of its convictions. Let us declare with Scharnhorst: 'Nation and army are one!'." *DN*'s idealistic militance compares interestingly with *BK*'s technocratic attitudes. The categories of the attitude scale are characterized by these types of statements:

+3—outright demand for reinstitution of pre-World War II traditional Wilhelmine or Nazi models of army or police (no instances of this category appeared);

+2—criticism of Innere Fuehrung and praise of Prussian tradition. Military and/or police should be provided with better equipment; these professions should be made more attractive; the Prussian soldier is a model to be emulated;

+1—the soldier, the policeman should receive more respect. "The NPD backs our Bundeswehr!" (*DN*, August 1, 1969). The American (John Birch Society) slogan "support your local police force" would fall into this category;

=0—neutral, uncritical mention: "Police arrested 15 demonstrators."

—1—mild or limited, or implied criticism: "The police did not try to keep the SDS from disrupting our rally."

—2—thoroughgoing criticism e.g., "the whole course of police training encourages police brutality."

—3—demand for reform in a left direction e.g., the draft should be abolished, police should no longer carry pistols . . .

Sample B shows at a glance that *DN* had far more to say about the army and the police, most of it in a positive or traditional direction, than did *DNZ* or certainly *BK*; here a statistical procedure for analysis of variance (the statistic F; see footnote 1 of this chapter and Chapter 16 of Hubert Blalock's *Social Statistics*) shows that the differences among the three papers in emphasis of this complex are significant at the .01 level (F for these date = 5.85 with 2 and 21 degrees of freedom). There is a marked difference not only between *DN* and *BK* with its small number of points but between *DN* and *DNZ* as well.[4] However, we note that well over half of all *DNZ* statements relating to police and army were distinctly favorable to the old-style army.

DNZ's taste for military history brings up another general point about differences in the type of material the three newspapers include: *DNZ* gives more space than do either *DN* or *BK* to partisan documentation of "things past"; one full page out of twelve in each issue is devoted to such topics as "September 1914", "Goering's last minutes in Nuremberg", "Resistance in Vienna", etc., as compared with the one out of *DN's* sixteen pages for "Dokumentation" of things like the Morgenthau Plan (October 5, 1969, p. 10) or "Guilt in the First World War" (August 8, 1969, p. 10). There is nothing comparable in *Bayern Kurier*.

DNZ also devotes comparatively little attention to current foreign affairs and economic developments, though it does usually have at least one article per issue on the political situation in Austria. *BK* is the only one of the three which really offers regular analyses of foreign military political developments; examples are a twelve-paragraph account of the re-establishment of Soviet-approved administration in Czechoslovakia (August 23, 1969, p. 5), "Ceausescu's Balancing Act", and "Legends about de Gaulle" (August 16, 1969, p. 6). The statistical comparison takes into account only direct references to German military matters, but 'scare' references to the Soviet Union and praise of de Gaulle fit a nationalist pattern as well. *DN* always mentions current developments in other countries at least on its economics and "European Security" pages: "250,000 unreliable 'Brothers in Arms' — the great purge in the Czech army has begun" (October 3, 1969, p. 11) or "Secret Plans by the Crate to Israel" (October 10, 1969, p. 11). However, on page 2 of *DN* for October 31 there are also articles about access to Libyan oil after the military coup in that country, and the Austrian state elections. The selection of foreign news for commentary, especially in newspapers primarily concerned with domestic affairs gives interesting insight into thought patterns although it is difficult to deal with statistically due to the paucity of references.

C. Orientation to technical and economic progress

On the complex economics-modernity, it is easy to classify *BK* in the pre-election issue of September 13; nearly every article in the twelve-page "BK-Report: Freedom and Prosperity" contains CDU–CSU self-congratulation on the grounds of the economic progress that comes from efficiency-oriented efforts in industrialization and expanding trade. In fact, *BK* is rather flat-footedly technocratic and materialistic; in the same issue there is an advertisement for the CSU filling the outer two columns of page 5, with a smug, benevolent-looking picture of Kiesinger and the text "You are well off — you live in Germany. No other country in the world provides so much social security: stable currency, economic growth, rising wages, full employment". On the last page of the September 20 issue, under the inch-high rubric "What Franz Josef Strauss has accomplished", 14 out of 14 points listed for domestic accomplishments have to do with Strauss' contribution to things like economic growth, financial stability and full employment. *DN*'s position on this complex is rather subtle; on the one hand it discusses largely such economically related problems as are likely to concern the economically less secure sectors of the population. "Many taxes are superfluous" reads the largest title on the economics page of the August 8, 1969 *DN*; the following week's economics page has titles including "Agriculture can't accumulate capital of its own any more", and "A real chance for export" (of agricultural goods). However, though abstract support and concern for the farmer is voiced occasionally including endorsement of the "family farm" and rejection of the Common Market's Mansholt Plan for rationalizing agricultural production, the *DN* never commits itself to any specific measures to protect farmers, skilled artisans, coal miners, etc., from further economic rationalization, and on page 15 of *DN* for October 3, 1969 one sees the sober headline "There is no way back to the basic professions", with the subtitle "Parallels between Agriculture and Mining: What's lost remains lost". Half of the next page is filled with an article titled "The distorted relationship to atomic energy" (it is the wave of the future and a desirable innovation), by a Dr. Walther Helm, physicist. *DN* also occasionally reports on West Germany's educational lag. It notes, for example, that not only the United States and Japan but (East) Germany has a higher percentage of people in higher educational institutions, and this portends a consequent technological lag that could be dangerous economically and militarily. This reflects the increasing influence of the "modern nationalists" and/or pragmatic Fascists in the NPD. Even the old-fashioned DRP stronghold of the *DN* is no longer immune.

As for the *Deutsche National Zeitung* it is hard to discern an even approximately complete view of economic life, technology, and achievement orientation. Like *Deutsche Nachrichten*, *DNZ* noted the American moon landing with considerable pride, that it was the "118 men from Peenemuende" who made it possible (August 1, 1969), thus trumpeting more rejoicing over German intelligence and accomplishments than a position on the significance of desirability of the trend toward technical advance in itself. There are articles dealing with specific economic nightmares of the lower middle class like the "World Economic Crisis" and inflation.

Attitudes toward the importance of validity of technical usefulness and efficiency criteria (more or less like Talcott Parson's pattern variable achievement versus ascription, see Chapter 1) were the focal point in an attempt to build a scale that really measured a single but basic underlying variable. It did not seem possible to distinguish validly and reliably among seven gradations, as was done in all the other cases. Hence this five-point scale was used:

+2—the value of something depends (almost) entirely on its efficiency or utility; something is good if it possesses large degrees of these characteristics;

+1—evaluation of achievement, technical advance, economic success, etc. is distinctly positive;

+0—neutral mention of achievement, technical advance, economic success;

—1—statement or implication that these things are not so important, or that technical progress also has distinct drawbacks;

—2—technical or "materialistic" values are false, dangerous, should be dropped and replaced by traditional (e.g. ascriptive) values.

Here a statistical analysis of variance shows very great differences in orientation among the three papers. *Bayern Kurier* has by far the most emphasis points — 620.9, to 255 for *DN* and 26.7 for *DNZ*. The difference between *BK* and *DN* is significant at the .005 level (t = 3.24 with 14 degrees of freedom) and the difference between each of them and *DNZ* is at least as big. In this case weighting for the size of each issue increases the differentiation between papers so that an enormous analysis of variance statistic results (F = 24.09, significant at more than a .001 level), but even with the raw scores one gets a statistic significant at the .01 level (F = 9.016).

D. Pre- and non-industrial and obsolescent economic sectors

As noted above, the *DN* issues examined contained suggestions of NPD backing for the maintenance of the healthy family farm; the government efforts of the past decade to get people to leave uneconomical farms are also denounced. An interesting sidelight on what the NPD regards as sound farm policy is the following note from the October 31, 1969 issue, p. 8: "The Swiss people recognizes . . . the dynamic family plant as the bearer of agricultural production . . . (its) socio-political purpose . . . consists not only in production of foodstuffs, but also in the maintenance of a well-tended, cultivated countryside as vacation and national recreation areas." Also a large factor in the NPD's rejection of the EEC's rationalization scheme for agriculture, the Mansholt plan, or any other scheme for an agricultural division of labour in Europe is that at present the Federal Republic of Germany can, according to *DN*, produce 70 percent of the essential foodstuffs it needs; that means it is already dependent on other countries for the other 30 percent, and it would be utter folly, strategically, to reduce still further Germany's ability to feed itself!

BK seems to have a no-nonsense, efficiency-first approach to farm policy. In the September 13 issue, pages 21–22, ex-Agriculture Minister Hoecherl writes about a "structural policy" to bring about a "comprehensive reordering of rural areas"; among the main items on the agenda were encouragement of migration from unproductive farms, higher old-age pensions and stipends for relinquishing one's land (*Landabgaberente*), and resettling of agriculturally related industry into rural areas. *DNZ* seems not to deal at all regularly with the problems of the farmer, although the same "DSZ-Verlag" that publishes it also puts out a monthly paper entitled *Der Deutsche Bauer* (The German Farmer).

In none of the newspaper issues analyzed were skilled craftsmen or small retailers mentioned more than fleetingly. One can probably assume, however, that they form an important part of the audience, for all three newspapers' tirades against inflation and SPD's economics minister Schiller's socialist irresponsible and/or inept experiments with the currency. The scale was as follows:

+3—proposal that some present trend or policy should be reversed for the benefit of traditional farm, crafts, or small retail sectors, etc.;

+2—suggestion of compensation for the effects of such developments e.g., proposal that the BRD should use the machinery of the EEC as fully for the benefit of their agricultural sector as France has done in the past;

+1—abstract declaration of support for the farmer, craftsman, etc.;

+0—neutral reference to "threatened" groups (farmers', craftsmen's, coal miners' problems . . .);

—1—statements like "We're for the farmer, but we've all got to realize the less efficient farms can't stay in business for ever";

—2—agreement with the Mansholt plan, positive attitudes towards "retionalization" and consolidation;

—3—advocacy of rapid and/or drastic measures in this direction.

We can see from Sample D that *DN* was the only paper that always said something about the economically weaker sectors, and *DN*'s references are the most supportive for the traditional non-industrial population. Nevertheless, there is not a statistically significant difference between *DN* and *BK*, and most of the total variance (F for the raw data is significant at the .05 level, while for the weighted data F = 3.099 and approaches significance at about the .09 level) is due to *DNZ*'s extremely low number of relevant statements.

E. National Emphasis

Probably the bulk of the references to Germanness and national pride in the eight weeks' sample of *DN*, *DNZ*, and *BK* come in the cultural sections and *DNZ*'s historical articles, although there were also several statements in *DNZ*'s coverage of the Defregger case (the Catholic bishop accused of committing atrocities during World War II) rejecting German war guilt and suggesting that this case was being used purposefully by Communist agents to defame Germany and the Catholic Church. *DNZ*'s emphasis on the German contribution to American space feats has already been mentioned. An example of *DNZ*'s treatment of cultural subjects for the purpose of bolstering national sentiment is the August 1 issue's article *Die Fackel brennt* (the Torch Burns) in praise of a nationalist poet. *DN*'s cultural pages sometimes only implicitly emphasize Germanism; the regularly featured cultural articles deal almost exclusively with German or Germanic writers, painters and composers.

Usually the connection between Germanness and genius is not formulated directly, but in the October 31 issue an article praising a contemporary German artist begins: "That art is 'international' is one of the most stupid phrases of the cultural anarchists. True art is rather the noblest expression of the national character . . . If the nations are destroyed, the pre-requisites of higher culture will also be eliminated. Therefore cultural policy must be national, and national policy in its highest purposes must always be cultural policy." On page six of the same issue Germany is called the "land of origin of the world's most valuable musical creations". (The composers are all pre-World War I vintage.) *DN* and *DNZ* very occasionally express explicitly the need to strengthen German nationalist consciousness e.g., as a pre-requisite to really solid defence against internal and external Communist onslaughts. On page three of *DN* for September 19 one reads ". . . therefore we National Democrats demand the creation of a natural state-consciousness of the Germans." *DNZ* also appeals to national "consciousness" of this sort in its endless headline references to Brandt as a traitor because of his emigration and assumption of Norwegian citizenship: *"Als Brandt Norweger war"* (When Brandt was a Norwegian), and Brandt as an "illegitimate" dubious character, *Brandt alias Frahm.*

Paragraphs including themes related to German national consciousness were classified according to this scale:

+3—something is superior because it is German; Germanness as a goal to be pursued;

+2—praise of "truly German" culture, accomplishments ascribed to German intelligence and diligence, etc.;

+1—linking of positively evaluated objects (e.g. moon landing) with Germanness;

+0—evaluatively unclassifiable mention of Germanness of national consciousness including such negative formulations as "Ulbricht's un-German state";

—1—mild criticism or rejection of German nationalism or German nation, suggestion that Germany has made mistakes too;

—2—serious criticism along these lines;

—3—the nation should be dissolved into some larger community.

Most of *BK*'s sparse comments of these sorts fall into the category of linking positively evaluated objects with Germanness e.g., German economic miracles, German financial stability as contrasted with the French or British financial problems. A statistical difference of means test comparing the mean number of emphasis points for national consciousness in *DNZ* and in *DN* shows that the difference between them in this respect is little more than chance (t = .708 with 14 degrees of freedom, for which a t-score of at least 1.345 is needed to reach even the .10 level). The difference between both of these papers and *BK*, on the other hand, is significant at better than the .001 confidence level (t for *DN* : *BK* was 4.545, for example, again with 14 degrees of freedom). *Bayern Kurier* does not hammer home old-fashioned nationalism.

F. Ingroup–outgroup, perception of threatening enemies, and fear mongering

This factor of right-wing paranoic seeing the ingroup constantly under attack had to be distinguished somehow from the complex obsession with left-wing radicalism. For generally "friend-enemy" themes the following scale was established with the provision that any statement that would otherwise fall under these categories but specifically contained the words "red", "Communist", "Bolschevik", etc., or other reference to the radical left would be classified under complex G instead. Paragraphs about the "Soviet threat" or other states as enemies without specific reference to their Communist political system went into the following "enemy categories along with hostile comments about the "Lizenz Presse" (those papers licensed during the occupation by the allies) and German politicians who were going to "sell out" Germany.

+3—threat is of catastrophic proportions, or reference to a conspiracy of enemies;

+2—is dangerous in itself, threat is serious; enemy atrocities;

+1—is linked to a negative symbol; statements that the "national" is being persecuted (DNZ publishers, NPD . . .);

+0—is "dangerous" because incompetent or imprudent or a stock enemy is mentioned without immediate reference to less dangerousness;

—1—is not such a big threat;

—2—(some stock enemy) has his good points; or "it will do the country good to have the SPD in office for a while" . . .

—3—there are no threats, things will turn out one way or the other.

The *DNZ* spent a tremendous amount of space in the Fall 1969 defaming SPD politicians. The series of articles trying to discredit Brandt under the general title "When Brandt was a Norwegian" began in August 1969 and ran well into 1970; "his 'textbook' on partisan warfare: appeal to fight against the Germans", concerns the August 22 edition. A small article on the first page of that paper notes that Podgorny sent red roses for Heinemann's birthday. Other notable themes from the *DNZ* are: "Wehner: Spy against Germany" (a serial account of Wehner's activities as a Communist); the iniquities of the mass media originally licensed by the Western allies and now systematically discriminating against the right; an SPD victory would be the end of Berlin; Schuetz (Berlin's SPD mayor) and Brandt are even falsifying history, trying to make Ernst Reuter into an ally in their campaign for an opening to the East.

In the August 1 *DN* special issue on the army, one finds the following ideas: the CDU is guilty of treating the Bundeswehr as a stepchild; "the NPD is against treason", safety from foreign enemies depends upon having one's internal affairs in order; there are agents and traitors in the "highest positions", and there are a total of at least 10,000 enemy agents in the Federal Republic of Germany; the external enemy is the USSR, and its allies and agents in the Federal Republic particularly concentrate on persecuting the NPD. Some of the pre-election issues give a great deal of space to blasts by prominent NPD men against people who had attacked the party verbally e.g., Kiesinger and the CSU; the *DN* of September 19 contains a frontpage denunciation of the "flood of lies by the re-education press."

If one of the *DNZ's* favourite techniques is the "exposé" of political opponents, *BK* has a characteristical technique of trying to discredit especially SPD-opponents by making them seem incompetent and ideologically out of touch with reality. On the economics page of the August 30 issue the CSU offers "Practical advice for theoretician Schiller"; the same technique is shown on the front page of the same issue when Strauss writes of "Schmidt and Co.: Senseless pilgrimage to Moscow — People who dance out their dreams and talk hot air." Another minor distinction between this "establishment" rightist paper and the others is that instead of the emphasis on impending disaster after the formation of the Brandt government *BK* simply notes, "The march into adventurism" (October 18) and "This majority won't last long" (October 25). It is something of a surprise therefore to find out that an analysis of variance in the data of Sample F shows no significant distinction among the three papers in amount and kind of threat and "enemy" ideas expressed.

Calculating an F score from the emphasis point totals shown —

where *DNZ's* extreme statements accusing Schuetz of arranging the takeover of Berlin by the GDR weigh four times as heavily as *BK's* snide comments about Schiller's ideological and/or technical competence — one gets a test statistic of 2.48, which is not significant at any level listed in most tables (for 2 and 21 degrees of freedom, one needs an F score of 3.47 or higher to reach the .05 significance level). However, noting the two cells of the table where *BK* had enormous numbers of the "snide comment" type of references, a recalculation was made, counting only the scale categories +1 through +3. Even so, *BK* turned out not to differ significantly from *DN* and *DNZ* in the amount and type of venom it spewed at its "enemies", and difference of means tests for all combinations showed that the one statistically significant difference in these data was that between *DNZ* (1359 points) and *DN* (651 points. With *BK* in the middle with 958 weighted points.) The difference, as is shown below, is even less in the specific case of concern about left radicalism.

G. *Exaggeration of left radicalism*

There are three principle targets here: the SPD, the trade union federation, DGB, and the new left. All three newspapers regard these political groups as either Communist or deluded tools of the Communists. *DNZ* issues of August 1 and August 8 have articles equating West Berlin leftist demonstrations with "separatist efforts" i.e., efforts to get Berlin's ties to the German Federal Republic severed; referring to the Berlin teachers' college as a factory for producing left radical teachers; and speculating about the harm leftist Protestant youth and leaders are doing to the Lutheran Church. Towards the end of August *DNZ* features a full page attack on the "left monopoly" in television. *DNZ* complains that the mass media systematically favor the left. The emphasis in the articles attacking Herbert Wehner is that he was an agent of international Communism, and *DNZ* does not see sufficient evidence to believe this is no longer the case.

DN talks about how the German Trade Union Association is full of Communists, and mentions again and again the "left radical and DGB campaign to produce disintegration in the Bundeswehr" (August 29; p. 4). DGB sponsored anti-NPD demonstrations and SPD city officials' (police chiefs, mayors) refusal to authorize NPD events at all instead of letting them take place under adequate police protection is taken as further evidence of the Communist control of unions and sections of the Social Democratic movement. References to the new left in *DN* often link it directly to outside Communist forces — the August 8 issue among others mentions "Ulbricht's fifth column, the APO." *DN* is preoccupied with the apparently rising rate of refusal to do military service, and suggests that the substitute non-military service should be made tougher. The following rationale (ideas *DN* shares with *DNZ* incidentally) is typical: Most people who refuse to serve in the army are leftists; one should teach them orderliness and respect for the law, among other things, but preferably not within the Bundeswehr itself, for they are likely to commit sabotage. Hence the need for a purposefully rigorous substitute civilian service period. Without using the old term "cultural Bolshevism" *DN* nevertheless makes "the left" responsible for "anarchy in today's theater" (August 8, 1969) and elsewhere.

It is important to specify that *BK*'s references to enemies and specifically those ones dubbed radical left differ in important detail from those in the other two papers. *BK* does not swing wildly in all directions, but directs its attacks at a single main political villain and electoral enemy: the SPD and its helpers, the DGB and its product, the leftist protestors and "neo-vandals". The amount and kind of invective against this enemy does not differ on the whole from the *DN*'s and *DNZ*'s allegations, with the one exception that *BK* never tries to create a St. Sebastian image by telling the reader that the CSU is being persecuted. There are a number of possible enemies which the *BK* did not bother to attack during this period — the mass media are hardly mentioned for example, and *BK* does not worry as constantly as *DN* does about "disintegration" in the Bundeswehr (which the CSU as a governing party, after all, helped to shape). However, *BK* too points to the "stir of disorder in the fighting forces" on the part of the public service and transportation union (September 6, p. 2). In any case, *BK* subjects SPD, DGB, and APO to its two characteristic forms of attack: New Left's offences against conventional standards of behaviour and the combined ideological and administrative ineptness and permissiveness of SPD politicians. But in both cases the more or less urbane or condescending attempt to discredit the opponent by belittling him frequently gives way to ominous predictions, especially in the back "Union Kurier" pages. "Slowly but surely the German Michel is to become red . . . the goal of SPD policies: a red totalitarian state . . .

This corresponds exactly to the socialist three pillar theory: organization of voting power in the SPD, organization of the labor forces in the SPD-directed union, organization of buying power in the SPD-determined socialized, and guided economy (*Gemeinwirtschaft*)" (September 13, 1969, last page).

Here is the scale constructed for specifically left-radical "enemy and threat" imagery:

+3—explicit reference to international Communist threat, conspiracy;
+2—is playing into the hands of the Communists, or domestic tendency will lead to Communism, totalitarian society, etc.;
+1—is creating disorder, is generally a disruptive, undesirable element;
—0—neutral mention of left, APO, socialist (not when used as neutral synonym for SPD);
—1—SPD, APO, DGB don't threaten anything essential;
—2— " " " have some good aspects:
—3—completely positive reference to DGB, APO, SPD, socialism . . .

Just from looking at the totals of emphasis points per issue(in Sample G) it was apparent that there would be even less variance between papers on pre-occupation with left radicalism than there was in the ingroup–outgroup data. The F score for variance between all three papers was a totally insignificant 1.102. It seemed nevertheless that there might be a significant difference between the paper's highest (*DN*) and lowest (*BK*) in total left radicalism emphasis points. This turned out to be not the case; the statistic for the difference of means between the *DN* and *BK* is 1.138 with 14 degrees of freedom, which does not even reach the .1 confidence level, much less the .05 level. In other words, what difference there is between the emphasis upon left radical threat and enemies in these two papers might well have been a matter of chance selection of issues etc., there is not strong enough evidence to assume they differ reliably and predictably on this complex.

H. Conventional morality

DNZ's August 1 issue has as its front page feature "Is Kennedy a murderer?" *DNZ* also mentions the "Falken scandal" at length in issues 32 and 36 — that is, the "Communist indoctrination, sex, and alcohol orgies" (p. 12, Sept. 5, 1969) that allegedly took place in the summer camp of the SPD youth organization, the Falken. This paper, though generally not adverse to sensationalism and despite its general opinion that encouragement of sexual freedom is a Communist tool for softening up the German people, displays less preoccupation with conventional standards and offences against them in the eight quantitatively analyzed issues than do *DN* or *BK*.

A good example of what *DN* thinks on this subject is the article on p. 6 of the July 25, 1969 issue: "Bonn finances Zadek's [an avant garde stage director] class hatred." On August 8 there is an article demanding preservation of "a clear distinction between masculine and feminine roles." The cultural section demands that the theater be cleansed of sex. *DN* also notes the latest folly of the would-be progressive penal authorities who allowed the performance by APO people for an audience of prisoners of a series of skits allegedly "ridiculing" the existing legal system. Increasing drug use provided material for 14 paragraphs in the October 31 issue. *BK* continually predicates moral offensiveness to the nation's new left enemies. Very nearly the same article on the APO demonstration at the Bamberg court house complete with sexual antics was printed twice, complete with picture, in the "Union Kurier" section of the *BK*. Each time a long list of APO sins against conventional sex standards left no doubt in the reader's mind just what goings-on had taken place. One gets the impression that the *BK*'s purpose in such articles is simply to discredit the youngsters and arouse middle-class support. It is sometimes implied that the weakening of conventional moral standards bodes social disintegration, and this is precisely what the Communists want. On the other hand not all change in moral custom and related law is bad; on August 30, page 2, Richard Jaeger claims credit for the changes in the laws regarding illegitimate children. Modern for him, since he supported reintroduction of the death penalty, but not a striking innovation in a country with an illegitimate child as chancellor.

The scale for classifying statements relating to conventional morality was:

+3—ruining moral standards is part of a deliberate plot;
+2—clear statement that loosening of moral standards is bad or dangerous, or statement of a standard as something the reader should act upon;
+1—linking person (or group) with conventionally disrespectable behaviors to discredit him (them);
+0—bland statements, like statistics on increasing criminality;
—1—customs including moral standards change with the times, some things that used to be punished probably should not be;

—2—particular aspect of the moral and/or legal code should be changed;
—3—conventional morality should be changed, challenged, undermined.

Analysis of variance on this case produces an F test statistic of 4.39, which means there is a considerable amount of variance between the three papers (.05 confidence level). With 223.3 weighted emphasis points to *Bayern Kurier's* 88.7, *Deutsche Nachrichten* holds the lead by a near-significant margin (for *DN* versus *BK*, t = 1.608, which is .07 significance level).[5]

I. Expellees, lost or threatened territory, fear mongering

Key words in this complex are "policy of self-denial" (*Verzichtpolitik*), Munich agreement, "reduction of tension" (*Entspannung*), and final German peace treaty. The government of a part of the former German Reich has neither the right nor the authority or power in terms of international law to give up German claims to former Reich territory. This includes the Sudetenland acquired by annexation as provided in the legally valid Munich Agreement of 1938. To give up rightful claims to the Sudetenland and the territories east of the Oder-Neisse-Line is thus on the one hand outside the Bonn government's legal competence, on the other hand utter folly resulting from false hopes of reducing tension with the East or from outright treasonous machinations. Any change in territorial claims must come only after the peace treaty between one German successor state (the GDR is of course not to be recognized) and all four Allied powers has finally been signed.

DN and *DNZ*, especially the latter, voice explicitly German claims to lost territories; an interesting note in *DN* of August 8, 1969 was, however, that the NPD finds it irresponsible and dishonest for politicians to promise refugees the return of their land. *DN* and *DNZ* both report favorably the activities of the *Landsmannschaften* (organizations of refugees according to their region of origin) and express moral — if rather abstract — support for the interests of Germans from lost territories and Sudetenland. Somewhat the same type of attitudes are extended to Berlin, and *DNZ* had several articles in August 1969 charging West Berlin's SPD Lord Mayor Schuetz with preparing the loss of Berlin to the GDR.

Instead of saying specifically "we're for . . .", *BK* simply criticizes and ridicules proponents of recognition of, for example, the Oder-

Neisse-Line. An article on page 4 of the September 13 issue criticizes left-liberal Professor Eugen Kogon's left-liberal *Bensberger Kreis* because they "want to give up the (demand for) settlement of the problem by a peace treaty and just leave everything up to Warsaw." An additional aspect of *BK*'s attitude, partially reflected in that article, is that it is simply irrational in terms of realistic power policy to make the concessions one's opponent wants without demanding concessions in return.

The scale used for this complex:

+3—explicit statement that the lost territories have to be regained;

+2—criticism of *Verzichtpolitik*, of 'sell-out' negotiations, 'atrocities' committed against German minorities in East Bloc countries;

+1—abstract defence of the interests of refugees; (expellees)

+0—neutral mention of "Eastern territories", Vertriebene, etc.;

—1—it's silly, pointless to try to maintain refugees' hopes, no prospect of regaining territories in foreseeable future;

—2—doubts about validity of Munich Agreement, soundness of maintaining claims to lost territories;

—3—statement for recognition of GDR, Oder-Neisse-Line . . .

Here again, the analysis of variance does not reveal a statistically significant overall difference in the amount of concern shown by the three papers with the problems of the refugees and claims to the lost territories. ($F = 2.19$ with 2 and 21 degrees of freedom; 3.47 is necessary for .05 significance level.) In any case, the "extremes" in this respect are *DN* with the most and *BK* with the fewest emphasis points, and the difference between *DN* and *BK* ($t = 2.269$) is significant at the .025 level.

J. European Unity

On the basis of a considerably more extensive reading of the three papers in question, their respective ideas about Germany's relationship to Europe can be summed up as follows: the real right extremist is deeply dissatisfied with the European status quo created by the Allies for their own benefit, and is almost more hostile to the "softening", re-education influences from the West than he is to the Soviet and other Communists whom he supposes can be met with military force if necessary. The aspect in which closer co-operation among European states is really necessary is military alliance because — specific anti-Americanism and general anti-Western liberalism aside — it seems at least risky to count on the United States to use its nuclear weapons to defend Europe. (This ties in with the cry in *DN, DNZ,* and *BK* that German signature of the anti-proliferation treaty would be foolish and dangerous and "reduce Germany to colonial status" i.e., make it vitally dependent upon a large non-European power). *DNZ* devotes very little attention to "European" themes at all. *DN* frequently mentions the need for a European military community but does not express any interest in closer co-operation in other areas. It does profess to accept the Common Market "in its original provisions" but objects to Germany always giving and other countries, i.e. France, always taking (Aug. 8, 1969, p. 12).

BK's issue 27 for 1969 contains a statement in which the CSU describes itself as "a Bavarian state party with a feeling of responsibility in matters concerning Germany in general and a clear commitment to a European federal state." *BK* has always evinced a sympathy for Gaullism i.e., de Gaulle's re-emphasis on his country's culture, his attempts to help the development of the national economy develop and to break certain dependencies on foreign countries, especially the United States. *BK* is for a European economic and defence community, as well as cultural exchanges and reflects Strauss' concern for managerial and military organization.

The following scale is used for this complex:

+3—for European supra-national political federation;
+2—European co-operation in some additional areas should be begun, like
    close European military cooperation and/or a separate pact;
+1—approval of EEC, for limited increase in EEC competence;
+0—neutral mention of EEC, defence community;
—1—EEC works to the disadvantage of Germany;
—2—ties and dependencies on other (European) countries should be reduced
    from their present level;
—3—autarchy must be achieved as nearly as possible;

It appears that *BK* does speak more often and more positively about European unification than do the other two papers.

On this European unity complex as well as the economic progress and old-fashioned nationalism variables a clear, significant difference between *BK* and the other two papers can be shown. The analysis of variance statistic F for these data is 6.99, which is significant at the .01 level or better. The difference of means between *BK* and second place *DN*, using the weighted data, is significant at the .05 level (t = 1.94).

What this content analysis has done is to confirm the trends noted in the political developments of the CSU and NPD, and indeed for the independent rightist group, especially in South Germany, which still maintains an attentist or at least ideologically differentiated position vis-à-vis the NPD. The *BK* is not a nationalistic paper in the same sense that *DNZ* and *DN* are. The glorification of Germany's past so evident in the latter two and especially in the historical paeans of *DNZ* are missing in the CSU organ. The *Kurier* seems mild when compared to the other two. It attempts to come to grips with socio-economic issues whereas *DNZ* and *DN* are filled with resentments; especially *DNZ*, which hardly concerns itself with any kind of serious functional analysis.

DNZ clubs the Federal Republic with big headlines and historical features that don't necessarily show up in a content analysis. On Oct. 24, 1969 *DNZ* shrieked: "Brandt's *Machtergreifung*" (Brandt's power seizure) — in German the word has an illicit flavor. For example — not the *DNZ* of course — one writes often of "Hitler's *Machtergreifung*", and *DNZ* trumpets "*Gott schuetze Deutschland und strafe die FDP*" (God save Germany and punish the FDP). Interestingly enough, "*Gott strafe England*" was a popular Protestant chancellory and mass-slogan during World War I. The *DNZ* headline clearly intimated that the SPD and its chancellor candidate Brandt had somehow illegally seized power and the FDP had completely prostituted itself morally in supporting this takeover. Brandt has always been a favorite enemy of *DNZ*. For years he was always called *Brandt alias Frahm*. This reference to Brandt's illegitimate birth and his emigration to Scandinavia as a young socialist in 1933 was harped upon and cunningly distorted over the years by *DNZ* in the most constant and serious attempt at character assassination in postwar German history. Interestingly enough, a pro-CSU Passau paper run by Strauss associate Kapfinger was not above the same type of allegation. *DNZ*'s style is typified by its matching pictures run of Israel Defence Minister Dayan and Hitler after the six day war (the copy was confiscated by the Federal Government but the damage was done). *DN* must be more careful. It is the official organ of the NPD, and the NPD keeps a wary eye out for the courts. *DN*'s headline (Oct. 10) *Was soll aus Deutschland werden?* (what shall become of Germany) is less volatile; nevertheless the new government is accused of planning to sell out Germany.

"Of course chancellor candidate Brandt . . . declared at once that he would concentrate mainly on 'internal reforms'. The field of foreign politics in turn would be left to the FDP gentlemen Scheel and Dahrendorf alone, so that they could get started with the sellout of Germany and bear the responsibility for it on their shoulders so that the SPD would not appear guilty in the eyes of the public. Mr. Scheel and Mr. Dahrendorf will: sign the non-proliferation treaty as quickly as possible in order to meet the wishes of Moscow . . .; give the de facto recognition of the Ulbricht regime and separation of West Berlin from the free part of Germany, as a so-called normalization of relations that will finally lead to the circumstance that has always been considered by the Communists as most desirable; the splitting of Germany into several states. Those are the results of that 28th of September (election day) 1969 which will go down as a black day in German history unless it is possible to halt this development and stop the sell out.

There is a kind of scale of intensity about the type of comment made depending on the socio-political position of the newspapers and the party they represent. *BK*'s attitude, as we have seen, differs in emotional intensity and language from that of *DN* and especially *DNZ*, but the quantitative scales bring the CSU organ into a similar statistical focus especially in regard to the utilization of security threats, the stress of the ingroup danger, and the diabolifying of "left-wing" radicalism. Nor is the *BK* always particular to maintain definite boundaries between forms of left radicalism and democratic elements in German society. The *Kurier* which seems so vitally right wing to many German observers really reflects the political tightrope that the CSU must walk. The paper is more cautious than *DN* in its pandering to threatened economic sectors and its attitude towards re-unification and the refugees.

The trends, however, are similar here with statistically valid differentiations not noted. *DNZ* is a truly volatile nationalist paper. It ignores functional issues and inveighs all the more on emotional ones. This is a luxury that the *Kurier* cannot and would not want to afford. The CSU is, after all, a party with excellent ties to Germany's managerial elite, and big capitalists are wary of extremist panegyrics. The *Kurier* reflects the new technocratic conservatism and openness towards a conservative Europe that characterizes Strauss and through him the CSU. It remains very much his broadsword. In its organization minded, efficiency oriented technocratism and "Europeanism" it differs from the old-fashioned extremism of the *DN* and the emotional know nothingness of *DNZ* the way the CSU under Strauss differs from the NPD and the independent rightists of various stripes. That is perhaps the most interesting result of this content analysis. It would be silly to maintain that our correlates really indicate, with mathematical exactness the relation of the CSU to the NPD. Or that they are even that accurate for longer periods of *BK* and the other two papers. On the other hand the fixing of propagandistic trends in a rigorous manner gives a mighty clue to party predelictions. This is especially true if the limited quantitative analysis, as this one seems to do, corroborates certain hypotheses made on the basis of broader traditional political analysis. The ambiguities in the political position of the CSU are too evident to ascribe them either to statistical error or analytical prejudice.

Notes

1. A Likert scale is a set of statements that represents the possible attitudes along some single dimension e.g., approval–disapproval about some given subject. Each step away from the neutral point is assigned a higher positive or negative number. A simple hypothetical example would be the following set of statements measuring evaluation of the Social Democratic Party (a given individual responding to a questionnaire or a survey interviewer would choose only one of the statements):

+3–I am strongly for the SPD.
+2–I am for the SPD.
—1–I disapprove mildly of the SPD.
+0–I don't care one way or the other about the SPD.
—1–I disapprove moldly of the SPD.
—2–I have definite objections to the SPD.
—3–I disapprove strongly of the SPD.

If one had an appropriately constructed sample of survey respondents one could work out statistics showing quantitatively how much more positive the attitude towards the SPD was in some social sectors than in others (assuming all the respondents had understood the answer alternatives in the same way, or at least that the social variables or categories were not related to differences in understanding). Similarly, one should be able to construct scales to differentiate systematically among attitudes expressed in newspapers about subjects whose treatment one wants to analyse. The central dimension of each scale (each is discussed under its respectve heading A through J) is either positive concern–unconcern or agreement–disagreement with traditional attitudes. About the scoring: an entry in the zero or neutral category is still an indication of concern with the subject; that is, the paper could have devoted that space to some other topic.

We want to include "neutral mentions" in our calculations, though certainly with less weight than positively or negatively charged statements; therefore, to calculate the number of "emphasis points" in each newspaper issue for some subject we multiply or weight each entry in the zero category by 1, each in the +1 or mildly positive category by 2, each entry in the +2 category by 3 and each in the +3 category by 4. (But entries in the −1, −2, and −3 categories are multiplied by −1, −2, and −3, respectively.) So a statement of a really extreme position counts 4 (or −3) times as much as a statement in which no particular attitude can be detected.

The scores on which the statistical operations are performed for each of the attitude variables are the eight totals of points per issue for each paper, or 3 sets of 8 scores each.

2. About the statistical terms in the text: "Significance levels" .05, .01, etc., show the proportion of all possible cases of a given type of problem in which a statistical relationship of such strength would occur as appeared in the problem at hand. That is, the smaller the "significance level" number, the higher the significance of the finding, for (and note that the statistics in this chapter are measuring degrees of *difference* among the 3 samples of newspapers) if a given difference is significant at the .001 level, that means such a large difference could have occurred by chance only once in 1,000 cases (with the same mean and standard deviation), while a difference significant at the .05 level could theoretically have occurred by chance in 5 cases out of 100. Usually in sociological and psychological research statistical results are considered significant if they are large enough to qualify at the .05 level. On the other hand, many writers report results "near-significant" at the .07, .08, or even .10 levels, for social science methods are often rather blunt, and one cannot be sure that one's indicators were measured with absolute precision and validity in the first place, and anyway, if there are ten chances out of one hundred that an apparent statistical relationship is mere coincidence, there are still a lot of chances that it is genuine.

The difference of means or t test and analysis of variance (the statistic F) show essentially the degree of probability that there is consistently more difference between the papers than there is within each one on a given subject, or the extent to which one can expect to be able to distinguish their positions on that matter. Analysis of variance compares the samples all at once, while the difference of means test compares two samples at a time. The calculations are based on the assumption that the samples of 8 issues each of DNZ, DN, and BK are typical or representative for those newspapers.

Another term which appears here is "degrees of freedom". This is important only if the reader wants to check up on the accuracy of the conclusions and looks at tables of t and F values, which vary according to degrees of freedom based on the number and size of samples in the problem. There are always one or more "degrees of freedom" fewer in a given problem than there are items in the sample(s). In our difference of means cases, for example, the N or number of entries per sample is 8 in each case, and there are always N + N − 2 or 14 d. f. The general idea is that in any problem, for any specific result, only a certain number of the cases are "free" to vary randomly. To take a very simple illustration, suppose there is an addition problem with four blanks and a place for the sum. For any given sum, however, three blanks can be filled with any random numbers but the fourth has to be the difference between the first three addends and the sum.

3. The Tables and Steps are too complicated for printing here. They are available upon request at the Otto Suhr Institute c/o Prof. A. Ashkenasi, I Berlin 33 Freie Univ. Berlin.

4. Since in each comparison the raw emphasis points for each paper were weighted, issue by issue, to compensate for the larger or smaller total number of paragraphs in each issue, there are no grounds to suspect that a statistical difference may be an artifact of one paper's greater length. That is, we took the total number of paragraphs for each week, e.g., 990 for week 8, and divided it by three to get a mean number, in this case 330. Then we figured out the number by which each paper's actual number of paragraphs for that week had to be multiplied (DNZ: 1.174, DN: .859, BK: 1.015) in order to equal this mean. The same was done for all the other weeks on the same principle.

On this army and police variable the weighting for size of the issues reduced the variance between *Deutsche Nachrichten* and *Deutsche National–Zeitung* from 254 versus 85 points to 197.6 versus 95.3 points. Still there was a difference (T score of 1.58) near-significant at the .08 or .07 level.

5. Sample H

SAMPLE H

Conventional morality — sample problem

Here every single step is illustrated for the reader's benefit.

The first step is arranging the totals for each issue into columns, and squaring each number:

DNZ		DN		BK		
12	144	70	4900	23	529	without weighting
16	256	25	625	4	16	
2	4	7	49	3	9	
	404					
0		41	1681	19	361	
0		4	16	0	0	
0		23	529	22	484	
0		3	9	0	0	
0		71	5041	6	36	
			12850		1435	
						grand total:
30	900	244	59536	77	5929	351 123201

Sample H

(2)

DNZ		DN		BK		
13.4	179.56	68.5	4692.25	21.1	445.21	with weighting
15.7	246.49	19.3	372.49	5.8	33.64	
2.6	6.76	7.8	60.84	2.2	4.84	
	432.81					
0		45.3	2052.09	15.8	249.64	
0		2.6	6.76	0	0	
0		16.7	278.89	37.7	1421.29	
0		2.1	4.41	0	0	
0		61.0	3721.00	6.1	37.21	
			11188.83		2191.83	

grand total:

31.7	1004.89	223.3	49862.89	88.7	7867.69	343.7
						111129.69

VIII

Modern German Nationalism

The chances for resuscitation of German nationalism as a key political determinant of Germany's internal and external policies depends on the categorical normative power that nationalism retains in modern Germany and on the attainment of levels of social conflict necessary to galvanize dormant and latent ideological excess. Nationalism's diffuse and chameleonlike character has been the major reason for its survival through the constant changes in political systems that have marked history's course since this ideology took its place as a central and decisive normative phenomenon. The establishment of the modern nation-state system is of course unthinkable without this chiliastic impetus.

One can postulate as has been done in this book that the modern state system and the essentially bourgeois society around which it revolves are on the wane. One can hypothesize that an enormous growth of internal social conflict has paralleled the extension of domestic into international strife and has resulted in an interplay of social or vertical, and international or horizontal conflict. That is, conflict groups on the national or domestic level unite ideologically if not organisationally on the international level. The horizontalization of social conflicts was apparent in the two world wars. Indeed these conflagrations are both symptomatic of the fact that the curve in this historical cycle has been turned, that new social and political forms are in development, and that they have accelerated the process. One must also question if the normative power of the central ideological conception for this historical era can retain its hold over the minds of enough men and/or elites so that it may be utilized with the manipulative strength that has been its historical characteristic.

Nationalism was an ideology that was always able to integrate. It held a unifying hand over the domestic social conflicts of the nineteenth and twentieth centuries. It was latent in all social groups. It had not only the integrative force that made it the manipulative vehicle par excellence for elite groups but it gave the political life of the modern era an explosive force and imminent irrationality which served really as a contradiction to the rational elements of the scientific revolution which accompanied the establishment of the nation-state system. It was this force and this irrationalism which made it an excellent tool for atavistic social elites and for the repression of theoretically more logical and more socially reformistic ideologies with which it competed, for example liberalism and socialism. This repression was not limited to the sphere of ideology. Politically, nationalism has been primarily utilized after its heady emancipatory phase as a politically manipulative tool of the conservative forces in society, and this factor of its development in the industrial societies of the Western world was nowhere better illustrated than in Germany.

German nationalism has been socially and politically conservative. One might have to qualify this statement in dealing with other Western nations but no qualification is necessary nor even thinkable in the German historical experience. Even an originally revolutionary, nationalistic movement like National Socialism, historically the most extreme extension of the nationalist idea, was not able to break out of this rule of the German nationalist experience. The Nazis remained socially conservative. The socialist verbiage of the movement was hopelessly outthundered by the nationalist ideology.

This extreme form of nationalism, part and parcel of the post-World War I shock and the fear of new social and cultural forms on the part of broad elements of German society, is dead in Germany today. It is altogether conceivable that one may encounter it in other areas of the world, but Germany having had the experience is probably immune. This is not only so because of the shattering aspects of defeat and the realization of the demonic character of extreme nationalism: the international balance of power, West German's historically new international political position, and the deep and constant changes in German social and economic structure have cut away any broad base for national extremism. Nationalism in Germany was always in a sense partly a function of the vagaries of the internatonal system in which Germany was an actor. There was always in Germany a strong feeling that the German state could reform or restructure the international system in which it operated. Essentially this was one of the critical aspects of the German nationalist experience and provided perhaps the only ostensibly realistic buttress of the entire complex. Although it is questionable whether even the powerful Germany of the Wilhelmine and Nationalist Socialist periods was really able to restructure the balance of power in the world in which it functioned, the internal appraisal of ability had a spurious *raison d'être*. Modern German nationalists are forced by the recent construction of the international system to seek out new elements in order to give the nationalist normative line a continuing justification — hence the concern with Europe.

The German nationalist sees Europe as a power block, as an economic force to achieve political parity with other world powers, to re-achieve independence of action for European leadership elites. The identification process between the national and the European is evident. Indeed the identification processes can easily be stretched to include regional areas within the nation. The chapters on the CSU illustrated this factor, and regionalism and the sister conception of homelandism buttress nationalism. It is perhaps not as surprising and paradoxical as it seems that nationalists and particularists stress the European idea. The important thing is to analyse the components of this European idea and to determine the role reserved for this Europe. Interestingly enough these German nationalists do not blanche at the British and especially French conservative nationalist application of the European idea. Essentially the Germans reflect the same view, but of course in a profoundly realistic hope of eventual dominance. Germany's economic base, the core of the European community and her dynamism give wings to this conception. Her past calls for verbal discretion.

The goal of the modern German nationalist is a Europe of economic concentration and military power. This is not really surprising. The essentials of the nation-state are simply transferred to the European idea. The identification process is then easy for those social groups still functionally and ideologically in need of the national vertical.

In Germany certain social groups in certain regions seem more susceptible to this type of modern German nationalism. The "pre-industrialists", categorical moralists, and groups of society which are psychologically dogmatically structured, and especially those with preference for hierarchical authority structures in their choice of occupation career have emerged in this study. This is especially true for the armed forces, a reservoir of nationalism. Other hierarchically structured groups such as the police and the Catholic church are susceptible as well but probably less so than the armed forces. The police in many German cities and lands are influenced by their own quite liberal labour union and are controlled by Social Democratic communal administrations. (As the Nuremberg situation showed, the police are vulnerable, but latent neo-nationalist activity can be nipped in the bud.) Although the Social Democrats can be individually nationalist and although they have tried to utilize nationalism in the past they are not the group in Germany that in our analysis has proved to be either the profiteers from, or the real manipulators of the nationalist idea. Indeed the policies of the current Social Democratic government perhaps unconsciously, and perhaps consciously, seem directed at weakening elements of the nationalist idea in Germany.

Social Democracy is neither the political movement of the farmer or of the old middle class or of the armed forces. It is a movement which contains a healthy fear of the ideological excess to which Germany has been so prone. Perhaps this is one of the reasons for its adoption of an essentially pragmatic reformistic approach to political affairs. This has certainly been the case since the death of its dynamic, essentially pre-World War II leader, Kurt Schuhmacher in 1952. Essentially the SPD wants Europe as well, but it wants a broader Europe which includes the social reformistic ideas of the Scandinavian countries, and it wants a Europe without any lasting juridical or normative claims on the East. It is also quite willing to sacrifice key elements of a military posture and seems far more willing than modern German nationalists to accept a security guaranteed by "area foreign" (*raumfremd*) powers. In its rejection of independent security, modern weaponry, and the Easternism of the past, and in its acceptance of social restructuring of German society and cultural permissiveness it is essentially the major political bulwark against resuscitation of German nationalism.

The latest security scandals and land elections showed how consistently vulnerable the SPD, as well as policies deviating from a nationalist normative pattern, are to organized nationalist criticism. In this case the criticism came from the CDU/CSU, but it was essentially the policies of the CSU which have captured the larger party. The elections, of course, are not absolutely accurate as indicators of anything. Certainly other issues were important. But it seems that the national question, couched in terms of "national security" and the familiar allusions to a reformist party's national insufficience and/or incompetence to provide security, fill the campaigns. Nevertheless neither the resuscitation of the national idea and its regeneration in the European model nor the appeal to ordered society coloured with attacks on cultural permissiveness in which lurks the threat of the "managerization" of the new middle class were able at this point to stampede the Germans. The country is essentially divided between those tending towards this security-oriented, moral type of nationalism and those tending tentatively towards future-oriented reformism and a rejection of the nationalist past.

The extremism of the NPD and even its pragmatic Facism remains suspect for overwhelming majorities in Germany. The postwar generation and especially its academic elite are probably less susceptible to nationalist arguments than any generation since 1848. And the percentage of German youth going to college is growing rapidly. Cosmopolitan and tolerance seem also to be a function of the urbanization which is also growing apace. Indeed, among the social pillars of the bourgeois nation-state, nationalism is the one most acute in functional jeopardy. Its ideological association with the entrepreneural aspect of life and with bourgeois social mores gives it a normative power that can certainly be galvanised.

It is doubtful if this regalvanisation process will arise out of the West German domestic political and social process. The level of social conflict in Germany seems lower than that of other Western nations, for example France or the United States, at least superficially. In addition, potentially conservative social groups in this country seem to be melting away faster than in other nations. Nevertheless international crises of either an economic or political nature will certainly strengthen modern nationalists in Germany as indeed they will strengthen all ideologies. And Germany is terribly susceptible to international developments. Increases in the level of Western European national intrasigence and a stiffening of the Eastern position are enough to start tiping 'tolerants' into the 'tough' camp. A sudden flare-up in the level of social conflict in Germany through student or worker unrest and/or economic crisis can certainly not be entirely excluded and could also inflame passions thought to be long burnt out. Political parties exist which would utilize these passions and powerful social groups exist which would support these parties to the fullest.

While time may be running out for any kind of functional nationalism, it is not running out for authoritarian conceptions of political control. The integrational aspects of the nationalist idea remain attractive for the manipulation of prone social groups and the damping of social reform. Modern German nationalism is certainly not going to die a sudden death. Germany may indeed be less threatened by the inherent danger of nationalism than most other industrial nations, but its past and its critical central position in Europe call for special care and exaggerated caution.